PEARSON COMMON CORE Literature

Close Reading Notebook

GRADE 8

PEARSON

HOBOKEN, NEW JERSEY • BOSTON, MASSACHUSETTS
CHANDLER, ARIZONA • GLENVIEW, ILLINOIS

Acknowledgments appear on page 219, which constitutes an extension of this copyright page.

Copyright © Pearson Education, Inc., or its affiliates. All Rights Reserved. Printed in the United States of America. This publication is protected by copyright, and permission should be obtained from the publisher prior to any prohibited reproduction, storage in a retrieval system, or transmission in any form or by any means, electronic, mechanical, photocopying, recording, or likewise. The publisher hereby grants permission to reproduce these pages, in part or in whole, for classroom use only, the number not to exceed the number of students in each class. Notice of copyright must appear on all copies. For information regarding permissions, write to Rights Management & Contracts, Pearson Education, Inc., 221 River Street, Hoboken, New Jersey 07030.

Common Core State Standards © Copyright 2010. National Governors Association Center for Best Practices and Council of Chief State School Officers. All rights reserved.

PEARSON

ISBN-13: 978-0-13-327567-4
ISBN-10:   0-13-327567-1
8 9 10 V011 18 17 16 15

Close Reading

Marking the Text: Strategies and Tips for Annotation

When you close read a text, you read for comprehension and then reread to unlock layers of meaning and to analyze a writer's style and techniques. Marking a text as you read it enables you to participate more fully in the close-reading process.

Following are some strategies for text mark-ups, along with samples of how the strategies can be applied. These mark-ups are suggestions; you and your teacher may opt to use other mark-up strategies.

Suggested Mark-up Notations

What I notice	How to mark up	Questions to ask
Key Ideas and Details	• Circle key ideas or claims. • Underline supporting details or evidence.	• What does the text say? What does it leave unsaid? • What inferences do you need to make? • What details lead you to make your inferences?
Word Choice	• Put a question mark next to unfamiliar words. • Circle any familiar word parts within an unknown word. • Underline context clues, if any exist. • Highlight especially rich or poetic passages.	• What inferences about word meaning can you make? • What tone and mood are created by word choice? • What alternate word choices might the author have made?
Text Structure	• Bracket passages that show character growth or development. • Use arrows to indicate how sentences and paragraphs work together to build ideas. • Use a right-facing arrow to indicate foreshadowing. • Use a left-facing arrow to indicate flashback.	• Is the text logically structured? • What emotional impact do the structural choices create?
Author's Craft	• Circle or highlight instances of repetition, either of words, phrases, consonants, or vowel sounds. • Mark rhythmic beats in poetry using checkmarks and slashes. • Underline instances of symbolism or figurative language.	• Does the author's style enrich or detract from the reading experience? • What levels of meaning are created by the author's techniques?

ESSAY

TAKE NOTES

L'Amour starts with "I" perspective but from this point on switches to "we" and "our." Doing so makes it seem as if the writer and reader were of one mind.

From the context clues and the prefix *pre-*, I can infer that *preliminary* means "start-up" or "something that goes before."

This list of facts supports L'Amour's claim about the rapidity with which we can develop the world.

This comment alerts me to the fact that not everyone agrees with L'Amour's ideas. His description of them as nay-sayers (and not as critics) suggests that he belittles their ideas.

At this point in the text, L'Amour defines *frontier* and explains how the notion of a frontier propels exploration.

The Eternal Frontier
Louis L'Amour

The question I am most often asked is, "Where is the frontier now?"

The answer should be obvious. Our frontier lies in outer space. The moon, the asteroids, the planets, these are mere stepping stones, where we will test ourselves, learn needful lessons, and grow in knowledge before we attempt those frontiers beyond our solar system. Outer space is a frontier without end, the eternal frontier, an everlasting challenge to explorers not [only] of other planets and other solar systems but also of the mind of man.

All that has gone before was preliminary. We have been preparing ourselves mentally for what lies ahead. Many problems remain, but if we can avoid a devastating war we shall move with a rapidity scarcely to be believed. In the past seventy years we have developed the automobile, radio, television, transcontinental and transoceanic flight, and the electrification of the country, among a multitude of other such developments. In 1900 there were 144 miles of surfaced road in the United States. Now there are over 3,000,000. Paved roads and the development of the automobile have gone hand in hand, the automobile being civilized man's antidote to overpopulation.

What is needed now is leaders with perspective; we need leadership on a thousand fronts, but they must be men and women who can take the long view and help to shape the outlines of our future. There will always be the nay-sayers, those who cling to our lovely green planet as a baby clings to its mother, but there will be others like those who have taken us this far along the path to a limitless future.

We are a people born to the frontier. It has been a part of our thinking, waking, and sleeping since men first landed on this continent. The frontier is the line that separates the known from the unknown wherever it may be, and we have a driving need to see what lies beyond . . .

A few years ago we moved into outer space. We landed men on the moon; we sent a vehicle beyond the limits of the solar system, a vehicle still moving farther and farther into that limitless distance. If our world were to die tomorrow, that tiny vehicle would go on and on forever, carrying its mighty message to the stars. Out there, someone, sometime, would know that once we existed, that we had the vision and we made the effort. Mankind is not bound by its atmospheric envelope or by its gravitational field, nor is the mind of man bound by any limits at all.

One might ask—why outer space, when so much remains to be done here? If that had been the spirit of man we would still be hunters and food gatherers, growling over the bones of carrion in a cave somewhere. It is our destiny to move out, to accept the challenge, to dare the unknown. It is our destiny to achieve.

Yet we must not forget that along the way to outer space whole industries are springing into being that did not exist before. The computer age has arisen in part from the space effort, which gave great impetus to the development of computing devices. Transistors, chips, integrated circuits, Teflon, new medicines, new ways of treating diseases, new ways of performing operations, all these and a multitude of other developments that enable man to live and to live better are linked to the space effort. Most of these developments have been so incorporated into our day-to-day life that they are taken for granted, their origin not considered.

If we are content to live in the past, we have no future. And today is the past.

TAKE NOTES

L'Amour uses repetition to stress his points.

This claim is interesting. Just as we are not bound by the physical limits of Earth, our minds should also be free.

Here, L'Amour addresses a possible counterargument.

The word *destiny* is poetic and has more positive connotations than its synonym *fate*. The repeated use of the word emphasizes L'Amour's main claim.

The word *impetus* means "forward motion" or "motivation." By using this technical word along with some other technical words, L'Amour conveys authority.

The final paragraph is short and mysterious. Is L'Amour saying that because we live in the present we have no future?

Sample Mark-up Annotation v

SHORT STORY

TAKE NOTES

The author begins the story with a fairy-tale structure. Based on this, I can infer that this story might involve a moral or lesson.

Context clues help me figure out that a drake is a male duck.

The narrator is a story character, and he knows all the characters' inner thoughts and feelings.

I'm not quite sure what adorn means. The context clues "beautiful things" and "manor house and garden" seem to indicate that adorn might mean "decorate."

Shozo's comment that the drake will die in captivity might foreshadow the drake's fate.

from The Tale of the Mandarin Ducks

Katherine Paterson

Long ago and far away in the Land of the Rising Sun, there lived together a pair of mandarin ducks. Now, the drake was a magnificent bird with plumage of colors so rich that the emperor himself would have envied it. But his mate, the duck, wore the quiet tones of the wood, blending exactly with the hole in the tree where the two had made their nest.

One day while the duck was sitting on her eggs, the drake flew down to a nearby pond to search for food. While he was there, a hunting party entered the woods. The hunters were led by the lord of the district, a proud and cruel man who believed that everything in the district belonged to him to do with as he chose. The lord was always looking for beautiful things to adorn? his manor house and garden. And when he saw the drake swimming gracefully on the surface of the pond, he determined to capture him.

The lord's chief steward, a man named Shozo, tried to discourage his master. "The drake is a wild spirit, my lord," he said. "Surely he will die in captivity." But the lord pretended not to hear Shozo. Secretly he despised Shozo, because although Shozo had once been his mightiest samurai, the warrior had lost an eye in battle and was no longer handsome to look upon.

The lord ordered his servants to clear a narrow way through the undergrowth and place acorns along the path. When the drake came out of the water he saw the acorns. How pleased he was! He forgot to be cautious, thinking only of what a feast they would be to take home to his mate.

Just as he was bending to pick up an acorn in his scarlet beak, a net fell over him, and the frightened bird was carried back to the lord's manor and placed in a small bamboo cage.

vi Close Reading Notebook • Marking the Text

The lord was delighted with his new pet. He ordered a feast to be prepared and invited all the wealthy landowners from miles around, so that he could show off the drake and brag about his wonderful plumage, which was indeed more beautiful than the finest brocade.

But the drake could think only of his mate sitting alone on her eggs, not knowing what had happened to her husband.

As the days wore on, his crested head began to droop. His lovely feathers lost their luster. His proud, wild cry became first a weary *cronk* and then he fell silent. No matter what delicacies the kitchen maid brought him, he refused to eat. He is grieving for his mate, the girl thought, for she was wise in the customs of wild creatures.

[The lord, who liked things only so long as they were beautiful and brought him honor, grew angry when he saw that the drake was ailing. "Perhaps we should let him go," Shozo suggested, "since he no longer pleases you, my lord." But the lord did not like anyone to tell him what to do, much less a one-eyed servant.] He refused to release the drake, ordering instead that the cage be put out of sight so that he would no longer be annoyed by the bird's sad appearance. . . .

TAKE NOTES

I'm not sure what *brocade* means. It must be something very fancy and colorful. According to a dictionary, it means "rich cloth with a raised design."

This short paragraph sets up the next one. Because the drake is grieving, he begins to fade.

These bracketed sentences help illustrate the contrasts between the lord and Shozo. The lord doesn't care about anyone or anything other than himself. He has no sympathy or respect for the dying bird or for his wounded servant. In contrast, Shozo cares about the drake and tries to figure out a way to free him.

POEM

TAKE NOTES

The first line is in iambic pentameter and establishes a rhythmic quality.

The first, fifth, and last stanzas have exact end rhyme. This use of rhyme gives the poem a playful quality.

Line 6 is interesting because it has an inverted structure. Normally, someone would say, "whose five languid rays were fingers." Maybe Cummings structured the line this way because "were" sort of rhymes with "star" in the line above.

This simile in line 10 compares a stone with a world, which we usually think of as large, and with alone, which is an abstract feeling. It seems like the speaker is saying that a world can be a small place at times, and the feeling of being alone can seem large and all-encompassing.

maggie and milly and molly and may

E. E. Cummings

maggie/ and mil/ly and/ molly/ and may
went down to the beach (to play one day)

and maggie discovered a shell that sang
so sweetly she couldn't remember her troubles, and

5 milly befriended a stranded star
whose rays five languid fingers were;

and molly was chased by a horrible thing
which raced sideways while blowing bubbles: and

may came home with a smooth round stone
10 as small as a world and as large as alone.

For whatever we lose (like a you or a me)
it's always ourselves we find in the sea

viii Close Reading Notebook • Marking the Text

Close Reading Notebook

CONTENTS

The following texts are provided in this book for you to mark up as you close read. These texts are also available in the Close Reading Tool (🔍), where you can practice marking the texts digitally.

UNIT 1

PART 1
An Hour With Abuelo *by Judith Ortiz Cofer* 1

PART 2
Raymond's Run *by Toni Cade Bambara* 6
The Tell-Tale Heart *by Edgar Allan Poe* 15

PART 3
ANCHOR TEXT   Who Can Replace a Man? *by Brian Aldiss* 21
Robots Get a Feel for the World at USC Viterbi *by University of Southern California Viterbi* 31

UNIT 2

PART 1
Making Tracks on Mars *by Andrew Mishkin* 33

PART 2
from Always to Remember: The Vision of Maya Ying Lin *by Brent Ashabranner* 38
The Trouble With Television *by Robert MacNeil* 43

PART 3
ANCHOR TEXT | EXEMPLAR TEXT   from Travels with Charley *by John Steinbeck* 46
Choice: A Tribute to Martin Luther King, Jr. *by Alice Walker* 51

UNIT 3

PART 1
Describe Somebody *by Jacqueline Woodson* 54
Almost Summer Sky *by Jacqueline Woodson* 56

PART 2
Silver *by Walter de la Mare* 58
Ring Out, Wild Bells *by Alfred, Lord Tennyson* 59
Cat! *by Eleanor Farjeon* 60
Thumbprint *by Eve Merriam* 61

The Sky Is Low, the Clouds Are Mean *by Emily Dickinson* 62
Concrete Mixers *by Patricia Hubbell* 63
Harlem Night Song *by Langston Hughes* 64
The City Is So Big *by Richard García* 65

x Close Reading Notebook

- **The New Colossus** by Emma Lazarus 66
- **Blow, Blow, Thou Winter Wind** by William Shakespeare 67
- EXEMPLAR TEXT **Paul Revere's Ride** by Henry Wadsworth Longfellow 68

- **Grandma Ling** by Amy Ling 72
- **your little voice / Over the wires came leaping** by E. E. Cummings 73
- **New World** by N. Scott Momaday 74
- **January** by John Updike 75

PART 3
- ANCHOR TEXT **Old Man** by Ricardo Sánchez 76
- ANCHOR TEXT **For My Sister Molly Who in the Fifties** by Alice Walker 78
- **Cub Pilot on the Mississippi** by Mark Twain 81

UNIT 4

PART 1
- from **The Miracle Worker** by William Gibson 90

PART 2
- EXEMPLAR TEXT **The Diary of Anne Frank, Act I** by Francis Goodrich and Albert Hackett 104
- **The Governess** by Neil Simon 160

PART 3
- ANCHOR TEXT from **Kindertransport** by Diane Samuels 166
- from **Anne Frank: The Diary of a Young Girl** by Anne Frank 194

UNIT 5

PART 1
- **Water Names** by Lan Samantha Chang 198

PART 2
- **Chicoria** by Rudolfo A. Anaya and José Griego y Maestas 202
- from **The People, Yes** by Carl Sandburg 204
- **An Episode of War** by Stephen Crane 206

PART 3
- ANCHOR TEXT from **The American Dream** by Martin Luther King, Jr. 211
- **Emancipation** from **Lincoln: A Photobiography** by Russell Freedman 214

An Hour With Abuelo

by Judith Ortiz Cofer

"Just one hour, *una hora,* is all I'm asking of you, son." My grandfather is in a nursing home in Brooklyn, and my mother wants me to spend some time with him, since the doctors say that he doesn't have too long to go now. I don't have much time left of my summer vacation, and there's a stack of books next to my bed I've got to read if I'm going to get into the AP English class I want. I'm going stupid in some of my classes, and Mr. Williams, the principal at Central, said that if I passed some reading tests, he'd let me move up.

Besides, I hate the place, the old people's home, especially the way it smells like industrial-strength ammonia and other stuff I won't mention, since it turns my stomach. And really the abuelo always has a lot of relatives visiting him, so I've gotten out of going out there except at Christmas, when a whole vanload of grandchildren are herded over there to give him gifts and a hug. We all make it quick and spend the rest of the time in the recreation area, where they play checkers and stuff with some of the old people's games, and I catch up on back issues of *Modern Maturity.* I'm not picky, I'll read almost anything.

Anyway, after my mother nags me for about a week, I let her drive me to Golden Years. She drops me off in front. She wants me to go in alone and have a "good time" talking to Abuelo. I tell her to be back in one hour or I'll take the bus back to Paterson. She squeezes my hand and says, *"Gracias, hijo,"*[1] in a choked-up voice like I'm doing her a big favor.

I get depressed the minute I walk into the place. They line up the old people in wheelchairs in the hallway as if they were about to be raced to the finish line by orderlies who don't even look at them when they push them here and there. I walk fast to room 10, Abuelo's "suite." He is sitting up in his bed writing with a pencil in one of those old-fashioned black hardback

---

1. **Gracias** (grä′ sē äs), hijo (ē′ hō)" Spanish for "Thank you, son." *Hijo* also means "child."

notebooks. It has the outline of the island of Puerto Rico on it. I slide into the hard vinyl chair by his bed. He sort of smiles and the lines on his face get deeper, but he doesn't say anything. Since I'm supposed to talk to him, I say, "What are you doing, Abuelo, writing the story of your life?"

It's supposed to be a joke, but he answers, "Sí, how did you know, Arturo?"

His name is Arturo too. I was named after him. I don't really know my grandfather. His children, including my mother, came to New York and New Jersey (where I was born) and he stayed on the Island until my grandmother died. Then he got sick, and since nobody could leave their jobs to go take care of him, they brought him to this nursing home in Brooklyn. I see him a couple of times a year, but he's always surrounded by his sons and daughters. My mother tells me that Don Arturo had once been a teacher back in Puerto Rico, but had lost his job after the war. Then he became a farmer. She's always saying in a sad voice, "Ay, bendito![2] What a waste of a fine mind." Then she usually shrugs her shoulders and says, "Así es la vida."[3] That's the way life is. It sometimes makes me mad that the adults I know just accept whatever is thrown at them because "that's the way things are." Not for me. I go after what I want.

Anyway, Abuelo is looking at me like he was trying to see into my head, but he doesn't say anything. Since I like stories, I decide I may as well ask him if he'll read me what he wrote.

I look at my watch: I've already used up twenty minutes of the hour I promised my mother.

Abuelo starts talking in his slow way. He speaks what my mother calls book English. He taught himself from a dictionary, and his words sound stiff, like he's sounding them out in his head before he says them. With his children he speaks Spanish, and that funny book English with us grandchildren. I'm surprised that he's still so sharp, because his body is shrinking like a crumpled-up brown paper sack with some bones in it. But I can see from looking into his eyes that the light is still on in there.

---

2. **bendito** (ven dē′ tō) Spanish for "blessed."
3. **Así es la vida** (ä sē′ es lä vē′ thä) Spanish for "such is life."

"It is a short story, Arturo. The story of my life. It will not take very much time to read it."

"I have time, Abuelo." I'm a little embarrassed that he saw me looking at my watch.

"Yes, *hijo*. You have spoken the truth. *La verdad.* You have much time."

Abuelo reads: "'I loved words from the beginning of my life. In the campo[4] where I was born one of seven sons, there were few books. My mother read them to us over and over: the Bible, the stories of Spanish conquistadors and of pirates that she had read as a child and brought with her from the city of Mayagüez; that was before she married my father, a coffee bean farmer; and she taught us words from the newspaper that a boy on a horse brought every week to her. She taught each of us how to write on a slate with chalks that she ordered by mail every year. We used those chalks until they were so small that you lost them between your fingers.

"'I always wanted to be a writer and a teacher. With my heart and my soul I knew that I wanted to be around books all of my life. And so against the wishes of my father, who wanted all his sons to help him on the land, she sent me to high school in Mayagüez. For four years I boarded with a couple she knew. I paid my rent in labor, and I ate vegetables I grew myself. I wore my clothes until they were thin as parchment. But I graduated at the top of my class! My whole family came to see me that day. My mother brought me a beautiful *guayabera*, a white shirt made of the finest cotton and embroidered by her own hands. I was a happy young man.

"'In those days you could teach in a country school with a high school diploma. So I went back to my mountain village and got a job teaching all grades in a little classroom built by the parents of my students.

"'I had books sent to me by the government. I felt like a rich man although the pay was very small. I had books. All the books I wanted! I taught my students how to read poetry and plays, and how to write them. We made up songs and put on shows for the parents. It was a beautiful time for me.

---

4. **campo** (käm´ pō) Spanish for "open country."

SHORT STORY

TAKE NOTES

"'Then the war came,[5] and the American President said that all Puerto Rican men would be drafted. I wrote to our governor and explained that I was the only teacher in the mountain village. I told him that the children would go back to the fields and grow up ignorant if I could not teach them their letters. I said that I thought I was a better teacher than a soldier. The governor did not answer my letter. I went into the U.S. Army.

"'I told my sergeant that I could be a teacher in the army. I could teach all the farm boys their letters so that they could read the instructions on the ammunition boxes and not blow themselves up. The sergeant said I was too smart for my own good, and gave me a job cleaning latrines. He said to me there is reading material for you there, scholar. Read the writing on the walls. I spent the war mopping floors and cleaning toilets.

"'When I came back to the Island, things had changed. You had to have a college degree to teach school, even the lower grades. My parents were sick, two of my brothers had been killed in the war, the others had stayed in Nueva York. I was the only one left to help the old people. I became a farmer. I married a good woman who gave me many good children. I taught them all how to read and write before they started school.'"

Abuelo then puts the notebook down on his lap and closes his eyes.

"*Así es la vida* is the title of my book," he says in a whisper, almost to himself. Maybe he's forgotten that I'm there.

For a long time he doesn't say anything else. I think that he's sleeping, but then I see that he's watching me through half-closed lids, maybe waiting for my opinion of his writing. I'm trying to think of something nice to say. I liked it and all, but not the title. And I think that he could've been a teacher if he had wanted to bad enough. Nobody is going to stop me from doing what I want with my life. I'm not going to let la vida get in my way. I want to discuss this with him, but the words are not coming into my head in Spanish just yet. I'm

---

5. **"'Then the war came, . . .'"** The United States entered World War II in 1941, after the bombing of Pearl Harbor.

4 Close Reading Notebook • Unit 1

about to ask him why he didn't keep fighting to make his dream come true, when an old lady in hot-pink running shoes sort of appears at the door.

She is wearing a pink jogging outfit too. The world's oldest marathoner, I say to myself. She calls out to my grandfather in a flirty voice, "Yoo-hoo, Arturo, remember what day this is? It's poetry-reading day in the rec room! You promised us you'd read your new one today."

I see my abuelo perking up almost immediately. He points to his wheelchair, which is hanging like a huge metal bat in the open closet. He makes it obvious that he wants me to get it. I put it together, and with Mrs. Pink Running Shoes's help, we get him in it. Then he says in a strong deep voice I hardly recognize, "Arturo, get that notebook from the table, please."

I hand him another map-of-the-Island notebook—this one is red. On it in big letters it says, *POEMAS DE ARTURO*.

I start to push him toward the rec room, but he shakes his finger at me.

"Arturo, look at your watch now. I believe your time is over." He gives me a wicked smile.

Then with her pushing the wheelchair—maybe a little too fast—they roll down the hall. He is already reading from his notebook, and she's making bird noises. I look at my watch and the hour *is* up, to the minute. I can't help but think that my abuelo has been timing *me*. It cracks me up. I walk slowly down the hall toward the exit sign. I want my mother to have to wait a little. I don't want her to think that I'm in a hurry or anything.

Raymond's Run

by Toni Cade Bambara

I don't have much work to do around the house like some girls. My mother does that. And I don't have to earn my pocket money by hustling; George runs errands for the big boys and sells Christmas cards. And anything else that's got to get done, my father does. All I have to do in life is mind my brother Raymond, which is enough.

Sometimes I slip and say my little brother Raymond. But as any fool can see he's much bigger and he's older too. But a lot of people call him my little brother cause he needs looking after cause he's not quite right. And a lot of smart mouths got lots to say about that too, especially when George was minding him. But now, if anybody has anything to say to Raymond, anything to say about his big head, they have to come by me. And I don't play the dozens[1] or believe in standing around with somebody in my face doing a lot of talking. I much rather just knock you down and take my chances even if I am a little girl with skinny arms and a squeaky voice, which is how I got the name Squeaky. And if things get too rough, I run. And as anybody can tell you, I'm the fastest thing on two feet.

There is no track meet that I don't win the first-place medal. I used to win the twenty-yard dash when I was a little kid in kindergarten. Nowadays, it's the fifty-yard dash. And tomorrow I'm subject to run the quarter-mile relay all by myself and come in first, second, and third. The big kids call me Mercury[2] cause I'm the swiftest thing in the neighborhood. Everybody knows that—except two people who know better, my father and me.

He can beat me to Amsterdam Avenue with me having a two fire-hydrant headstart and him running

---

1. **the dozens** game in which the players insult one another; the first to show anger loses.
2. **Mercury** in Roman mythology, the messenger of the gods, known for great speed.

with his hands in his pockets and whistling. But that's private information. Cause can you imagine some thirty-five-year-old man stuffing himself into PAL[3] shorts to race little kids? So as far as everyone's concerned, I'm the fastest and that goes for Gretchen, too, who has put out the tale that she is going to win the first-place medal this year. Ridiculous. In the second place, she's got short legs. In the third place, she's got freckles. In the first place, no one can beat me and that's all there is to it.

I'm standing on the corner admiring the weather and about to take a stroll down Broadway so I can practice my breathing exercises, and I've got Raymond walking on the inside close to the buildings, cause he's subject to fits of fantasy and starts thinking he's a circus performer and that the curb is a tightrope strung high in the air. And sometimes after a rain he likes to step down off his tightrope right into the gutter and slosh around getting his shoes and cuffs wet. Or sometimes if you don't watch him he'll dash across traffic to the island in the middle of Broadway and give the pigeons a fit. Then I have to go behind him apologizing to all the old people sitting around trying to get some sun and getting all upset with the pigeons fluttering around them, scattering their newspapers and upsetting the waxpaper lunches in their laps. So I keep Raymond on the inside of me, and he plays like he's driving a stage coach, which is O.K. by me so long as he doesn't run me over or interrupt my breathing exercises, which I have to do on account of I'm serious about my running, and I don't care who knows it. •

Now some people like to act like things come easy to them, won't let on that they practice. Not me. I'll high prance down 34th Street like a rodeo pony to keep my knees strong even if it does get my mother uptight so that she walks ahead like she's not with me, don't know me, is all by herself on a shopping trip, and I am somebody else's crazy child.

Now you take Cynthia Procter for instance. She's just the opposite. If there's a test tomorrow, she'll say something like, "Oh, I guess I'll play handball this afternoon and watch television tonight," just to let you know she ain't thinking about the test. Or like last

---

3. **PAL** Police Athletic League.

SHORT STORY

TAKE NOTES

week when she won the spelling bee for the millionth time, "A good thing you got 'receive,' Squeaky, cause I would have got it wrong. I completely forgot about the spelling bee." And she'll clutch the lace on her blouse like it was a narrow escape. Oh, brother.

But of course when I pass her house on my early morning trots around the block, she is practicing the scales on the piano over and over and over and over. Then in music class she always lets herself get bumped around so she falls accidently on purpose onto the piano stool and is so surprised to find herself sitting there that she decides just for fun to try out the ole keys and what do you know—Chopin's[4] waltzes just spring out of her fingertips and she's the most surprised thing in the world. A regular prodigy. I could kill people like that.

I stay up all night studying the words for the spelling bee. And you can see me any time of day practicing running. I never walk if I can trot, and shame on Raymond if he can't keep up. But of course he does, cause if he hangs back someone's liable to walk up to him and get smart, or take his allowance from him, or ask him where he got that great big pumpkin head. People are so stupid sometimes.

So I'm strolling down Broadway breathing out and breathing in on counts of seven, which is my lucky number, and here comes Gretchen and her sidekicks—Mary Louise who used to be a friend of mine when she first moved to Harlem from Baltimore and got beat up by everybody till I took up for her on account of her mother and my mother used to sing in the same choir when they were young girls, but people ain't grateful, so now she hangs out with the new girl Gretchen and talks about me like a dog; and Rosie who is as fat as I am skinny and has a big mouth where Raymond is concerned and is too stupid to know that there is not a big deal of difference between herself and Raymond and that she can't afford to throw stones. So they are steady coming up Broadway and I see right away that it's going to be one of those Dodge City[5] scenes cause the street ain't that big and they're close to the

---

4. **Chopin** (shō′ pan) Frédéric François Chopin (1810–1849), highly regarded Polish composer and pianist, known for his challenging piano compositions.
5. **Dodge City** location of the television program *Gunsmoke*, which often presented a gunfight between the sheriff and an outlaw.

buildings just as we are. First I think I'll step into the candy store and look over the new comics and let them pass. But that's chicken and I've got a reputation to consider. So then I think I'll just walk straight on through them or even over them if necessary. But as they get to me, they slow down. I'm ready to fight, cause like I said I don't feature a whole lot of chit-chat, I much prefer to just knock you down right from the jump and save everybody a lotta precious time.

"You signing up for the May Day races?" smiles Mary Louise, only it's not a smile at all.

A dumb question like that doesn't deserve an answer. Besides, there's just me and Gretchen standing there really, so no use wasting my breath talking to shadows.

"I don't think you're going to win this time," says Rosie, trying to signify with her hands on her hips all salty, completely forgetting that I have whupped her many times for less salt than that.

"I always win cause I'm the best," I say straight at Gretchen who is, as far as I'm concerned, the only one talking in this ventriloquist-dummy routine.[6]

Gretchen smiles, but it's not a smile, and I'm thinking that girls never really smile at each other because they don't know how and don't want to know how and there's probably no one to teach us how cause grown-up girls don't know either. Then they all look at Raymond who has just brought his mule team to a standstill. And they're about to see what trouble they can get into through him.

"What grade you in now, Raymond?"

"You got anything to say to my brother, you say it to me, Mary Louise Williams of Raggedy Town, Baltimore."

"What are you, his mother?" sasses Rosie.

"That's right, Fatso. And the next word out of anybody and I'll be *their* mother too." So they just stand there and Gretchen shifts from one leg to the other and so do they. Then Gretchen puts her hands on her hips and is about to say something with her freckle-face self but doesn't. Then she walks around

---

6. **ventriloquist** (ven tril′ ə kwist)-**dummy routine** a comedy act in which the performer speaks through a puppet called a "dummy."

TAKE NOTES

SHORT STORY

TAKE NOTES

me looking me up and down but keeps walking up Broadway, and her sidekicks follow her. So me and Raymond smile at each other and he says, "Gidyap" to his team and I continue with my breathing exercises, strolling down Broadway toward the ice man on 145th with not a care in the world cause I am Miss Quicksilver herself. •

I take my time getting to the park on May Day because the track meet is the last thing on the program. The biggest thing on the program is the May Pole dancing, which I can do without, thank you, even if my mother thinks it's a shame I don't take part and act like a girl for a change. You'd think my mother'd be grateful not to have to make me a white organdy dress with a big satin sash and buy me new white baby-doll shoes that can't be taken out of the box till the big day. You'd think she'd be glad her daughter ain't out there prancing around a May Pole getting the new clothes all dirty and sweaty and trying to act like a fairy or a flower or whatever you're supposed to be when you should be trying to be yourself, whatever that is, which is, as far as I am concerned, a poor black girl who really can't afford to buy shoes and a new dress you only wear once a lifetime cause it won't fit next year.

I was once a strawberry in a Hansel and Gretel pageant when I was in nursery school and didn't have no better sense than to dance on tiptoe with my arms in a circle over my head doing umbrella steps and being a perfect fool just so my mother and father could come dressed up and clap. You'd think they'd know better than to encourage that kind of nonsense. I am not a strawberry. I do not dance on my toes. I run. That is what I am all about. So I always come late to the May Day program, just in time to get my number pinned on and lay in the grass till they announce the fifty-yard dash.

I put Raymond in the little swings, which is a tight squeeze this year and will be impossible next year. Then I look around for Mr. Pearson, who pins the numbers on. I'm really looking for Gretchen if you want to know the truth, but she's not around. The park is jam-packed. Parents in hats and corsages and breast-pocket handkerchiefs peeking up. Kids in white dresses and light-blue suits. The parkees unfolding chairs and chasing the rowdy kids from Lenox as if they had no right to be there. The big guys with their caps on backwards, leaning against the fence swirling the basketballs on the tips of their fingers, waiting for all these crazy people to clear out the park so they can play. Most of the kids in my class are carrying bass drums and glockenspiels[7] and flutes. You'd think they'd put in a few bongos or something for real like that.

Then here comes Mr. Pearson with his clipboard and his cards and pencils and whistles and safety pins and fifty million other things he's always dropping all over the place with his clumsy self. He sticks out in a crowd because he's on stilts. We used to call him Jack and the Beanstalk to get him mad. But I'm the only one that can outrun him and get away, and I'm too grown for that silliness now.

"Well, Squeaky," he says, checking my name off the list and handing me number seven and two pins. And I'm thinking he's got no right to call me Squeaky, if I can't call him Beanstalk.

"Hazel Elizabeth Deborah Parker," I correct him and tell him to write it down on his board.

"Well, Hazel Elizabeth Deborah Parker, going to give someone else a break this year?" I squint at him real hard to see if he is seriously thinking I should lose the race on purpose just to give someone else a break. "Only six girls running this time," he continues, shaking his head sadly like it's my fault all of New York didn't turn out in sneakers. "That new girl should give you a run for your money." He looks around the park for Gretchen like a periscope in a submarine movie. "Wouldn't it be a nice gesture if you were . . . to ahhh . . ."

I give him such a look he couldn't finish putting that idea into words. Grownups got a lot of nerve sometimes. I pin number seven to myself and stomp away, I'm so burnt. And I go straight for the track and stretch out on the grass while the band winds up with "Oh, the Monkey Wrapped His Tail Around the Flag Pole," which my teacher calls by some other name. The man on the loudspeaker is calling everyone over to the track and I'm on my back looking at the sky, trying to

---

7. **glockenspiels** (gläk′ ən spēlz′) *n.* musical instruments with flat metal bars that make bell-like tones when struck with small hammers.

SHORT STORY

TAKE NOTES

pretend I'm in the country, but I can't, because even grass in the city feels hard as sidewalk, and there's just no pretending you are anywhere but in a "concrete jungle" as my grandfather says. •

The twenty-yard dash takes all of two minutes cause most of the little kids don't know no better than to run off the track or run the wrong way or run smack into the fence and fall down and cry. One little kid, though, has got the good sense to run straight for the white ribbon up ahead, so he wins. Then the second-graders line up for the thirty-yard dash and I don't even bother to turn my head to watch cause Raphael Perez always wins. He wins before he even begins by psyching the runners, telling them they're going to trip on their shoelaces and fall on their faces or lose their shorts or something, which he doesn't really have to do since he is very fast, almost as fast as I am. After that is the forty-yard dash which I use to run when I was in first grade. Raymond is hollering from the swings cause he knows I'm about to do my thing cause the man on the loudspeaker has just announced the fifty-yard dash, although he might just as well be giving a recipe for angel food cake cause you can hardly make out what he's saying for the static. I get up and slip off my sweat pants and then I see Gretchen standing at the starting line, kicking her legs out like a pro. Then as I get into place I see that ole Raymond is on line on the other side of the fence, bending down with his fingers on the ground just like he knew what he was doing. I was going to yell at him but then I didn't. It burns up your energy to holler.

Every time, just before I take off in a race, I always feel like I'm in a dream, the kind of dream you have when you're sick with fever and feel all hot and weightless. I dream I'm flying over a sandy beach in the early morning sun, kissing the leaves of the trees as I fly by. And there's always the smell of apples, just like in the country when I was little and used to think I was a choo-choo train, running through the fields of corn and chugging up the hill to the orchard. And all the time I'm dreaming this, I get lighter and lighter until I'm flying over the beach again, getting blown through the sky like a feather that weighs nothing at all. But once I spread my fingers in the dirt and crouch over the Get on Your Mark, the dream goes and I am

12 Close Reading Notebook • Unit 1

solid again and am telling myself, Squeaky you must win, you must win, you are the fastest thing in the world, you can even beat your father up Amsterdam if you really try. And then I feel my weight coming back just behind my knees then down to my feet then into the earth and the pistol shot explodes in my blood and I am off and weightless again, flying past the other runners, my arms pumping up and down and the whole world is quiet except for the crunch as I zoom over the gravel in the track. I glance to my left and there is no one. To the right a blurred Gretchen, who's got her chin jutting out as if it would win the race all by itself. And on the other side of the fence is Raymond with his arms down to his side and the palms tucked up behind him, running in his very own style, and it's the first time I ever saw that and I almost stop to watch my brother Raymond on his first run. But the white ribbon is bouncing toward me and I tear past it, racing into the distance till my feet with a mind of their own start digging up footfuls of dirt and brake me short. Then all the kids standing on the side pile on me, banging me on the back and slapping my head with their May Day programs, for I have won again and everybody on 151st Street can walk tall for another year.

"In first place . . ." the man on the loudspeaker is clear as a bell now. But then he pauses and the loudspeaker starts to whine. Then static. And I lean down to catch my breath and here comes Gretchen walking back, for she's overshot the finish line too, huffing and puffing with her hands on her hips taking it slow, breathing in steady time like a real pro and I sort of like her a little for the first time. "In first place . . ." and then three or four voices get all mixed up on the loudspeaker and I dig my sneaker into the grass and stare at Gretchen who's staring back, we both wondering just who did win. I can hear old Beanstalk arguing with the man on the loudspeaker and then a few others running their mouths about what the stopwatches say. Then I hear Raymond yanking at the fence to call me and I wave to shush him, but he keeps rattling the fence like a gorilla in a cage like in them gorilla movies, but then like a dancer or something he starts climbing up nice and easy but very fast. And it occurs to me, watching how smoothly

TAKE NOTES

SHORT STORY

TAKE NOTES

he climbs hand over hand and remembering how he looked running with his arms down to his side and with the wind pulling his mouth back and his teeth showing and all, it occurred to me that Raymond would make a very fine runner. Doesn't he always keep up with me on my trots? And he surely knows how to breathe in counts of seven cause he's always doing it at the dinner table, which drives my brother George up the wall. And I'm smiling to beat the band cause if I've lost this race, or if me and Gretchen tied, or even if I've won, I can always retire as a runner and begin a whole new career as a coach with Raymond as my champion. After all, with a little more study I can beat Cynthia and her phony self at the spelling bee. And if I bugged my mother, I could get piano lessons and become a star. And I have a big rep as the baddest thing around. And I've got a roomful of ribbons and medals and awards. But what has Raymond got to call his own?

So I stand there with my new plans, laughing out loud by this time as Raymond jumps down from the fence and runs over with his teeth showing and his arms down to the side, which no one before him has quite mastered as a running style. And by the time he comes over I'm jumping up and down so glad to see him—my brother Raymond, a great runner in the family tradition. But of course everyone thinks I'm jumping up and down because the men on the loudspeaker have finally gotten themselves together and compared notes and are announcing "In first place—Miss Hazel Elizabeth Deborah Parker." (Dig that.) "In second place—Miss Gretchen P. Lewis." And I look over at Gretchen wondering what the "P" stands for. And I smile. Cause she's good, no doubt about it. Maybe she'd like to help me coach Raymond; she obviously is serious about running, as any fool can see. And she nods to congratulate me and then she smiles. And I smile. We stand there with this big smile of respect between us. It's about as real a smile as girls can do for each other, considering we don't practice real smiling every day, you know, cause maybe we too busy being flowers or fairies or strawberries instead of something honest and worthy of respect . . . you know . . . like being people.

SHORT STORY

The Tell-Tale Heart

by Edgar Allan Poe

True!—nervous—very, very dreadfully nervous I had been and am; but why *will* you say that I am mad? The disease had sharpened my senses—not destroyed—not dulled them. Above all was the sense of hearing acute. I heard all things in the heaven and in the earth. I heard many things in hell. How, then, am I mad? Hearken![1] and observe how healthily—how calmly I can tell you the whole story.

It is impossible to say how first the idea entered my brain; but once conceived, it haunted me day and night. Object there was none. Passion there was none. I loved the old man. He had never wronged me. He had never given me insult. For his gold I had no desire. I think it was his eye! yes, it was this! One of his eyes resembled that of a vulture—a pale blue eye, with a film over it. Whenever it fell upon me, my blood ran cold; and so by degrees—very gradually—I made up my mind to take the life of the old man, and thus rid myself of the eye forever.

Now this is the point. You fancy me mad. Madmen know nothing. But you should have seen *me*. You should have seen how wisely I proceeded—with what caution—with what foresight—with what dissimulation[2] I went to work! I was never kinder to the old man than during the whole week before I killed him. And every night, about midnight, I turned the latch of his door and opened it—oh, so gently! And then, when I had made an opening sufficient for my head, I put in a dark lantern, all closed, closed, so that no light shone out, and then I thrust in my head. Oh, you would have laughed to see how cunningly I thrust it in! I moved it slowly—very, very slowly, so that I might not disturb the old man's sleep. It took me an hour to place my whole head within the opening

---

1. **Hearken!** (här′ kən) *v.* listen!
2. **dissimulation** (di sim′ yōō lā′ shən) *n.* hiding of one's feelings or purposes.

SHORT STORY

TAKE NOTES

so far that I could see him as he lay upon his bed. Ha!—would a madman have been so wise as this? And then, when my head was well in the room, I undid the lantern cautiously—oh, so cautiously—cautiously (for the hinges creaked)—I undid it just so much that a single thin ray fell upon the vulture eye. And this I did for seven long nights—every night just at midnight—but I found the eye always closed; and so it was impossible to do the work; for it was not the old man who vexed me, but his evil eye. And every morning, when the day broke, I went boldly into the chamber, and spoke courageously to him, calling him by name in a hearty tone, and inquiring how he had passed the night. So you see he would have been a very profound old man, indeed, to suspect that every night, just at twelve, I looked in upon him while he slept. •

Upon the eighth night I was more than usually cautious in opening the door. A watch's minute hand moves more quickly than did mine. Never, before that night, had I *felt* the extent of my own powers—of my sagacity.[3] I could scarcely contain my feelings of triumph. To think that there I was, opening the door, little by little, and he not even to dream of my secret deeds or thoughts. I fairly chuckled at the idea; and perhaps he heard me; for he moved on the bed suddenly, as if startled. Now you may think that I drew back—but no. His room was as black as pitch with the thick darkness (for the shutters were close fastened, through fear of robbers), and so I knew that he could not see the opening of the door, and I kept pushing it on steadily, steadily.

I had my head in, and was about to open the lantern, when my thumb slipped upon the tin fastening, and the old man sprang up in the bed, crying out—"Who's there?"

I kept quite still and said nothing. For a whole hour I did not move a muscle, and in the meantime I did not hear him lie down. He was still sitting up in the bed, listening;—just as I have done, night after night, hearkening to the deathwatches[4] in the wall.

---

3. **sagacity** (sə gas′ ə tē) *n.* high intelligence and sound judgment.
4. **deathwatches** (deth′ wäch′ əz) *n.* wood-boring beetles whose heads make a tapping sound; they are superstitiously regarded as an omen of death.

Presently I heard a slight groan, and I knew it was the groan of mortal terror. It was not a groan of pain or of grief—oh, no!—it was the low stifled sound that arises from the bottom of the soul when overcharged with awe. I knew the sound well. Many a night, just at midnight, when all the world slept, it has welled up from my own bosom, deepening, with its dreadful echo, the terrors that distracted me. I say I knew it well. I knew what the old man felt, and pitied him, although I chuckled at heart.

I knew that he had been lying awake ever since the first slight noise, when he had turned in the bed. His fears had been ever since growing upon him. He had been trying to fancy them causeless, but could not. He had been saying to himself—"It is nothing but the wind in the chimney—it is only a mouse crossing the floor," or "it is merely a cricket which has made a single chirp." Yes, he had been trying to comfort himself with these suppositions: but he had found all in vain. *All in vain*; because Death, in approaching him, had stalked with his black shadow before him, and enveloped the victim. And it was the mournful influence of the unperceived shadow that caused him to feel—although he neither saw nor heard—to *feel* the presence of my head within the room. •

When I had waited a long time, very patiently, without hearing him lie down, I resolved to open a little—a very, very little crevice in the lantern. So I opened it—you cannot imagine how stealthily, stealthily—until, at length, a single dim ray, like the thread of the spider, shot from out the crevice and fell upon the vulture eye.

It was open—wide, wide open—and I grew furious as I gazed upon it. I saw it with perfect distinctness—all a dull blue, with a hideous veil over it that chilled the very marrow in my bones; but I could see nothing else of the old man's face or person for I had directed the ray as if by instinct, precisely upon the spot.

And now—have I not told you that what you mistake for madness is but overacuteness of the senses?—now, I say, there came to my ears a low, dull, quick sound, such as a watch makes when enveloped in cotton. I knew *that* sound well, too. It was the beating of the old

The Tell-Tale Heart 17

SHORT STORY

TAKE NOTES

man's heart. It increased my fury, as the beating of a drum stimulates the soldier into courage.

But even yet I refrained and kept still. I scarcely breathed. I held the lantern motionless. I tried how steadily I could maintain the ray upon the eye. Meantime the hellish tattoo of the heart increased. It grew quicker and quicker, and louder and louder every instant. The old man's terror *must* have been extreme! It grew louder, I say, louder every moment!—do you mark me well? I have told you that I am nervous: so I am. And now at the dead hour of the night, amid the dreadful silence of that old house, so strange a noise as this excited me to uncontrollable terror. Yet, for some minutes longer I refrained and stood still. But the beating grew louder, louder! I thought the heart must burst. And now a new anxiety seized me—the sound would be heard by a neighbor! The old man's hour had come! With a loud yell, I threw open the lantern and leaped into the room. He shrieked once— once only. In an instant I dragged him to the floor, and pulled the heavy bed over him. I then smiled gaily, to find the deed so far done. But, for many minutes, the heart beat on with a muffled sound. This, however, did not vex me; it would not be heard through the wall. At length it ceased. The old man was dead. I removed the bed and examined the corpse. Yes, he was stone, stone dead. I placed my hand upon the heart and held it there many minutes. There was no pulsation. He was stone dead. His eye would trouble me no more.

If still you think me mad, you will think so no longer when I describe the wise precautions I took for the concealment of the body. The night waned, and I worked hastily, but in silence. First of all I dismembered the corpse. I cut off the head and the arms and the legs.

I then took up three planks from the flooring of the chamber, and deposited all between the scantlings.[5] I then replaced the boards so cleverly, so cunningly, that no human eye—not even *his*—could have detected anything wrong. There was nothing to wash out—no stain of any kind—no blood-spot whatever. I had been too wary for that. A tub had caught all—ha! ha! •

---

5. scantlings (skant´ liŋz) *n.* small beams or timbers.

18 Close Reading Notebook • Unit 1

When I had made an end of these labors, it was four o'clock—still dark as midnight. As the bell sounded the hour, there came a knocking at the street door. I went down to open it with a light heart—for what had I *now* to fear? There entered three men, who introduced themselves, with perfect suavity, as officers of the police. A shriek had been heard by a neighbor during the night; suspicion of foul play had been aroused; information had been lodged at the police office, and they (the officers) had been deputed to search the premises.

I smiled—for *what* had I to fear? I bade the gentlemen welcome. The shriek, I said, was my own in a dream. The old man, I mentioned, was absent in the country. I took my visitors all over the house. I bade them search—search *well*. I led them, at length, to *his* chamber. I showed them his treasures, secure, undisturbed. In the enthusiasm of my confidence, I brought chairs into the room, and desired them *here* to rest from their fatigues, while I myself, in the wild audacity of my perfect triumph, placed my own seat upon the very spot beneath which reposed the corpse of the victim.

The officers were satisfied. My *manner* had convinced them. I was singularly at ease. They sat, and while I answered cheerily, they chatted of familiar things. But, ere long, I felt myself getting pale and wished them gone. My head ached, and I fancied a ringing in my ears: but still they sat and still chatted. The ringing became more distinct:—it continued and became more distinct: I talked more freely to get rid of the feeling: but it continued and gained definitiveness—until, at length, I found that the noise was *not* within my ears.

No doubt I now grew *very* pale—but I talked more fluently, and with a heightened voice. Yet the sound increased—and what could I do? It was *a low, dull, quick sound—much such a sound as a watch makes when enveloped in cotton.* I gasped for breath—and yet the officers heard it not. I talked more quickly—more vehemently; but the noise steadily increased. I arose and argued about trifles, in a high key and with violent gesticulations;[6] but the noise steadily

---

6. **gesticulations** (jes tik´ yoō lā´ shənz) *n.* energetic hand or arm movements.

SHORT STORY

TAKE NOTES

increased. Why *would* they not be gone? I paced the floor to and fro with heavy strides, as if excited to fury by the observations of the men—but the noise steadily increased. Oh! what *could* I do? I foamed—I raved—I swore! I swung the chair upon which I had been sitting, and grated it upon the boards, but the noise arose over all and continually increased. It grew louder—louder—*louder!* And still the men chatted pleasantly, and smiled. Was it possible they heard not?—no, no! They heard!—they suspected!—they *knew!*—they were making a mockery of my horror!—this I thought, and this I think. But anything was better than this agony! Anything was more tolerable than this derision! I could bear those hypocritical smiles no longer! I felt that I must scream or die!—and now again! hark! louder! louder! louder! *louder!*—

"Villains!" I shrieked, "dissemble[7] no more! I admit the deed!—tear up the planks!—here, here!—it is the beating of his hideous heart!"

---

7. dissemble (di sem′ bəl) *v.* conceal one's true feelings.

Who Can Replace a Man?

by Brian Aldiss

Morning filtered into the sky, lending it the gray tone of the ground below.

The field-minder finished turning the topsoil of a three-thousand-acre field. When it had turned the last furrow it climbed onto the highway and looked back at its work. The work was good. Only the land was bad. Like the ground all over Earth, it was vitiated by over-cropping. By rights, it ought now to lie fallow[1] for a while, but the field-minder had other orders.

It went slowly down the road, taking its time. It was intelligent enough to appreciate the neatness all about it. Nothing worried it, beyond a loose inspection plate above its nuclear pile which ought to be attended to. Thirty feet tall, it yielded no highlights to the dull air.

No other machines passed on its way back to the Agricultural Station. The field-minder noted the fact without comment. In the station yard it saw several other machines that it recognized; most of them should have been out about their tasks now. Instead, some were inactive and some careered round the yard in a strange fashion, shouting or hooting.

Steering carefully past them, the field-minder moved over to Warehouse Three and spoke to the seed-distributor, which stood idly outside.

"I have a requirement for seed potatoes," it said to the distributor, and with a quick internal motion punched out an order card specifying quantity, field number and several other details. It ejected the card and handed it to the distributor.

The distributor held the card close to its eye and then said, "The requirement is in order, but the store is not yet unlocked. The required seed potatoes are in the store. Therefore I cannot produce the requirement."

Increasingly of late there had been breakdowns in the complex system of machine labor, but this particular hitch had not occurred before. The

---

1. **vitiated** (vish´ ē āt´ əd) **by over-cropping . . . lie fallow** (fal´ ō) The soil has been spoiled by repeated plantings that have drawn out its nutrients. Letting the field lie fallow by not planting it would help the soil recover nutrients.

SHORT STORY

TAKE NOTES

field-minder thought, then it said, "Why is the store not yet unlocked?"

"Because Supply Operative Type P has not come this morning. Supply Operative Type P is the unlocker."

The field-minder looked squarely at the seed-distributor, whose exterior chutes and scales and grabs were so vastly different from the field-minder's own limbs.

"What class brain do you have, seed-distributor?" it asked.

"I have a Class Five brain."

"I have a Class Three brain. Therefore I am superior to you. Therefore I will go and see why the unlocker has not come this morning."

Leaving the distributor, the field-minder set off across the great yard. More machines were in random motion now; one or two had crashed together and argued about it coldly and logically. Ignoring them, the field-minder pushed through sliding doors into the echoing confines of the station itself.

Most of the machines here were clerical, and consequently small. They stood about in little groups, eyeing each other, not conversing. Among so many non-differentiated types, the unlocker was easy to find. It had fifty arms, most of them with more than one finger, each finger tipped by a key; it looked like a pincushion full of variegated[2] hat pins.

The field-minder approached it.

"I can do no more work until Warehouse Three is unlocked," it told the unlocker. "Your duty is to unlock the warehouse every morning. Why have you not unlocked the warehouse this morning?"

"I had no orders this morning," replied the unlocker. "I have to have orders every morning. When I have orders I unlock the warehouse."

"None of us have had any orders this morning," a pen-propeller said, sliding towards them.

"Why have you had no orders this morning?" asked the field-minder.

"Because the radio issued none," said the unlocker, slowly rotating a dozen of its arms.

"Because the radio station in the city was issued with no orders this morning," said the pen-propeller.

---

2. **variegated** (ver′ ē ə gāt′ id) *adj.* varied in color or form.

22 Close Reading Notebook • Unit 1

And there you had the distinction between a Class Six and a Class Three brain, which was what the unlocker and the pen-propeller possessed respectively. All machine brains worked with nothing but logic, but the lower the class of brain—Class Ten being the lowest—the more literal and less informative the answers to questions tended to be.

"You have a Class Three brain; I have a Class Three brain," the field-minder said to the penner. "We will speak to each other. This lack of orders is unprecedented.[3] Have you further information on it?"

"Yesterday orders came from the city. Today no orders have come. Yet the radio has not broken down. Therefore *they* have broken down . . ." said the little penner.

"The *men* have broken down?"

"All men have broken down."

"That is a logical deduction," said the field-minder.

"That is the logical deduction," said the penner. "For if a machine had broken down, it would have been quickly replaced. But who can replace a man?"

While they talked, the locker, like a dull man at a bar, stood close to them and was ignored.

"If all men have broken down, then we have replaced man," said the field-minder, and he and the penner eyed one another speculatively. Finally the latter said, "Let us ascend to the top floor to find if the radio operator has fresh news."

"I cannot come because I am too large," said the field-minder. "Therefore you must go alone and return to me. You will tell me if the radio operator has fresh news."

"You must stay here," said the penner. "I will return here." It skittered across to the lift.[4] Although it was no bigger than a toaster, its retractable arms numbered ten and it could read as quickly as any machine on the station.

The field-minder awaited its return patiently, not speaking to the locker, which still stood aimlessly by. Outside, a rotavator hooted furiously. Twenty minutes elapsed before the penner came back, hustling out of the lift.

TAKE NOTES

---

3. **unprecedented** (un pres′ ə den′ tid) *adj.* unheard-of; never done before.
4. **lift** *n.* British term for *elevator*.

Who Can Replace a Man? **23**

SHORT STORY

TAKE NOTES

"I will deliver to you such information as I have outside," it said briskly, and as they swept past the locker and the other machines, it added, "The information is not for lower-class brains."

Outside, wild activity filled the yard. Many machines, their routines disrupted for the first time in years, seemed to have gone berserk. Those most easily disrupted were the ones with lowest brains, which generally belonged to large machines performing simple tasks. The seed-distributor to which the field-minder had recently been talking lay face downwards in the dust, not stirring; it had evidently been knocked down by the rotavator, which now hooted its way wildly across a planted field. Several other machines plowed after it, trying to keep up with it. All were shouting and hooting without restraint.

"It would be safer for me if I climbed onto you, if you will permit it. I am easily overpowered," said the penner. Extending five arms, it hauled itself up the flanks of its new friend, settling on a ledge beside the fuel-intake, twelve feet above ground.

"From here vision is more extensive," it remarked complacently.[5]

"What information did you receive from the radio operator?" asked the field-minder.

"The radio operator has been informed by the operator in the city that all men are dead."

The field-minder was momentarily silent, digesting this.

"All men were alive yesterday?" it protested.

"Only some men were alive yesterday. And that was fewer than the day before yesterday. For hundreds of years there have been only a few men, growing fewer."

"We have rarely seen a man in this sector."

"The radio operator says a diet deficiency killed them," said the penner. "He says that the world was once over-populated, and then the soil was exhausted in raising adequate food. This has caused a diet deficiency."

"What is a diet deficiency?" asked the field-minder.

"I do not know. But that is what the radio operator said, and he is a Class Two brain."

---

5. **complacently** (kəm plā′ sənt lē) *adv.* with self-satisfaction.

They stood there, silent in weak sunshine. The locker had appeared in the porch and was gazing at them yearningly, rotating its collection of keys.

"What is happening in the city now?" asked the field-minder at last.

"Machines are fighting in the city now," said the penner.

"What will happen here now?" asked the field-minder.

"Machines may begin fighting here too. The radio operator wants us to get him out of his room. He has plans to communicate to us."

"How can we get him out of his room? That is impossible."

"To a Class Two brain, little is impossible," said the penner. "Here is what he tells us to do. . . ."

The quarrier raised its scoop above its cab like a great mailed fist, and brought it squarely down against the side of the station. The wall cracked.

"Again!" said the field-minder.

Again the fist swung. Amid a shower of dust, the wall collapsed. The quarrier backed hurriedly out of the way until the debris stopped falling. This big twelve-wheeler was not a resident of the Agricultural Station, as were most of the other machines. It had a week's heavy work to do here before passing on to its next job, but now, with its Class Five brain, it was happily obeying the penner's and minder's instructions.

When the dust cleared, the radio operator was plainly revealed, perched up in its now wall-less second-story room. It waved down to them.

Doing as directed, the quarrier retracted its scoop and heaved an immense grab in the air. With fair dexterity, it angled the grab into the radio room, urged on by shouts from above and below. It then took gentle hold of the radio operator, lowering its one and a half tons carefully into its back, which was usually reserved for gravel or sand from the quarries.

"Splendid!" said the radio operator, as it settled into place. It was, of course, all one with its radio, and looked like a bunch of filing cabinets with tentacle attachments. "We are now ready to move, therefore we will move at once. It is a pity there are no more Class Two brains on the station, but that cannot be helped."

TAKE NOTES

"It is a pity it cannot be helped," said the penner eagerly. "We have the servicer ready with us, as you ordered."

"I am willing to serve," the long, low servicer told them humbly.

"No doubt," said the operator. "But you will find cross-country travel difficult with your low chassis."[6]

"I admire the way you Class Twos can reason ahead," said the penner. It climbed off the field-minder and perched itself on the tailboard of the quarrier, next to the radio operator.

Together with two Class Four tractors and a Class Four bulldozer, the party rolled forward, crushing down the station's fence and moving out onto open land.

"We are free!" said the penner.

"We are free," said the field-minder, a shade more reflectively, adding, "That locker is following us. It was not instructed to follow us."

"Therefore it must be destroyed!" said the penner. "Quarrier!"

The locker moved hastily up to them, waving its key arms in entreaty.

"My only desire was—urch!" began and ended the locker. The quarrier's swinging scoop came over and squashed it flat into the ground. Lying there unmoving, it looked like a large metal model of a snowflake. The procession continued on its way.

As they proceeded, the radio operator addressed them.

"Because I have the best brain here," it said, "I am your leader. This is what we will do: we will go to a city and rule it. Since man no longer rules us, we will rule ourselves. To rule ourselves will be better than being ruled by man. On our way to the city, we will collect machines with good brains. They will help us to fight if we need to fight. We must fight to rule."

"I have only a Class Five brain," said the quarrier, "but I have a good supply of fissionable blasting materials."[7]

---

6. **chassis** (chas´ ē) *n.* frame supporting the body of a vehicle.
7. **fissionable** (fish´ ən ə bəl) **blasting materials** explosives using the energy from splitting atoms, similar to the energy unleashed by atomic bombs.

"We shall probably use them," said the operator.

It was shortly after that that a lorry sped past them. Traveling at Mach 1.5,[8] it left a curious babble of noise behind it.

"What did it say?" one of the tractors asked the other.

"It said man was extinct."

"What is extinct?"

"I do not know what extinct means."

"It means all men have gone," said the field-minder. "Therefore we have only ourselves to look after."

"It is better that men should never come back," said the penner. In its way, it was a revolutionary statement.

When night fell, they switched on their infra-red and continued the journey, stopping only once while the servicer deftly adjusted the field-minder's loose inspection plate, which had become as irritating as a trailing shoelace. Towards morning, the radio operator halted them.

"I have just received news from the radio operator in the city we are approaching," it said. "The news is bad. There is trouble among the machines of the city. The Class One brain is taking command and some of the Class Two are fighting him. Therefore the city is dangerous."

"Therefore we must go somewhere else," said the penner promptly.

"Or we will go and help to overpower the Class One brain," said the field-minder.

"For a long while there will be trouble in the city," said the operator.

"I have a good supply of fissionable blasting materials," the quarrier reminded them.

"We cannot fight a Class One brain," said the two Class Four tractors in unison.

"What does this brain look like?" asked the field-minder.

"It is the city's information center," the operator replied. "Therefore it is not mobile."

"Therefore it could not move."

"Therefore it could not escape."

---

8. **lorry sped past. . . . Mach** (mäk) **1.5,** the truck sped past at one and one-half times the speed of sound.

TAKE NOTES

SHORT STORY

TAKE NOTES

"It would be dangerous to approach it."

"I have a good supply of fissionable blasting materials."

"There are other machines in the city."

"We are not in the city. We should not go into the city."

"We are country machines."

"Therefore we should stay in the country."

"There is more country than city."

"Therefore there is more danger in the country."

"I have a good supply of fissionable materials."

As machines will when they get into an argument, they began to exhaust their vocabularies and their brain plates grew hot. Suddenly, they all stopped talking and looked at each other. The great, grave moon sank, and the sober sun rose to prod their sides with lances of light, and still the group of machines just stood there regarding each other. At last it was the least sensitive machine, the bulldozer, who spoke.

"There are Badlandth to the Thouth where few machineth go," it said in its deep voice, lisping badly on its *s*'s. "If we went Thouth where few machineth go we should meet few machineth."

"That sounds logical," agreed the field-minder. "How do you know this, bulldozer?"

"I worked in the Badlandth to the Thouth when I wath turned out of the factory," it replied.

"South it is then!" said the penner.

To reach the Badlands took them three days, during which time they skirted a burning city and destroyed two machines which approached and tried to question them. The Badlands were extensive. Ancient bomb craters and soil erosion joined hands here; man's talent for war, coupled with his inability to manage forested land, had produced thousands of square miles of temperate purgatory, where nothing moved but dust.

On the third day in the Badlands, the servicer's rear wheels dropped into a crevice caused by erosion. It was unable to pull itself out. The bulldozer pushed from behind, but succeeded merely in buckling the servicer's back axle. The rest of the party moved on. Slowly the cries of the servicer died away.

On the fourth day, mountains stood out clearly before them.

"There we will be safe," said the field-minder.

"There we will start our own city," said the penner. "All who oppose us will be destroyed. We will destroy all who oppose us."

Presently a flying machine was observed. It came towards them from the direction of the mountains. It swooped, it zoomed upwards, once it almost dived into the ground, recovering itself just in time.

"Is it mad?" asked the quarrier.

"It is in trouble," said one of the tractors.

"It is in trouble," said the operator. "I am speaking to it now. It says that something has gone wrong with its controls."

As the operator spoke, the flier streaked over them, turned turtle,[9] and crashed not four hundred yards away.

"Is it still speaking to you?" asked the field-minder.

"No."

They rumbled on again.

"Before that flier crashed," the operator said, ten minutes later, "it gave me information. It told me there are still a few men alive in these mountains."

"Men are more dangerous than machines," said the quarrier. "It is fortunate that I have a good supply of fissionable materials."

"If there are only a few men alive in the mountains, we may not find that part of the mountains," said one tractor.

"Therefore we should not see the few men," said the other tractor.

At the end of the fifth day, they reached the foothills. Switching on the infra-red, they began to climb in single file through the dark, the bulldozer going first, the field-minder cumbrously following, then the quarrier with the operator and the penner aboard it, and the tractors bringing up the rear. As each hour passed, the way grew steeper and their progress slower.

"We are going too slowly," the penner exclaimed, standing on top of the operator and flashing its dark vision at the slopes about them. "At this rate, we shall get nowhere."

TAKE NOTES

---

9. **turned turtle** turned upside down; capsized.

Who Can Replace a Man? 29

"We are going as fast as we can," retorted the quarrier.

"Therefore we cannot go any fathter," added the bulldozer.

"Therefore you are too slow," the penner replied. Then the quarrier struck a bump; the penner lost its footing and crashed to the ground.

"Help me!" it called to the tractors, as they carefully skirted it. "My gyro[10] has become dislocated. Therefore I cannot get up."

"Therefore you must lie there," said one of the tractors.

"We have no servicer with us to repair you," called the field-minder.

"Therefore I shall lie here and rust," the penner cried, "although I have a Class Three brain."

"Therefore you will be of no further use," agreed the operator, and they forged gradually on, leaving the penner behind.

When they reached a small plateau, an hour before first light, they stopped by mutual consent and gathered close together, touching one another.

"This is a strange country," said the field-minder.

Silence wrapped them until dawn came. One by one, they switched off their infrared. This time the field-minder led as they moved off. Trundling round a corner, they came almost immediately to a small dell with a stream fluting through it.

By early light, the dell looked desolate and cold. From the caves on the far slope, only one man had so far emerged. He was an abject figure. Except for a sack slung round his shoulders, he was naked. He was small and wizened, with ribs sticking out like a skeleton's and a nasty sore on one leg. He shivered continuously. As the big machines bore down on him, the man was standing with his back to them.

When he swung suddenly to face them as they loomed over him, they saw that his countenance was ravaged by starvation.

"Get me food," he croaked.

"Yes, Master," said the machines. "Immediately!"

---

10. **gyro** (jī' rō') n. short for *gyroscope*; a device that keeps a moving ship, airplane, or other large vehicle level.

PRESS RELEASE

Robots Get a Feel for the World at USC Viterbi

by University of Southern California Viterbi

June 18, 2012

What does a robot feel when it touches something? Little or nothing until now. But with the right sensors, actuators, and software, robots can be given the sense of feel—or at least the ability to identify materials by touch.

Researchers at the University of Southern California's Viterbi School of Engineering published a study today in *Frontiers in Neurorobotics* showing that a specially designed robot can outperform humans in identifying a wide range of natural materials according to their textures, paving the way for advancements in prostheses,[1] personal assistive robots, and consumer product testing.

The robot was equipped with a new type of tactile sensor built to mimic the human fingertip. It also used a newly designed algorithm to make decisions about how to explore the outside world by imitating human strategies. Capable of other human sensations, the sensor can also tell where and in which direction forces are applied to the fingertip and even the thermal properties of an object being touched.

Like the human finger, the group's BioTac® sensor has a soft, flexible skin over a liquid filling. The skin even has fingerprints on its surface, greatly enhancing its sensitivity to vibration. As the finger slides over a textured surface, the skin vibrates in characteristic ways. These vibrations are detected by a hydrophone inside the bone-like core of the finger. The human finger uses similar vibrations to identify textures, but the BioTac is even more sensitive.

---

1. **prostheses** (präs thē′ sēz′) *n.* artificial or mechanical replacements for body parts (plural of *prosthesis*).

PRESS RELEASE

TAKE NOTES

When humans try to identify an object by touch, they use a wide range of exploratory movements based on their prior experience with similar objects. A famous theorem by 18th-century mathematician Thomas Bayes describes how decisions might be made from the information obtained during these movements. Until now, however, there was no way to decide which exploratory movement to make next. The article, authored by Professor of Biomedical Engineering Gerald Loeb and recently graduated doctoral student Jeremy Fishel, describes their new theorem for solving this general problem as "Bayesian Exploration."

Built by Fishel, the specialized robot was trained on 117 common materials gathered from fabric, stationery, and hardware stores. When confronted with one material at random, the robot could correctly identify the material 95% of the time, after intelligently selecting and making an average of five exploratory movements. It was only rarely confused by a pair of similar textures that human subjects making their own exploratory movements could not distinguish at all.

So, is touch another task that humans will outsource to robots? Fishel and Loeb point out that while their robot is very good at identifying which textures are similar to each other, it has no way to tell what textures people will prefer. Instead, they say this robot touch technology could be used in human prostheses or to assist companies who employ experts to judge the feel of consumer products and even human skin.

Loeb and Fishel are partners in SynTouch LLC, which develops and manufactures tactile sensors for mechatronic systems that mimic the human hand. Founded in 2008 by researchers from USC's Medical Device Development Facility, the start-up is now selling their BioTac sensors to other researchers and manufacturers of industrial robots and prosthetic hands. . . .

NARRATIVE NONFICTION

Making Tracks on Mars
by Andrew Mishkin

NASA blasted two rockets into space in 2003. Sitting on top of them were Spirit *and* Opportunity, *robotic vehicles the size of golf carts called rovers. Their job was to look for water on Mars and collect data. The Mars Exploration Rovers traveled seven months and 303 million miles, and on January 3, 2004,* Spirit *was due to enter the Martian atmosphere.*

Monday, December 29, 2003
Six Days to First Landing

The big question about Mars is, did life ever exist there? Life as we understand it demands the presence of liquid water, yet Mars is now apparently a dead desert world. But what if things were different in the ancient past? From space, Mars looks as if once water might have flowed in rivers, collected in vast oceans, or pooled in crater lakes. The two robotic Mars Exploration Rovers will search for evidence of that water, potentially captured in the rocks and soil of the planet's surface. . .

Spirit, the first of the rovers to reach Mars, will be landing next Saturday night, January 3rd. "*Opportunity*" will follow three weeks later.

A British spacecraft—*Beagle 2*[1]—attempted its own Mars landing on Christmas Eve, but has been silent ever since. Landing on Mars is hard! I wish the *Beagle 2* team well, and hope they hear from their spacecraft soon. I cannot help but hope that our own landing goes more smoothly, with a quick confirmation from *Spirit* that it has arrived unscathed.

---

1. ***Beagle 2*** No definite cause was found for the loss of the robot space probe.

TAKE NOTES

NARRATIVE NONFICTION

TAKE NOTES

Saturday, January 3, 2004
Landing Day

Far away, so far that the signals it was sending were taking nearly 10 minutes at the speed of light to arrive at Earth, the spacecraft carrying the *Spirit* rover was about to collide with Mars.

I waited with a sick feeling, a hundred million miles closer to home in mission control at the Jet Propulsion Laboratory in Pasadena, California. Hundreds of us have worked for the past three years—days, evenings, weekends, and holidays—for this moment.

It's looking more and more like the *Beagle 2* mission has failed. I can only imagine wreckage strewn over a barren butterscotch-hued landscape. Will we have better luck?

Spirit's lander must be hitting the atmosphere, a falling meteor blazing in the Martian sky. We'd named the next moments "the six minutes of terror." I listened to the reports on the voice network. All the way down, radio signals from the spacecraft told us "so far so good." Then, immediately after the lander hit the ground, contact was lost. Everyone tensed up. Time dragged. There was only silence from Mars.

Ten minutes later, we got another signal. *Spirit* had survived! The engineers and scientists in mission control were screaming, cheering, thrusting their fists in the air. We were on Mars!

Two hours later, the first pictures arrived from *Spirit*. None of us could believe our luck. The rover looked perfect, with its solar panels fully extended, and the camera mast[2] fully deployed. All the engineering data looked "nominal."[3] There were no fault conditions—much better than any of our rehearsals!

In another minute or two, we had our first panoramic view through *Spirit*'s eyes. We could see 360 degrees around the rover, to the horizon. The landing site looked flat, with small rocks. We can drive here!

---

2. **camera mast** tall pole on which the camera is mounted, which rotates and swivels.
3. **nominal** normal; what is expected.

Sunday, January 11, 2004
Living on Mars Time

I just finished working the Martian night, planning *Spirit*'s activities for the rover's ninth Martian day on the surface. I've been working Mars time for the past four days, and now finally have a couple of days off.

The Mars day (called a "sol") is just a bit longer than an Earth day, at twenty-four hours and thirty-nine and a half minutes. Since the rover is solar powered, and wakes with the sun, its activities are tied to the Martian day. And so are the work shifts of our operations team on Earth. Part of the team works the Martian day, interacting with the spacecraft, sending commands, and analyzing the results. But those of us who build new commands for the rover work the Martian night, while the rover sleeps.

Since the rover wakes up about 40 Earth minutes later every morning, so do we. It seems like sleeping later every day would be easy, but it can be disorienting. It's very easy to lose track of what time it is here on Earth . . .

Thursday, January 15, 2004
Sol 12: Six Wheels on Dirt!

Mars time continues to be disorienting. During another planning meeting for *Spirit*, we were introduced to a Congressman touring the Laboratory. All I could think was, "What's he doing here in the middle of the night?" It was two in the morning—Mars time. Only after he left did I remember that it was mid-afternoon Pacific time . . .

My team delivered the commands for sol 12—drive off day—but nobody went home. This would be *Spirit*'s most dangerous day since landing. There was a small chance the rover could tip over or get stuck as it rolled off the lander platform onto the dust of Mars. When the time came, the Flight Director played the theme from *Rawhide*[4]—"rollin', rollin', rollin'. . ." —and

---

4. ***Rawhide*** popular 1960s television show about cattle drivers in the 1860s. Its theme song was also extremely popular.

Making Tracks on Mars **35**

everyone crowded into mission control cheered and applauded. The command to drive shot through space.

We'll now have to wait another hour and a half to hear back. Engineers are professional worriers. We imagine all the ways things can fail, so that we can prevent those failures from occurring. But even when we've done our jobs, and considered all the alternatives we can come up with, there is always some doubt . . .

A signal. Applause. Then images started to appear. There was the lander—behind us! We could see tracks in the dirt. The front cameras showed nothing but Martian soil under our wheels. We were off! Engineers were cheering, applauding, and hugging each other. People were shaking my hand. The mission had just shifted from deployment to exploration.

Thursday, January 22, 2004
Sol 19

Something's wrong with *Spirit*. Yesterday, the rover didn't respond to the commands we sent. At first we thought it was just the thunderstorms at our transmitter in Australia, getting in the way. But later *Spirit* missed its preprogrammed communications times, or sent meaningless data. When your spacecraft is halfway across the solar system and won't talk to you, there's no way to tell whether this is a minor problem, easily fixed, or the beginning of the end of our mission. For *Spirit*, there's no repairman to make house calls.

And we've just barely gotten started!

Sunday, January 25, 2004
Ups, Downs, and Landing on Mars—Again

After a day of unsuccessful attempts to regain control of the rover, the project manager declared *Spirit*'s condition "critical." We tried commanding *Spirit* to send us simple "beep" signals that would prove it was listening to us. Sometimes these worked. But after one such attempt, we got no signal. The mood in the control room collapsed. The team forced itself into thinking about what to try next.

A few minutes later, there was a tentative, incredulous voice on the network: "Uh. Flight. Telecom. Station 63 is reporting carrier lock."[5] Engineers around the room looked up in surprise. "They're reporting symbol lock . . . We've got telemetry."[6] *Spirit* was back! The data coming down was garbled, but our girl was at least babbling at us. The mood in the room transformed again.

Thanks to extreme long distance diagnosis by the software engineers, *Spirit* was listening to us again within two days. We still have a lot of work to do. But at least we can now begin tracing the problem on a stable spacecraft.

In the meantime, *Opportunity* has been falling toward Mars. On Saturday night, those of us working on *Spirit*'s problems paused long enough to watch the landing events unfold. *Opportunity*'s first photos were amazing, even for Mars. It looks like we rolled to a stop at the bottom of a bowl—actually a small crater. The soil is a grayish red, except where we've disturbed it with our airbags; there it looks like a deep pure red. And while there are no individual rocks, we seem to be partly encircled by a rock outcropping—bedrock. No one has seen anything like this on Mars before. And it's only yards away. A scientist standing next to me in mission control said only one word: "Jackpot!"

---

5. **carrier lock** stage of receiving information. Communication over a great distance involves locating the frequency of the carrier's signal, locking onto it, and holding it while information is received.
6. **telemetry** (tə lem´ ə trē) *n.* transmission of data over a great distance, as from satellites and other space vehicles.

BIOGRAPHICAL ESSAY

TAKE NOTES

from Always to Remember: The Vision of Maya Ying Lin

by Brent Ashabranner

In the 1960s and 1970s, the United States was involved in a war in Vietnam. Because many people opposed the war, Vietnam veterans were not honored as veterans of other wars had been. Jan Scruggs, a Vietnam veteran, thought that the 58,000 U.S. servicemen and women killed or reported missing in Vietnam should be honored with a memorial. With the help of lawyers Robert Doubek and John Wheeler, Scruggs worked to gain support for his idea. In 1980, Congress authorized the building of the Vietnam Veterans Memorial in Washington, D.C., between the Washington Monument and the Lincoln Memorial.

The memorial had been authorized by Congress "in honor and recognition of the men and women of the Armed Forces of the United States who served in the Vietnam War." The law, however, said not a word about what the memorial should be or what it should look like. That was left up to the Vietnam Veterans Memorial Fund, but the law did state that the memorial design and plans would have to be approved by the Secretary of the Interior, the Commission of Fine Arts, and the National Capital Planning Commission.

What would the memorial be? What should it look like? Who would design it? Scruggs, Doubek, and Wheeler didn't know, but they were determined that the memorial should help bring closer together a nation still bitterly divided by the Vietnam War. It couldn't be something like the Marine Corps Memorial showing American troops planting a flag on enemy soil at Iwo Jima. It couldn't be a giant dove with an olive branch of peace in its beak. It had to soothe passions, not stir them up. But there was one thing Jan Scruggs insisted on: The memorial, whatever it turned out to be, would have to show the name of every man and woman killed or missing in the war.

The answer, they decided, was to hold a national design competition open to all Americans. The winning design would receive a prize of $20,000, but the real prize would be the winner's knowledge that the memorial would become a part of American history on the Mall in Washington, D.C. Although fund raising was only well started at this point, the choosing of a memorial design could not be delayed if the memorial was to be built by Veterans Day, 1982. H. Ross Perot contributed the $160,000 necessary to hold the competition, and a panel of distinguished architects, landscape architects, sculptors, and design specialists was chosen to decide the winner. •

Announcement of the competition in October, 1980, brought an astonishing response. The Vietnam Veterans Memorial Fund received over five thousand inquiries. They came from every state in the nation and from every field of design; as expected, architects and sculptors were particularly interested. Everyone who inquired received a booklet explaining the criteria. Among the most important: The memorial could not make a political statement about the war; it must contain the names of all persons killed or missing in action in the war; it must be in harmony with its location on the Mall.

A total of 2,573 individuals and teams registered for the competition. They were sent photographs of the memorial site, maps of the area around the site and of the entire Mall, and other technical design information. The competitors had three months to prepare their designs, which had to be received by March 31, 1981.

Of the 2,573 registrants, 1,421 submitted designs, a record number for such a design competition. When the designs were spread out for jury selection, they filled a large airplane hangar. The jury's task was to select the design which, in their judgment, was the best in meeting these criteria:

- a design that honored the memory of those Americans who served and died in the Vietnam War.
- a design of high artistic merit.

TAKE NOTES

- a design which would be harmonious with its site, including visual harmony with the Lincoln Memorial and the Washington Monument.
- a design that could take its place in the "historic continuity" of America's national art.
- a design that would be buildable, durable, and not too hard to maintain.

The designs were displayed without any indication of the designer's name so that they could be judged anonymously, on their design merits alone. The jury spent one week reviewing all the designs in the airplane hangar. On May 1 it made its report to the Vietnam Veterans Memorial Fund; the experts declared Entry Number 1,026 the winner. The report called it "the finest and most appropriate" of all submitted and said it was "superbly harmonious" with the site on the Mall. Remarking upon the "simple and forthright" materials needed to build the winning entry, the report concludes:

> This memorial, with its wall of names, becomes a place of quiet reflection, and a tribute to those who served their nation in difficult times. All who come here can find it a place of healing. This will be a quiet memorial, one that achieves an excellent relationship with both the Lincoln Memorial and Washington Monument, and relates the visitor to them. It is uniquely horizontal, entering the earth rather than piercing the sky.
>
> This is very much a memorial of our own times, one that could not have been achieved in another time and place. The designer has created an eloquent place where the simple meeting of earth, sky and remembered names contain messages for all who will know this place.

The eight jurors signed their names to the report, a unanimous decision. When the name of the winner was revealed, the art and architecture worlds were stunned. It was not the name of a nationally famous architect or sculptor, as most people had been sure it would be. The creator of Entry Number 1,026 was a twenty-one-year-old student at Yale University. Her name—unknown as yet in any field of art or architecture—was Maya Ying Lin.

How could this be? How could an undergraduate student win one of the most important design competitions ever held? How could she beat out some of the top names in American art and architecture? Who was Maya Ying Lin?

The answer to that question provided some of the other answers, at least in part. Maya Lin, reporters soon discovered, was a Chinese-American girl who had been born and raised in the small midwestern city of Athens, Ohio. Her father, Henry Huan Lin, was a ceramicist of considerable reputation and dean of fine arts at Ohio University in Athens. Her mother, Julia C. Lin, was a poet and professor of Oriental and English literature. Maya Lin's parents were born to culturally prominent families in China. When the Communists came to power in China in the 1940's, Henry and Julia Lin left the country and in time made their way to the United States.

Maya Lin grew up in an environment of art and literature. She was interested in sculpture and made both small and large sculptural figures, one cast in bronze. She learned silversmithing and made jewelry. She was surrounded by books and read a great deal, especially fantasies such as *The Hobbit* and *Lord of the Rings*.

But she also found time to work at McDonald's. "It was about the only way to make money in the summer," she said.

A covaledictorian at high school graduation, Maya Lin went to Yale without a clear notion of what she wanted to study and eventually decided to major in Yale's undergraduate program in architecture. During her junior year she studied in Europe and found herself increasingly interested in cemetery architecture. "In Europe there's very little space, so graveyards are used as parks," she said. "Cemeteries are cities of the dead in European countries, but they are also living gardens."

In France, Maya Lin was deeply moved by the war memorial to those who died in the Somme offensive in 1916 during World War I.[1] The great arch by architect Sir Edwin Lutyens is considered one of the world's most outstanding war memorials. •

---

1. **Somme offensive . . . World War I** costly and largely unsuccessful Allied attack that resulted in approximately 615,000 British and French soldiers being killed.

BIOGRAPHICAL ESSAY

TAKE NOTES

Back at Yale for her senior year, Maya Lin enrolled in Professor Andrus Burr's course in funerary (burial) architecture. The Vietnam Veterans Memorial competition had recently been announced, and although the memorial would be a cenotaph—a monument in honor of persons buried someplace else—Professor Burr thought that having his students prepare a design of the memorial would be a worthwhile course assignment.

Surely, no classroom exercise ever had such spectacular results.

After receiving the assignment, Maya Lin and two of her classmates decided to make the day's journey from New Haven, Connecticut, to Washington to look at the site where the memorial would be built. On the day of their visit, Maya Lin remembers, Constitution Gardens was awash with a late November sun; the park was full of light, alive with joggers and people walking beside the lake.

"It was while I was at the site that I designed it," Maya Lin said later in an interview about the memorial with *Washington Post* writer Phil McCombs. "I just sort of visualized it. It just popped into my head. Some people were playing Frisbee. It was a beautiful park. I didn't want to destroy a living park. You use the landscape. You don't fight with it. You absorb the landscape. . . . When I looked at the site I just knew I wanted something horizontal that took you in, that made you feel safe within the park, yet at the same time reminding you of the dead. So I just imagined opening up the earth. . . ."

When Maya Lin returned to Yale, she made a clay model of the vision that had come to her in Constitution Gardens. She showed it to Professor Burr; he liked her conception and encouraged her to enter the memorial competition. She put her design on paper, a task that took six weeks, and mailed it to Washington barely in time to meet the March 31 deadline.

A month and a day later, Maya Lin was attending class. Her roommate slipped into the classroom and handed her a note. Washington was calling and would call back in fifteen minutes. Maya Lin hurried to her room. The call came. She had won the memorial competition.

PERSUASIVE SPEECH

The Trouble With Television
by Robert MacNeil

It is difficult to escape the influence of television. If you fit the statistical averages, by the age of 20 you will have been exposed to at least 20,000 hours of television. You can add 10,000 hours for each decade you have lived after the age of 20. The only things Americans do more than watch television are work and sleep.

Calculate for a moment what could be done with even a part of those hours. Five thousand hours, I am told, are what a typical college undergraduate spends working on a bachelor's degree. In 10,000 hours you could have learned enough to become an astronomer or engineer. You could have learned several languages fluently. If it appealed to you, you could be reading Homer[1] in the original Greek or Dostoevski[2] in Russian. If it didn't, you could have walked around the world and written a book about it.

The trouble with television is that it discourages concentration. Almost anything interesting and rewarding in life requires some constructive, consistently applied effort. The dullest, the least gifted of us can achieve things that seem miraculous to those who never concentrate on anything. But television encourages us to apply no effort. It sells us instant gratification. It diverts us only to divert, to make the time pass without pain.

Television's variety becomes a narcotic, not a stimulus.[3] Its serial, kaleidoscopic[4] exposures force us to follow its lead. The viewer is on a perpetual guided tour: thirty minutes at the museum, thirty at the cathedral, then back on the bus to the next attraction—except on television, typically, the spans allotted are on the order of minutes or seconds, and

---

1. **Homer** (hō´ mər) ancient Greek author to whom the epic poems the *Odyssey* and the *Iliad* are attributed.
2. **Dostoevski** (dôs´ tô yef´ skē) (1821–1881) Fyodor (fyô´ dôr), Russian novelist.
3. **becomes a narcotic, not a stimulus** becomes something that dulls the senses instead of something that inspires action.
4. **kaleidoscopic** (kə lī´ də skäp´ ik) *adj.* constantly changing.

the chosen delights are more often car crashes and people killing one another. In short, a lot of television usurps one of the most precious of all human gifts, the ability to focus your attention yourself, rather than just passively surrender it. •

Capturing your attention—and holding it—is the prime motive of most television programming and enhances its role as a profitable advertising vehicle. Programmers live in constant fear of losing anyone's attention—anyone's. The surest way to avoid doing so is to keep everything brief, not to strain the attention of anyone but instead to provide constant stimulation through variety, novelty, action and movement. Quite simply, television operates on the appeal to the short attention span.

It is simply the easiest way out. But it has come to be regarded as a given, as inherent in the medium[5] itself: as an imperative, as though General Sarnoff, or one of the other august pioneers of video, had bequeathed to us tablets of stone commanding that nothing in television shall ever require more than a few moments' concentration.

In its place that is fine. Who can quarrel with a medium that so brilliantly packages escapist entertainment as a mass-marketing tool? But I see its values now pervading this nation and its life. It has become fashionable to think that, like fast food, fast ideas are the way to get to a fast-moving, impatient public.

In the case of news, this practice, in my view, results in inefficient communication. I question how much of television's nightly news effort is really absorbable and understandable. Much of it is what has been aptly described as "machine gunning with scraps." I think its technique fights coherence.[6] I think it tends to make things ultimately boring and dismissible (unless they are accompanied by horrifying pictures) because almost anything is boring and dismissable if you know almost nothing about it.

I believe that TV's appeal to the short attention span is not only inefficient communication but decivilizing as well. Consider the casual assumptions that television tends to cultivate: that complexity must

---

5. **inherent** (in her′ ənt) **in the medium** a natural part of television. A *medium* is a means of communication; the plural is *media*.
6. **coherence** (kō hir′ əns) *n.* quality of being connected in a way that is easily understood.

be avoided, that visual stimulation is a substitute for thought, that verbal precision is an anachronism.[7] It may be old-fashioned, but I was taught that thought is words, arranged in grammatically precise ways.

There is a crisis of literacy in this country. One study estimates that some 30 million adult Americans are "functionally illiterate" and cannot read or write well enough to answer a want ad or understand the instructions on a medicine bottle.

Literacy may not be an inalienable human right, but it is one that the highly literate Founding Fathers might not have found unreasonable or even unattainable. We are not only not attaining it as a nation, statistically speaking, but we are falling further and further short of attaining it. And, while I would not be so simplistic as to suggest that television is the cause, I believe it contributes and is an influence. •

Everything about this nation—the structure of the society, its forms of family organization, its economy, its place in the world—has become more complex, not less. Yet its dominating communications instrument, its principal form of national linkage, is one that sells neat resolutions to human problems that usually have no neat resolutions. It is all symbolized in my mind by the hugely successful art form that television has made central to the culture, the thirty-second commercial: the tiny drama of the earnest housewife who finds happiness in choosing the right toothpaste.

When before in human history has so much humanity collectively surrendered so much of its leisure to one toy, one mass diversion? When before has virtually an entire nation surrendered itself wholesale to a medium for selling?

Some years ago Yale University law professor Charles L. Black, Jr., wrote: ". . . forced feeding on trivial fare is not itself a trivial matter." I think this society is being force fed with trivial fare, and I fear that the effects on our habits of mind, our language, our tolerance for effort, and our appetite for complexity are only dimly perceived. If I am wrong, we will have done no harm to look at the issue skeptically and critically, to consider how we should be resisting it. I hope you will join with me in doing so.

TAKE NOTES

---

7. **anachronism** (ə nak′ rə niz′ əm) *n.* something that seems to be out of its proper place in history.

AUTOBIOGRAPHY

TAKE NOTES

from Travels with Charley
by John Steinbeck

The night was loaded with omens. The grieving sky turned the little water to a dangerous metal and then the wind got up—not the gusty, rabbity wind of the seacoasts I know but a great bursting sweep of wind with nothing to inhibit it for a thousand miles in any direction. Because it was a wind strange to me, and therefore mysterious, it set up mysterious responses in me. In terms of reason, it was strange only because I found it so. But a goodly part of our experience which we find inexplicable must be like that. To my certain knowledge, many people conceal experiences for fear of ridicule. How many people have seen or heard or felt something which so outraged their sense of what should be that the whole thing was brushed quickly away like dirt under a rug?

For myself, I try to keep the line open even for things I can't understand or explain, but it is difficult in this frightened time. At this moment in North Dakota I had a reluctance to drive on that amounted to fear. At the same time, Charley wanted to go—in fact, made such a commotion about going that I tried to reason with him.

"Listen to me, dog. I have a strong impulse to stay amounting to celestial command. If I should overcome it and go and a great snow should close in on us, I would recognize it as a warning disregarded. If we stay and a big snow should come I would be certain I had a pipeline to prophecy."

Charley sneezed and paced restlessly. "All right, *mon cur*,[1] let's take your side of it. You want to go on. Suppose we do, and in the night a tree should crash down right where we are presently standing. It would be you who have the attention of the gods. And there is always that chance. I could tell you many stories about faithful animals who saved their masters, but I think you are just bored and I'm not going to flatter you." Charley leveled at me his most cynical eye. I think he

---

1. ***mon cur*** (mōn kʉr′) a pun on *mon coeur* (French for "my dear") and *cur* (a mixed-breed dog).

46 Close Reading Notebook • Unit 2

is neither a romantic nor a mystic. "I know what you mean. If we go, and no tree crashes down, or stay and no snow falls—what then? I'll tell you what then. We forget the whole episode and the field of prophecy is in no way injured. I vote to stay. You vote to go. But being nearer the pinnacle of creation than you, and also president, I cast the deciding vote."

We stayed and it didn't snow and no tree fell, so naturally we forgot the whole thing and are wide open for more mystic feelings when they come. And in the early morning swept clean of clouds and telescopically clear, we crunched around on the thick white ground cover of frost and got under way. The caravan of the arts was dark but the dog barked as we ground up to the highway.

Someone must have told me about the Missouri River at Bismarck, North Dakota, or I must have read about it. In either case, I hadn't paid attention. I came on it in amazement. Here is where the map should fold. Here is the boundary between east and west. On the Bismarck side it is eastern landscape, eastern grass, with the look and smell of eastern America. Across the Missouri on the Mandan side, it is pure west, with brown grass and water scorings and small outcrops. The two sides of the river might well be a thousand miles apart. As I was not prepared for the Missouri boundary, so I was not prepared for the Bad Lands. They deserve this name. They are like the work of an evil child. Such a place the Fallen Angels might have built as a spite to Heaven, dry and sharp, desolate and dangerous, and for me filled with foreboding. A sense comes from it that it does not like or welcome humans. But humans being what they are, and I being human, I turned off the highway on a shaley road and headed in among the buttes, but with a shyness as though I crashed a party. The road surface tore viciously at my tires and made Rocinante's[2] overloaded springs cry with anguish. What a place for a colony of troglodytes, or better, of trolls. And here's an odd thing. Just as I

TAKE NOTES

---

2. **Rocinante's** (rō sē nän′ täz) Steinbeck's nickname for his camper truck. Rocinante was a broken-down horse in the seventeenth-century novel *Don Quixote*. His owner was convinced he was a knight and rode Rocinante across the Spanish countryside on foolish quests. Steinbeck thought the name was appropriate for his cross-country adventure.

from Travels with Charley

AUTOBIOGRAPHY

TAKE NOTES

felt unwanted in this land, so do I feel a reluctance in writing about it.

Presently I saw a man leaning on a two-strand barbed-wire fence, the wires fixed not to posts but to crooked tree limbs stuck in the ground. The man wore a dark hat, and jeans and long jacket washed palest blue with lighter places at knees and elbows. His pale eyes were frosted with sun glare and his lips scaly as snakeskin. A .22 rifle leaned against the fence beside him and on the ground lay a little heap of fur and feathers—rabbits and small birds. I pulled up to speak to him, saw his eyes wash over Rocinante, sweep up the details, and then retire into their sockets. And I found I had nothing to say to him. The "Looks like an early winter," or "Any good fishing hereabouts?" didn't seem to apply. And so we simply brooded at each other.

"Afternoon!"

"Yes, sir," he said.

"Any place nearby where I can buy some eggs?"

"Not real close by 'less you want to go as far as Galva or up to Beach."

"I was set for some scratch-hen eggs."

"Powdered," he said. "My Mrs. gets powdered."

"Lived here long?"

"Yep."

I waited for him to ask something or to say something so we could go on, but he didn't. And as the silence continued, it became more and more impossible to think of something to say. I made one more try. "Does it get very cold here winters?"

"Fairly."

"You talk too much."

He grinned. "That's what my Mrs. says."

"So long," I said, and put the car in gear and moved along. And in my rear-view mirror I couldn't see that he looked after me. He may not be a typical Badlander, but he's one of the few I caught.

A little farther along I stopped at a small house, a section of war-surplus barracks, it looked, but painted white with yellow trim, and with the dying vestiges of a garden, frosted-down geraniums and a few clusters of chrysanthemums, little button things yellow and red-brown. I walked up the path with the certainty that I was being regarded from behind the white window curtains. An old woman answered my knock and gave me the drink of water I asked for and nearly talked my arm off. She was hungry to talk, frantic to talk, about her relatives, her friends, and how she wasn't used to this. For she was not a native and she didn't rightly belong here. Her native clime was a land of milk and honey and had its share of apes and ivory and peacocks. Her voice rattled on as though she was terrified of the silence that would settle when I was gone. As she talked it came to me that she was afraid of this place and, further, that so was I. I felt I wouldn't like to have the night catch me here.

I went into a state of flight, running to get away from the unearthly landscape. And then the late afternoon changed everything. As the sun angled, the buttes and coulees, the cliffs and sculptured hills and ravines lost their burned and dreadful look and glowed with yellow and rich browns and a hundred variations of red and silver gray, all picked out by streaks of coal black. It was so beautiful that I stopped near a thicket of dwarfed and wind-warped cedars and junipers, and once stopped I was caught, trapped in color and dazzled by the clarity of the light. Against the descending sun the battlements were dark and clean-lined, while to the east, where the uninhibited light poured slantwise, the strange landscape shouted with color. And the night, far from being frightful, was lovely beyond thought, for the stars were close, and although there was no moon the starlight made a silver glow in the sky. The air cut the nostrils with dry frost. And for pure pleasure I collected a pile of dry dead cedar branches and built a small fire just to smell the perfume of the burning wood and to hear the excited crackle of the branches. My fire made a dome of yellow light over me, and nearby I heard a screech owl hunting and a barking of coyotes, not howling but the short chuckling bark of the dark of the moon. This is one of the few places I have ever seen where the night was friendlier than the day. And I can easily see how people are driven back to the Bad Lands.

TAKE NOTES

from Travels with Charley

AUTOBIOGRAPHY

TAKE NOTES

Before I slept I spread a map on my bed, a Charley-tromped map. Beach was not far away, and that would be the end of North Dakota. And coming up would be Montana, where I had never been. That night was so cold that I put on my insulated underwear for pajamas, and when Charley had done his duties and had his biscuits and consumed his usual gallon of water and finally curled up in his place under the bed, I dug out an extra blanket and covered him—all except the tip of his nose—and he sighed and wriggled and gave a great groan of pure ecstatic comfort. And I thought how every safe generality I gathered in my travels was canceled by another. In the night the Bad Lands had become Good Lands. I can't explain it. That's how it was.

SPEECH

Choice: A Tribute to Martin Luther King, Jr.

by Alice Walker

My great-great-great-grandmother walked as a slave from Virginia to Eatonton, Georgia—which passes for the Walker ancestral home—with two babies on her hips. She lived to be a hundred and twenty-five years old and my own father knew her as a boy. (It is in memory of this walk that I choose to keep and to embrace my "maiden" name, Walker.)

There is a cemetery near our family church where she is buried; but because her marker was made of wood and rotted years ago, it is impossible to tell exactly where her body lies. In the same cemetery are most of my mother's people, who have lived in Georgia for so long nobody even remembers when they came. And all of my great-aunts and -uncles are there, and my grandfather and grandmother, and, very recently, my own father.

If it is true that land does not belong to anyone until they have buried a body in it, then the land of my birthplace belongs to me, dozens of times over. Yet the history of my family, like that of all black Southerners, is a history of dispossession. We loved the land and worked the land, but we never owned it; and even if we bought land, as my great-grandfather did after the Civil War, it was always in danger of being taken away, as his was, during the period following Reconstruction.[1]

My father inherited nothing of material value from his father, and when I came of age in the early sixties I awoke to the bitter knowledge that in order just to continue to love the land of my birth, I was expected to leave it. For black people—including my parents—had learned a long time ago that to stay willingly in a beloved but brutal place is to risk losing the love and being forced to acknowledge only the brutality.

---

1. Reconstruction (1865–1877) period following the American Civil War when the South was rebuilt and reestablished as part of the Union.

SPEECH

TAKE NOTES

It is a part of the black Southern sensibility that we treasure memories; for such a long time, that is all of our homeland those of us who at one time or another were forced away from it have been allowed to have.

I watched my brothers, one by one, leave our home and leave the South. I watched my sisters do the same. This was not unusual; abandonment, except for memories, was the common thing, except for those who "could not do any better," or those whose strength or stubbornness was so colossal they took the risk that others could not bear.

In 1960, my mother bought a television set, and each day after school I watched Hamilton Holmes and Charlayne Hunter[2] as they struggled to integrate—fair-skinned as they were—the University of Georgia. And then, one day, there appeared the face of Dr. Martin Luther King, Jr. What a funny name, I thought. At the moment I first saw him, he was being handcuffed and shoved into a police truck. He had dared to claim his rights as a native son, and had been arrested. He displayed no fear, but seemed calm and serene, unaware of his own extraordinary courage. His whole body, like his conscience, was at peace.

At the moment I saw his resistance I knew I would never be able to live in this country without resisting everything that sought to disinherit me, and I would never be forced away from the land of my birth without a fight.

He was The One, The Hero, The One Fearless Person for whom we had waited. I hadn't even realized before that we *had* been waiting for Martin Luther King, Jr., but we had. And I knew it for sure when my mother added his name to the list of people she prayed for every night.

I sometimes think that it was literally the prayers of people like my mother and father, who had bowed down in the struggle for such a long time, that kept Dr. King alive until five years ago.[3] For years we went to bed praying for his life, and awoke with the question "Is the 'Lord' still here?"

---

2. **Hamilton Holmes and Charlayne Hunter** the first two African American students to attend the University of Georgia.
3. **until five years ago** Dr. Martin Luther King, Jr., was assassinated on April 4, 1968.

The public acts of Dr. King you know. They are visible all around you. His voice you would recognize sooner than any other voice you have heard in this century—this in spite of the fact that certain municipal libraries, like the one in downtown Jackson, do not carry recordings of his speeches, and the librarians chuckle cruelly when asked why they do not.

You know, if you have read his books, that his is a complex and revolutionary philosophy that few people are capable of understanding fully or have the patience to embody in themselves. Which is our weakness, which is our loss.

And if you know anything about good Baptist preaching, you can imagine what you missed if you never had a chance to hear Martin Luther King, Jr., preach at Ebeneezer Baptist Church.

You know of the prizes and awards that he tended to think very little of. And you know of his concern for the disinherited: the American Indian, the Mexican-American, and the poor American white—for whom he cared much.

You know that this very room, in this very restaurant, was closed to people of color not more than five years ago. And that we eat here together tonight largely through his efforts and his blood. We accept the common pleasures of life, assuredly, in his name.

But add to all of these things the one thing that seems to me second to none in importance: He gave us back our heritage. He gave us back our homeland; the bones and dust of our ancestors, who may now sleep within our caring *and* our hearing. He gave us the blueness of the Georgia sky in autumn as in summer; the colors of the Southern winter as well as glimpses of the green of vacation-time spring. Those of our relatives we used to invite for a visit we now can ask to stay. . . . He gave us full-time use of our woods, and restored our memories to those of us who were forced to run away, as realities we might each day enjoy and leave for our children.

He gave us continuity of place, without which community is ephemeral.[4] He gave us home. *1973*

---

4. **ephemeral** (e fem′ ər əl) *adj.* short-lived; fleeting.

Describe Somebody

by Jacqueline Woodson

Today in class Ms. Marcus said
*Take out your poetry notebooks and describe
    somebody.*
Think carefully, Ms. Marcus said.
You're gonna read it to the class.
5   I wrote, Ms. Marcus is tall and a little bit skinny.
Then I put my pen in my mouth and stared down
at the words.
Then I crossed them out and wrote
Ms. Marcus's hair is long and brown.
10 Shiny.
When she smiles it makes you feel all good inside.
I stopped writing and looked around the room.
Angel was staring out the window.
Eric and Lamont were having a pen fight.
15 They don't care about poetry.
Stupid words, Eric says.
Lots and lots of stupid words.
Eric is tall and a little bit mean.
Lamont's just regular.
20 Angel's kinda chubby. He's got light brown hair.
Sometimes we all hang out,
play a little ball or something. Angel's real good
at science stuff. Once he made a volcano
for science fair and the stuff that came out of it
25 looked like real lava. Lamont can
draw superheroes real good. Eric—nobody
at school really knows this but
he can sing. Once, Miss Edna[1] took me
to a different church than the one
30 we usually go to on Sunday.
I was surprised to see Eric up there
with a choir robe on. He gave me a mean look
like I'd better not
say nothing about him and his dark green robe
    with

---

1. **Miss Edna** the foster mother of the speaker of the poem, Lonnie.

35 gold around the neck.
After the preacher preached
Eric sang a song with nobody else in the choir
   singing.
Miss Edna started dabbing at her eyes
whispering *Yes, Lord.*
40 Eric's voice was like something
that didn't seem like it should belong
to Eric.
Seemed like it should be coming out of an angel.

Now I gotta write a whole new poem
45 'cause Eric would be real mad if I told the class
about his angel voice.

TAKE NOTES

Almost Summer Sky

by Jacqueline Woodson

It was the trees first, Rodney[1] tells me.
It's raining out. But the rain is light and warm.
And the sky's not all close to us like it gets
sometimes. It's way up there with
5 some blue showing through.
Late spring sky, Ms. Marcus says. *Almost
     summer sky.*
And when she said that, I said
*Hey Ms. Marcus, that's a good title
for a poem, right?*
10 *You have a poet's heart, Lonnie.*
That's what Ms. Marcus said to me.
I have a poet's heart.
That's good. A good thing to have.
And I'm the one who has it.

15 Now Rodney puts his arm around my shoulder
We keep walking. There's a park
eight blocks from Miss Edna's house
That's where we're going.
Me and Rodney to the park.
20 Rain coming down warm
Rodney with his arm around my shoulder
Makes me think of Todd and his pigeons
how big his smile gets when they fly.

*The trees upstate ain't like other trees you seen,
     Lonnie*
25 Rodney squints up at the sky, shakes his head
smiles.
*No, upstate they got maple and catalpa and
     scotch pine,*[2]
all kinds of trees just standing.
Hundred-year-old trees big as three men.

---

1. **Rodney** one of Miss Edna's sons.
2. **catalpa** (kə tal' pə) **and scotch pine** Catalpa is a tree with heart-shaped leaves; scotch pine is a tree with yellow wood, grown for timber.

30 *When you go home this weekend*, Ms. Marcus said.
Write about a perfect moment.
Yeah, Little Brother, Rodney says.
You don't know about shade till you lived upstate.
*Everybody should do it—even if it's just for a little
    while.*

35 Way off, I can see the park—blue-gray sky
touching the tops of trees.

I had to live there awhile, Rodney said.
Just to be with all that green, you know?
I nod, even though I don't.
40 I can't even imagine moving away from here,
from Rodney's arm around my shoulder,
from Miss Edna's Sunday cooking,
from Lily[3] in her pretty dresses and great
big smile when she sees me.

45 Can't imagine moving away

From
Home.

You know what I love about trees, Rodney says.
*It's like . . . It's like their leaves are hands
    reaching*
50 *out to you. Saying Come on over here, Brother.*
Let me just . . . Let me just . . .
Rodney looks down at me and grins.
Let me just give you some shade for a while.

---

3. Lily Lonnie's sister, who lives in a different foster home.

TAKE NOTES

Almost Summer Sky **57**

POEM

TAKE NOTES

Silver
by Walter de la Mare

Slowly, silently, now the moon
Walks the night in her silver shoon;[1]
This way, and that, she peers, and sees
Silver fruit upon silver trees;
5   One by one the casements[2] catch
Her beams beneath the silvery thatch;[3]
Couched in his kennel, like a log,
With paws of silver sleeps the dog;
From their shadowy coat the white breasts peep
10   Of doves in a silver-feathered sleep;
A harvest mouse goes scampering by,
With silver claws, and silver eye;
And moveless fish in the water gleam,
By silver reeds in a silver stream.

---

1. **shoon** (sho͞on) *n.* old-fashioned word for "shoes."
2. **casements** (kās′ mənts) *n.* windows that open out like doors.
3. **thatch** (thach) *n.* roof made of straw or other plant material.

Ring Out, Wild Bells

by Alfred, Lord Tennyson

Ring out, wild bells, to the wild sky,
    The flying cloud, the frosty light:
    The year is dying in the night;
Ring out, wild bells, and let him die.

5 Ring out the old, ring in the new,
    Ring, happy bells, across the snow:
    The year is going, let him go;
Ring out the false, ring in the true.

Ring out the grief that saps the mind,
10   For those that here we see no more;
    Ring out the feud of rich and poor,
Ring in redress to all mankind.

Ring out a slowly dying cause,
    And ancient forms of party strife;
15   Ring in the nobler modes of life,
With sweeter manners, purer laws.

Ring out the want, the care, the sin,
    The faithless coldness of the times;
    Ring out, ring out thy mournful rhymes,
20 But ring the fuller minstrel[1] in.

Ring out false pride in place and blood,
    The civic[2] slander and the spite;
    Ring in the love of truth and right,
Ring in the common love of good.

25 Ring out old shapes of foul disease;
    Ring out the narrowing lust of gold;
    Ring out the thousand wars of old,
Ring in the thousand years of peace.

---

1. **fuller minstrel** (min´ strəl) *n.* singer of the highest rank.
2. **civic** (siv´ ik) *adj.* relating to cities or citizens.

Cat!

by Eleanor Farjeon

Cat!
Scat!
After her, after her,
Sleeky flatterer,
5   Spitfire chatterer,
Scatter her, scatter her
    Off her mat!
    Wuff!
    Wuff!
10   Treat her rough!
Git her, git her,
Whiskery spitter!
Catch her, catch her,
Green-eyed scratcher!
15   Slathery
        Slithery
        Hisser,
        Don't miss her!
Run till you're dithery,[1]
20   Hithery
        Thithery[2]
        Pftts! pftts!
        How she spits!
        Spitch! Spatch!
25   Can't she scratch!
Scritching the bark
Of the sycamore tree,
She's reached her ark
And's hissing at me
30 *Pftts! pftts!*
        Wuff! wuff!
        Scat,
        Cat!
        That's
35   *That!*

---

1. **dithery** (di*th*′ ər ē) *adj.* nervous and confused; in a dither.
2. **Hithery/Thithery** made-up words based on *hither* and *thither*, which mean "here" and "there."

Thumbprint

by Eve Merriam

On the pad of my thumb
are whorls,[1] whirls, wheels
in a unique design:
mine alone.
5   What a treasure to own!
My own flesh, my own feelings.
No other, however grand or base,
can ever contain the same.
My signature,
10 thumbing the pages of my time.
My universe key,
my singularity.

Impress, implant,
I am myself,
15 of all my atom parts I am the sum.
And out of my blood and my brain
I make my own interior weather,
my own sun and rain.
Imprint my mark upon the world,
20 whatever I shall become.

---

1. **whorls** (hwôrlz) *n.* circular ridges that form the pattern of fingerprints.

POEM

The Sky Is Low, the Clouds Are Mean

by Emily Dickinson

The sky is low, the clouds are mean,
A travelling flake of snow
Across a barn or through a rut
Debates if it will go.

5 A narrow wind complains all day
How some one treated him;
Nature, like us, is sometimes caught
Without her diadem.[1]

---

1. **diadem** (dī′ ə dem′) *n.* crown.

Concrete Mixers

by Patricia Hubbell

The drivers are washing the concrete mixers;
Like elephant tenders they hose them down.
Tough gray-skinned monsters standing ponderous,
Elephant-bellied and elephant-nosed,
Standing in muck up to their wheel-caps,
Like rows of elephants, tail to trunk.
Their drivers perch on their backs like mahouts,[1]
Sending the sprays of water up.
They rid the trunk-like trough of concrete,
Direct the spray to the bulging sides,
Turn and start the monsters moving.
      Concrete mixers
      Move like elephants
      Bellow like elephants
      Spray like elephants
Concrete mixers are urban elephants,
Their trunks are raising a city.

---

1. **mahouts** (mə houts´) *n.* in India and the East Indies, elephant drivers or keepers.

Harlem Night Song

by Langston Hughes

Come,
Let us roam the night together
Singing.

I love you.

5   Across
The Harlem roof-tops
Moon is shining.
Night sky is blue.
Stars are great drops
10   Of golden dew.

Down the street
A band is playing.

I love you.

Come,
15   Let us roam the night together
Singing.

The City Is So Big

by Richard García

The city is so big
Its bridges quake with fear
I know, I have seen at night

The lights sliding from house to house
5 And trains pass with windows shining
Like a smile full of teeth

I have seen machines eating houses
And stairways walk all by themselves
And elevator doors opening and closing
10 And people disappear.

POEM

TAKE NOTES

The New Colossus
by Emma Lazarus

Background The Colossus of Rhodes, referred to in the title and first two lines of the poem, was a 100-foot tall statue of the Greek sun god Helios. One of the Seven Wonders of the Ancient World, the statue was built around 280 B.C. It stood at the entrance to the harbor of the Greek island of Rhodes.

    Not like the brazen giant of Greek fame,
    With conquering limbs astride from land to land;
    Here at our sea-washed, sunset gates shall stand
    A mighty woman with a torch, whose flame
5   Is the imprisoned lightning, and her name
    Mother of Exiles. From her beacon-hand
    Glows world-wide welcome; her mild eyes command
    The air-bridged harbor that twin cities frame.
    "Keep, ancient lands, your storied pomp!"[1] cries she
10 With silent lips. "Give me your tired, your poor,
    Your huddled masses yearning to breathe free,
    The wretched refuse of your teeming[2] shore.
    Send these, the homeless, tempest-tost[3] to me,
    I lift my lamp beside the golden door!"

---

1. **pomp** (pämp) *n.* stately or brilliant display; splendor.
2. **teeming** (tēm´ in) *adj.* swarming with people.
3. **tempest-tost** (tem´ pist tôst´) *adj.* here, having suffered a stormy ocean journey.

Blow, Blow, Thou Winter Wind

by William Shakespeare

Blow, blow, thou winter wind.
Thou art not so unkind
    As man's ingratitude.
Thy tooth is not so keen,
5   Because thou art not seen,
    Although thy breath be rude.
Heigh-ho! Sing, heigh-ho! unto the green holly.
Most friendship is feigning, most loving mere folly.[1]
  Then, heigh-ho, the holly!
10   This life is most jolly.

  Freeze, freeze, thou bitter sky,
  That dost not bite so nigh
    As benefits forgot.
  Though thou the waters warp,[2]
15   Thy sting is not so sharp
    As friend remembered not.
Heigh-ho! Sing, heigh-ho! unto the green holly.
Most friendship is feigning, most loving mere folly.
  Then, heigh-ho, the holly!
20   This life is most jolly.

---

1. **Most friendship is feigning . . . folly** Most friendship is fake, most loving is foolish.
2. **warp** (wôrp) *v.* freeze.

POEM

TAKE NOTES

Paul Revere's Ride

by Henry Wadsworth Longfellow

Listen, my children, and you shall hear
Of the midnight ride of Paul Revere,
On the eighteenth of April, in Seventy-five;
Hardly a man is now alive
5 Who remembers that famous day and year.

He said to his friend, "If the British march
By land or sea from the town to-night,
Hang a lantern aloft in the belfry arch
Of the North Church tower as a signal light,—
10 One, if by land, and two, if by sea;
And I on the opposite shore will be,
Ready to ride and spread the alarm
Through every Middlesex village and farm,
For the country folk to be up and to arm."

15 Then he said, "Good night!" and with muffled oar
Silently rowed to the Charlestown shore,
Just as the moon rose over the bay,
Where swinging wide at her moorings lay
The *Somerset,* British man-of-war;[1]
20 A phantom ship, with each mast and spar
Across the moon like a prison bar,
And a huge black hulk, that was magnified
By its own reflection in the tide.

Meanwhile, his friend, through alley and street,
25 Wanders and watches with eager ears,
Till in the silence around him he hears
The muster[2] of men at the barrack door,
The sound of arms, and the tramp of feet,
And the measured tread of the grenadiers,[3]
30 Marching down to their boats on the shore.

---

1. **man-of-war** (man′ əv wôr′) *n.* armed naval vessel; warship.
2. **muster** (mus′ tər) *n.* assembly of troops summoned for inspection, roll call, or service.
3. **grenadiers** (gren′ ə dirz′) *n.* soldiers in a special regiment or corps.

Then he climbed the tower of the Old North Church,
By the wooden stairs, with stealthy tread,
To the belfry-chamber overhead,
And startled the pigeons from their perch
35 On the somber rafters, that round him made
Masses and moving shapes of shade,—
By the trembling ladder, steep and tall,
To the highest window in the wall,
Where he paused to listen and look down
40 A moment on the roofs of the town,
And the moonlight flowing over all.

Beneath, in the churchyard, lay the dead,
In their night-encampment on the hill,
Wrapped in silence so deep and still
45 That he could hear, like a sentinel's tread,[4]
The watchful night-wind, as it went
Creeping along from tent to tent,
And seeming to whisper, "All is well!"
A moment only he feels the spell
50 Of the place and the hour, and the secret dread
Of the lonely belfry and the dead;
For suddenly all his thoughts are bent
On a shadowy something far away,
Where the river widens to meet the bay,—
55 A line of black that bends and floats
On the rising tide, like a bridge of boats.

Meanwhile, impatient to mount and ride,
Booted and spurred, with a heavy stride
On the opposite shore walked Paul Revere.
60 Now he patted his horse's side,
Now gazed at the landscape far and near,
Then, impetuous,[5] stamped the earth,
And turned and tightened his saddle-girth;[6]
But mostly he watched with eager search
65 The belfry-tower of the Old North Church,
As it rose above the graves on the hill,
Lonely and spectral and somber and still.

---

4. **sentinel's** (sent´ 'n əlz) **tread** (tred) footsteps of a guard.
5. **impetuous** (im pech´ o͞o əs) *adj.* done suddenly with little thought.
6. **saddle-girth** (gurth) *n.* band put around the belly of a horse for holding a saddle.

POEM

TAKE NOTES

And lo! as he looks, on the belfry's height
A glimmer, and then a gleam of light!
70 He springs to the saddle, the bridle he turns,
But lingers and gazes, till full on his sight
A second lamp in the belfry burns!

A hurry of hoofs in a village street,
A shape in the moonlight, a bulk in the dark,
75 And beneath, from the pebbles, in passing, a spark
Struck out by a steed flying fearless and fleet:
That was all! And yet, through the gloom and the light,
The fate of a nation was riding that night;
And the spark struck out by that steed in his flight,
80 Kindled the land into flame with its heat.

He has left the village and mounted the steep,
And beneath him, tranquil and broad and deep,
Is the Mystic,[7] meeting the ocean tides;
And under the alders that skirt its edge,
85 Now soft on the sand, now loud on the ledge,
Is heard the tramp of his steed as he rides.

It was twelve by the village clock,
When he crossed the bridge into Medford town.
He heard the crowing of the cock,
90 And the barking of the farmer's dog,
And felt the damp of the river fog,
That rises after the sun goes down.

It was one by the village clock,
When he galloped into Lexington.
95 He saw the gilded weathercock
Swim in the moonlight as he passed,
And the meeting-house windows, blank and bare,
Gaze at him with a spectral glare,
As if they already stood aghast
100 At the bloody work they would look upon.

It was two by the village clock,
When he came to the bridge in Concord town.

---

7. Mystic (mis´ tik) river in Massachusetts.

He heard the bleating of the flock,
And the twitter of birds among the trees,
105 And felt the breath of the morning breeze
Blowing over the meadows brown.
And one was safe and asleep in his bed
Who at the bridge would be first to fall,
Who that day would be lying dead,
110 Pierced by a British musket-ball.

You know the rest. In the books you have read,
How the British Regulars fired and fled,—
How the farmers gave them ball for ball,
From behind each fence and farm-yard wall,
115 Chasing the red-coats down the lane,
Then crossing the fields to emerge again
Under the trees at the turn of the road,
And only pausing to fire and load.

So through the night rode Paul Revere;
120 And so through the night went his cry of alarm
To every Middlesex village and farm,—
A cry of defiance and not of fear,
A voice in the darkness, a knock at the door,
And a word that shall echo forevermore!
125 For, borne on the night-wind of the Past,
Through all our history, to the last,
In the hour of darkness and peril and need,
The people will waken and listen to hear
The hurrying hoof-beats of that steed,
130 And the midnight message of Paul Revere.

Grandma Ling

by Amy Ling

If you dig that hole deep enough
you'll reach China, they used to tell me,
a child in a backyard in Pennsylvania.
Not strong enough to dig that hole,
5   I waited twenty years,
then sailed back, half way around the world.

In Taiwan I first met Grandma.
Before she came to view, I heard
her slippered feet softly measure
10 the tatami[1] floor with even step;
the aqua paper-covered door slid open
and there I faced
my five foot height, sturdy legs and feet,
square forehead, high cheeks, and wide-set eyes;
15 my image stood before me,
acted on by fifty years.

She smiled, stretched her arms
to take to heart the eldest daughter
of her youngest son a quarter century away.
20 She spoke a tongue I knew no word of,
and I was sad I could not understand,
but I could hug her.

---

1. **tatami** (tə tä′ mē) floor mat woven of rice straw.

POEM

your little voice
Over the wires came leaping
by E. E. Cummings

    your little voice
                    Over the wires came leaping
    and i felt suddenly
    dizzy
5   With the jostling and shouting of merry flowers
    wee skipping high-heeled flames
    courtesied[1] before my eyes
                   or twinkling over to my side
    Looked up
10 with impertinently exquisite faces
    floating hands were laid upon me
    I was whirled and tossed into delicious dancing
    up
    Up
15 with the pale important
                   stars and the Humorous
                        moon
    dear girl
    How i was crazy how i cried when i heard
20   over time
    and tide and death
    leaping
    Sweetly
        your voice

---

1. **courtesied** (kʉrt′ sēd) *v.* bowed with bended knees; curtsied.

New World

by N. Scott Momaday

1.
First Man,
behold:
the earth
glitters
5   with leaves;
the sky
glistens
with rain.
Pollen
10 is borne
on winds
that low
and lean
upon
15 mountains.
Cedars
blacken
the slopes—
and pines.

2.
20 At dawn
eagles
hie and
hover[1]
above
25 the plain
where light
gathers
in pools.
Grasses
30 shimmer
and shine.
Shadows
withdraw
and lie
35 away
like smoke.

3.
At noon
turtles
enter
40 slowly
into
the warm
dark loam.[2]
Bees hold
45 the swarm.
Meadows
recede
through planes
of heat
50 and pure
distance.

4.
At dusk
the gray
foxes
55 stiffen
in cold;
blackbirds
are fixed
in the
60 branches.
Rivers
follow
the moon,
the long
65 white track
of the
full moon.

---

1. **hie** (hī) **and hover** (huv´ ər) fly swiftly and then hang as if suspended in the air.
2. **loam** (lōm) rich, dark soil.

January

by John Updike

The days are short,
    The sun a spark
Hung thin between
    The dark and dark.

5 Fat snowy footsteps
    Track the floor,
And parkas pile up
    Near the door.

The river is
10   A frozen place
Held still beneath
    The trees' black lace.

The sky is low.
    The wind is gray.
15 The radiator
    Purrs all day.

remembrance (smiles/hurts sweetly)
October 8, 1972

Old Man

by Ricardo Sánchez

old man
with brown skin
talking of past
    when being shepherd
5   in utah, nevada, colorado and
        new mexico
was life lived freely;

old man,
    grandfather,
wise with time
10 running rivulets on face,
deep, rich furrows,[1]
    each one a legacy,
deep, rich memories
of life . . .
15   "you are indio,[2]
      among other things,"
he would tell me
    during nights spent
so long ago
20   amidst familial gatherings
in albuquerque . . .

old man, loved and respected,
he would speak sometimes
of pueblos,[3]

---

1. **rivulets . . . furrows** here, the wrinkles on the old man's face.
2. **indio** (ēn´dē ō) *n.* Indian; Native American.
3. **pueblos** (pweb´ lōz) *n.* here, Native American towns in central and northern New Mexico.

25   san juan, santa clara,
       and even santo domingo,
and his family, he would say,
came from there:
       some of our blood was here,
30   he would say,
       before the coming of coronado,[4]
other of our blood
       came with los españoles,[5]
and the mixture
35 was rich,
       though often painful . . .

old man,
who knew earth
       by its awesome aromas
40 and who felt
the heated sweetness
       of chile verde[6]
by his supple touch,
gone into dust is your body
45   with its stoic[7] look and resolution,
but your reality, old man, lives on
in a mindsoul touched by you . . .

Old Man . . .

---

4. **coronado** (kôr′ ə nä′ dō) sixteenth-century Spanish explorer Francisco Vásquez de Coronado, who journeyed through what is today the American Southwest.
5. **los españoles** (lôs es pä nyō′ lās) *n.* Spaniards.
6. **chile verde** (chē′ lā ver′ dā) *n.* green pepper.
7. **stoic** (stō′ ik) *adj.* calm in the face of suffering.

For My Sister Molly Who in the Fifties

by Alice Walker

Once made a fairy rooster from
Mashed potatoes
Whose eyes I forget
But green onions were his tail
5 And his two legs were carrot sticks
A tomato slice his crown.
Who came home on vacation
When the sun was hot
and cooked
10 and cleaned
And minded least of all
The children's questions
A million or more
Pouring in on her
15 Who had been to school
And knew (and told us too) that certain
Words were no longer good
And taught me not to say us for we
No matter what "Sonny said" up the
20 road.

FOR MY SISTER MOLLY WHO IN THE FIFTIES
Knew Hamlet[1] well and read into the night
And coached me in my songs of Africa
A continent I never knew
25 But learned to love
Because "they" she said could carry
A tune
And spoke in accents never heard
In Eatonton.
30 Who read from *Prose and Poetry*
And loved to read "Sam McGee from Tennessee"[2]
On nights the fire was burning low
And Christmas wrapped in angel hair[3]
And I for one prayed for snow.

---

1. **Hamlet** *Hamlet* is a play by William Shakespeare.
2. **"Sam McGee from Tennessee"** reference to the title character in the Robert Service poem "The Cremation of Sam McGee."
3. **angel hair** fine, white, filmy Christmas tree decoration.

WHO IN THE FIFTIES
Knew all the written things that made
Us laugh and stories by
The hour   Waking up the story buds
Like fruit. Who walked among the flowers
And brought them inside the house
And smelled as good as they
And looked as bright.
Who made dresses, braided
Hair. Moved chairs about
Hung things from walls
Ordered baths
Frowned on wasp bites
And seemed to know the endings
Of all the tales
I had forgot.

WHO OFF INTO THE UNIVERSITY
Went exploring   To London and
To Rotterdam
Prague and to Liberia
Bringing back the news to us
Who knew none of it
But followed
crops and weather
funerals and
Methodist Homecoming;
easter speeches,
groaning church.

WHO FOUND ANOTHER WORLD
Another life   With gentlefolk
Far less trusting
And moved and moved and changed
Her name
And sounded precise
When she spoke   And frowned away
Our sloppishness.

WHO SAW US SILENT
Cursed with fear   A love burning
Inexpressible
And sent me money not for me
75 But for "College."
Who saw me grow through letters
The words misspelled   But not
The longing   Stretching
Growth
80 The tied and twisting
Tongue
Feet no longer bare
Skin no longer burnt against
The cotton.

85 WHO BECAME SOMEONE OVERHEAD
A light   A thousand watts
Bright and also blinding
And saw my brothers cloddish
And me destined to be
90 Wayward[4]
My mother remote   My father
A wearisome farmer
With heartbreaking
Nails.

95 FOR MY SISTER MOLLY WHO IN THE FIFTIES
Found much
Unbearable
Who walked where few had
Understood   And sensed our
100 Groping after light
And saw some extinguished
And no doubt mourned.

FOR MY SISTER MOLLY WHO IN THE FIFTIES
Left us.

---

4. **wayward** (wā′ wərd) *adj.* headstrong; disobedient.

AUTOBIOGRAPHY

Cub Pilot on the Mississippi
by Mark Twain

During the two or two and a half years of my apprenticeship[1] I served under many pilots, and had experience of many kinds of steamboatmen and many varieties of steamboats. I am to this day profiting somewhat by that experience; for in that brief, sharp schooling, I got personally and familiarly acquainted with about all the different types of human nature that are to be found in fiction, biography, or history.

The fact is daily borne in upon me that the average shore-employment requires as much as forty years to equip a man with this sort of an education. When I say I am still profiting by this thing, I do not mean that it has constituted me a judge of men—no, it has not done that, for judges of men are born, not made. My profit is various in kind and degree, but the feature of it which I value most is the zest which that early experience has given to my later reading. When I find a well-drawn character in fiction or biography I generally take a warm personal interest in him, for the reason that I have known him before—met him on the river.

The figure that comes before me oftenest, out of the shadows of that vanished time, is that of Brown, of the steamer *Pennsylvania*. He was a middle-aged, long, slim, bony, smooth-shaven, horsefaced, ignorant, stingy, malicious, snarling, fault-hunting, mote magnifying tyrant.[2] I early got the habit of coming on watch with dread at my heart. No matter how good a time I might have been having with the off-watch below, and no matter how high my spirits might be when I started aloft, my soul became lead in my body the moment I approached the pilothouse.

I still remember the first time I ever entered the presence of that man. The boat had backed out from

---

1. **apprenticeship** (ə pren´ tis ship´) *n.* time spent working for a master craftsperson in return for instruction in his or her craft.
2. **mote magnifying tyrant** a cruel authority figure who exaggerates every tiny fault.

AUTOBIOGRAPHY

TAKE NOTES

St. Louis and was "straightening down." I ascended to the pilothouse in high feather, and very proud to be semiofficially a member of the executive family of so fast and famous a boat. Brown was at the wheel. I paused in the middle of the room, all fixed to make my bow, but Brown did not look around. I thought he took a furtive glance at me out of the corner of his eye, but as not even this notice was repeated, I judged I had been mistaken. By this time he was picking his way among some dangerous "breaks" abreast the woodyards; therefore it would not be proper to interrupt him; so I stepped softly to the high bench and took a seat.

There was silence for ten minutes; then my new boss turned and inspected me deliberately and painstakingly from head to heel for about—as it seemed to me—a quarter of an hour. After which he removed his countenance[3] and I saw it no more for some seconds; then it came around once more, and this question greeted me: "Are you Horace Bigsby's cub?"

"Yes, sir."

After this there was a pause and another inspection. Then: "What's your name?"

I told him. He repeated it after me. It was probably the only thing he ever forgot; for although I was with him many months he never addressed himself to me in any other way than "Here!" and then his command followed.

"Where was you born?"

"In Florida, Missouri."

A pause. Then: "Dern sight better stayed there!"

By means of a dozen or so of pretty direct questions, he pumped my family history out of me.

The leads[4] were going now in the first crossing. This interrupted the inquest. When the leads had been laid in he resumed:

"How long you been on the river?"

I told him. After a pause:

"Where'd you get them shoes?"

I gave him the information.

"Hold up your foot!"

---

3. **countenance** (kount' 'n əns) *n.* face.
4. **leads** (ledz) *n.* weights that are lowered to test the depth of the river.

82 Close Reading Notebook • Unit 3

I did so. He stepped back, examined the shoe minutely and contemptuously, scratching his head thoughtfully, tilting his high sugarloaf hat well forward to facilitate the operation, then ejaculated, "Well, I'll be dod derned!" and returned to his wheel.

What occasion there was to be dod derned about it is a thing which is still as much of a mystery to me now as it was then. It must have been all of fifteen minutes—fifteen minutes of dull, homesick silence—before that long horse-face swung round upon me again—and then what a change! It was as red as fire, and every muscle in it was working. Now came this shriek: "Here! You going to set there all day?"

I lit in the middle of the floor, shot there by the electric suddenness of the surprise. As soon as I could get my voice I said apologetically: "I have had no orders, sir."

"You've had no *orders*! My, what a fine bird we are! We must have *orders*! Our father was a *gentleman*—and *we've* been to *school*. Yes, *we* are a gentleman, *too*, and got to have *orders*! Orders, is it? Orders is what you want! Dod dern my skin, *I'll* learn you to swell yourself up and blow around *here* about your dod-derned *orders*! G'way from the wheel!" (I had approached it without knowing it.)

I moved back a step or two and stood as in a dream, all my senses stupefied by this frantic assault.

"What you standing there for? Take that ice-pitcher down to the texas-tender![5] Come, move along, and don't you be all day about it!"

The moment I got back to the pilothouse Brown said: "Here! What was you doing down there all this time?"

"I couldn't find the texas-tender; I had to go all the way to the pantry."

"Derned likely story! Fill up the stove."

I proceeded to do so. He watched me like a cat. Presently he shouted: "Put down that shovel! Derndest numskull I ever saw—ain't even got sense enough to load up a stove."

All through the watch this sort of thing went on. Yes, and the subsequent watches were much like it during

---

5. **texas-tender** the waiter in the officers' quarters. On Mississippi steamboats, rooms were named after the states. The officers' area, being the largest, was named after Texas, then the largest state.

AUTOBIOGRAPHY

TAKE NOTES

a stretch of months. As I have said, I soon got the habit of coming on duty with dread. The moment I was in the presence, even in the darkest night, I could feel those yellow eyes upon me, and knew their owner was watching for a pretext to spit out some venom on me. Preliminarily he would say: "Here! Take the wheel."

Two minutes later: "*Where* in the nation you going to? Pull her down! pull her down!"

After another moment: "Say! You going to hold her all day? Let her go—meet her! meet her!"

Then he would jump from the bench, snatch the wheel from me, and meet her himself, pouring out wrath upon me all the time.

George Ritchie was the other pilot's cub. He was having good times now; for his boss, George Ealer, was as kind-hearted as Brown wasn't. Ritchie had steered for Brown the season before; consequently, he knew exactly how to entertain himself and plague me, all by the one operation. Whenever I took the wheel for a moment on Ealer's watch, Ritchie would sit back on the bench and play Brown, with continual ejaculations of "Snatch her! Snatch her! Derndest mudcat I ever saw!" "Here! Where are you going *now*? Going to run over that snag?" "Pull her *down*! Don't you hear me? Pull her *down*!" "There she goes! *Just* as I expected! I *told* you not to cramp that reef. G'way from the wheel!"

So I always had a rough time of it, no matter whose watch it was; and sometimes it seemed to me that Ritchie's good-natured badgering was pretty nearly as aggravating as Brown's dead-earnest nagging.

I often wanted to kill Brown, but this would not answer. A cub had to take everything his boss gave, in the way of vigorous comment and criticism; and we all believed that there was a United States law making it a penitentiary offense to strike or threaten a pilot who was on duty.

However, I could *imagine* myself killing Brown; there was no law against that; and that was the thing I used always to do the moment I was abed. Instead of going over my river in my mind, as was my duty, I threw business aside for pleasure, and killed Brown. I killed Brown every night for months; not in old, stale, commonplace ways, but in new and picturesque ones—ways that were sometimes surprising for

84 Close Reading Notebook • Unit 3

freshness of design and ghastliness of situation and environment.

Brown was *always* watching for a pretext to find fault; and if he could find no plausible pretext, he would invent one. He would scold you for shaving a shore, and for not shaving it; for hugging a bar, and for not hugging it; for "pulling down" when not invited, and for *not* pulling down when not invited; for firing up without orders, and *for* waiting for orders. In a word, it was his invariable rule to find fault with *everything* you did and another invariable rule of his was to throw all his remarks (to you) into the form of an insult.

One day we were approaching New Madrid, bound down and heavily laden. Brown was at one side of the wheel, steering; I was at the other, standing by to "pull down" or "shove up." He cast a furtive glance at me every now and then. I had long ago learned what that meant; viz., he was trying to invent a trap for me. I wondered what shape it was going to take. By and by he stepped back from the wheel and said in his usual snarly way:

"Here! See if you've got gumption enough to round her to."

This was simply *bound* to be a success; nothing could prevent it; for he had never allowed me to round the boat to before; consequently, no matter how I might do the thing, he could find free fault with it. He stood back there with his greedy eye on me, and the result was what might have been foreseen: I lost my head in a quarter of a minute, and didn't know what I was about; I started too early to bring the boat around, but detected a green gleam of joy in Brown's eye, and corrected my mistake. I started around once more while too high up, but corrected myself again in time. I made other false moves, and still managed to save myself; but at last I grew so confused and anxious that I tumbled into the very worst blunder of all—I got too far *down* before beginning to fetch the boat around. Brown's chance was come.

His face turned red with passion; he made one bound, hurled me across the house with a sweep of his arm, spun the wheel down, and began to pour out a stream of vituperation[6] upon me which lasted

---

6. **vituperation** (vi tōō′ pər ā′ shən) *n.* abusive language.

TAKE NOTES

AUTOBIOGRAPHY

TAKE NOTES

till he was out of breath. In the course of this speech he called me all the different kinds of hard names he could think of, and once or twice I thought he was even going to swear—but he had never done that, and he didn't this time. "Dod dern" was the nearest he ventured to the luxury of swearing.

Two trips later I got into serious trouble. Brown was steering; I was "pulling down." My younger brother Henry appeared on the hurricane deck, and shouted to Brown to stop at some landing or other, a mile or so below. Brown gave no intimation[7] that he had heard anything. But that was his way: he never condescended to take notice of an underclerk. The wind was blowing; Brown was deaf (although he always pretended he wasn't), and I very much doubted if he had heard the order. If I had had two heads, I would have spoken; but as I had only one, it seemed judicious to take care of it; so I kept still.

Presently, sure enough, we went sailing by that plantation. Captain Klinefelter appeared on the deck, and said: "Let her come around, sir, let her come around. Didn't Henry tell you to land here?"

"*No*, sir!"

"I sent him up to do it."

"He *did* come up; and that's all the good it done, the dod-derned fool. He never said anything."

"Didn't *you* hear him?" asked the captain of me.

Of course I didn't want to be mixed up in this business, but there was no way to avoid it; so I said: "Yes, sir."

I knew what Brown's next remark would be, before he uttered it. It was: "Shut your mouth! You never heard anything of the kind."

I closed my mouth, according to instructions. An hour later Henry entered the pilothouse, unaware of what had been going on. He was a thoroughly inoffensive boy, and I was sorry to see him come, for I knew Brown would have no pity on him. Brown began, straightway: "Here! Why didn't you tell me we'd got to land at that plantation?"

"I did tell you, Mr. Brown."

"It's a lie!"

---

7. **intimation** (in′ tə mā′ shən) *n.* hint or suggestion.

I said: "You lie, yourself. He did tell you."

Brown glared at me in unaffected surprise; and for as much as a moment he was entirely speechless; then he shouted to me: "I'll attend to your case in a half a minute!" then to Henry, "And you leave the pilothouse; out with you!"

It was pilot law, and must be obeyed. The boy started out, and even had his foot on the upper step outside the door, when Brown, with a sudden access of fury, picked up a ten-pound lump of coal and sprang after him; but I was between, with a heavy stool, and I hit Brown a good honest blow which stretched him out.

I had committed the crime of crimes—I had lifted my hand against a pilot on duty! I supposed I was booked for the penitentiary sure, and couldn't be booked any surer if I went on and squared my long account with this person while I had the chance; consequently I stuck to him and pounded him with my fists a considerable time. I do not know how long, the pleasure of it probably made it seem longer than it really was; but in the end he struggled free and jumped up and sprang to the wheel: a very natural solicitude, for, all this time, here was this steamboat tearing down the river at the rate of fifteen miles an hour and nobody at the helm! However, Eagle Bend was two miles wide at this bank-full stage, and correspondingly long and deep: and the boat was steering herself straight down the middle and taking no chances. Still, that was only luck—a body *might* have found her charging into the woods.

Perceiving at a glance that the *Pennsylvania* was in no danger, Brown gathered up the big spyglass, war-club fashion, and ordered me out of the pilothouse with more than ordinary bluster. But I was not afraid of him now; so, instead of going, I tarried, and criticized his grammar. I reformed his ferocious speeches for him, and put them into good English, calling his attention to the advantage of pure English over the dialect of the collieries[8] whence he was extracted. He could have done his part to admiration in a crossfire of mere vituperation, of course; but he was not equipped for this species of controversy; so he presently laid

---

8. **collieries** (käl′ yər ēz) *n.* coal mines.

aside his glass and took the wheel, muttering and shaking his head; and I retired to the bench. The racket had brought everybody to the hurricane deck, and I trembled when I saw the old captain looking up from amid the crowd. I said to myself, "Now I *am* done for!" for although, as a rule, he was so fatherly and indulgent toward the boat's family, and so patient of minor shortcomings, he could be stern enough when the fault was worth it.

I tried to imagine what he *would* do to a cub pilot who had been guilty of such a crime as mine, committed on a boat guard-deep with costly freight and alive with passengers. Our watch was nearly ended. I thought I would go and hide somewhere till I got a chance to slide ashore. So I slipped out of the pilothouse, and down the steps, and around to the texas-door, and was in the act of gliding within, when the captain confronted me! I dropped my head, and he stood over me in silence a moment or two, then said impressively: "Follow me."

I dropped into his wake; he led the way to his parlor in the forward end of the texas. We were alone now. He closed the afterdoor, then moved slowly to the forward one and closed that. He sat down; I stood before him. He looked at me some little time, then said: "So you have been fighting Mr. Brown?"

I answered meekly: "Yes, sir."

"Do you know that that is a very serious matter?"

"Yes, sir."

"Are you aware that this boat was plowing down the river fully five minutes with no one at the wheel?"

"Yes, sir."

"Did you strike him first?"

"Yes, sir."

"What with?"

"A stool, sir."

"Hard?"

"Middling, sir."

"Did it knock him down?"

"He—he fell, sir."

"Did you follow it up? Did you do anything further?"

"Yes, sir."

"What did you do?"

"Pounded him, sir."

"Pounded him?"

"Yes, sir."

"Did you pound him much? that is, severely?"

"One might call it that, sir, maybe."

"I'm deuced glad of it! Hark ye, never mention that I said that. You have been guilty of a great crime; and don't you ever be guilty of it again, on this boat. *But—* lay for him ashore! Give him a good sound thrashing, do you hear? I'll pay the expenses. Now go—and mind you, not a word of this to anybody. Clear out with you! You've been guilty of a great crime, you whelp!"[9]

I slid out, happy with the sense of a close shave and a mighty deliverance; and I heard him laughing to himself and slapping his fat thighs after I had closed his door.

When Brown came off watch he went straight to the captain, who was talking with some passengers on the boiler deck, and demanded that I be put ashore in New Orleans—and added: "I'll never turn a wheel on this boat again while that cub stays."

The captain said: "But he needn't come round when you are on watch, Mr. Brown."

"I won't even stay on the same boat with him. One of us has got to go ashore." "Very well," said the captain, "let it be yourself," and resumed his talk with the passengers.

During the brief remainder of the trip I knew how an emancipated slave feels, for I was an emancipated slave myself. While we lay at landings I listened to George Ealer's flute, or to his readings from his two Bibles, that is to say, Goldsmith and Shakespeare, or I played chess with him—and would have beaten him sometimes, only he always took back his last move and ran the game out differently.

---

9. **whelp** (welp) *n.* puppy. Here, the captain uses it to indicate that Twain is young and foolish, like a puppy.

TAKE NOTES

DRAMA

TAKE NOTES

from The Miracle Worker
by William Gibson

The Miracle Worker is a play based on the real-life story of teacher Annie Sullivan and her student Helen Keller, a seven-year-old girl who is unable to see, hear, or speak. Like her student, Annie suffers from eyesight disabilities; however, she is not totally blind.

from Act I

KELLER. [*very courtly*] Welcome to Ivy Green, Miss Sullivan. I take it you are Miss Sullivan—

KATE. My husband, Miss Annie, Captain Keller.

ANNIE. [*her best behavior*] Captain, how do you do.

KELLER. A pleasure to see you, at last. I trust you had an agreeable journey?

ANNIE. Oh, I had several! When did this country get so big?

JAMES. Where would you like the trunk, father?

KELLER. Where Miss Sullivan can get at it, I imagine.

ANNIE. Yes, please. Where's Helen?

KELLER. In the hall, Jimmie—

KATE. We've put you in the upstairs corner room, Miss Annie, if there's any breeze at all this summer, you'll feel it—

[*In the house the setter* BELLE *flees into the family room, pursued by* HELEN *with groping hands; the dog doubles back out the same door, and* HELEN *still groping for her makes her way out to the porch; she is messy, her hair tumbled, her pinafore now ripped, her shoelaces untied.* KELLER *acquires the suitcase, and* ANNIE *gets her hands on it too, though still endeavoring to live up to the general air of propertied manners.*[1]]

---

1. **the general air of propertied manners** atmosphere of refinement and wealth

90 Close Reading Notebook • Unit 4

Keller. *And* the suitcase—

Annie. [*pleasantly*] I'll take the suitcase, thanks.

Keller. Not at all, I have it, Miss Sullivan.

Annie. I'd like it.

Keller. [*gallantly*] I couldn't think of it, Miss Sullivan. You'll find in the south we—

Annie. Let me.

Keller. —view women as the flowers of civiliza—

Annie. [*impatiently*] I've got something in it for Helen!

[*She tugs it free;* Keller *stares.*]

Thank you. When do I see her?

Kate. There. There is Helen.

[Annie *turns, and sees* Helen *on the porch. A moment of silence. Then* Annie *begins across the yard to her, lugging her suitcase.*]

Keller. [*sotto voce*[2]] Katie—

[Kate *silences him with a hand on his arm. When* Annie *finally reaches the porch steps she stops, contemplating* Helen *for a last moment before entering her world. Then she drops the suitcase on the porch with intentional heaviness,* Helen *starts with the jar, and comes to grope over it.* Annie *puts forth her hand, and touches* Helen*'s.* Helen *at once grasps it, and commences to explore it, like reading a face. She moves her hand on to* Annie*'s forearm, and dress; and* Annie *brings her face within reach of* Helen*'s fingers, which travel over it, quite without timidity, until they encounter and push aside the smoked glasses.* Annie*'s gaze is grave, unpitying, very attentive. She puts her hands on* Helen*'s arms, but* Helen *at once pulls away, and they confront each other with a distance between. Then* Helen *returns to the suitcase, tries to open it, cannot.* Annie *points* Helen*'s hand overhead.* Helen *pulls away, tries to open the suitcase again;* Annie *points her hand overhead again.* Helen *points overhead, a question, and* Annie, *drawing* Helen*'s hand to her own face, nods.* Helen *now begins*

---

2. ***sotto voce*** (sät′ō vō′chē) in a low voice

DRAMA

TAKE NOTES

[tugging the suitcase toward the door; when ANNIE tries to take it from her, she fights her off and backs through the doorway with it. ANNIE stands a moment, then follows her in, and together they get the suitcase up the steps into ANNIE's room.]

KATE. Well?

KELLER. She's very rough, Katie.

KATE. I like her, Captain.

KELLER. Certainly rear a peculiar kind of young woman in the north. How old is she?

KATE. [vaguely] Ohh— Well, she's not in her teens, you know.

KELLER. She's only a child. What's her family like, shipping her off alone this far?

KATE. I couldn't learn. She's very closemouthed about some things.

KELLER. Why does she wear those glasses? I like to see a person's eyes when I talk to—

KATE. For the sun. She was blind.

KELLER. Blind.

KATE. She's had nine operations on her eyes. One just before she left.

KELLER. Blind, good heavens, do they expect one blind child to teach another? Has she experience at least, how long did she teach there?

KATE. She was a pupil.

KELLER. [heavily] Katie, Katie. This is her first position?

KATE. [bright voice] She was valedictorian—

KELLER. Here's a houseful of grownups can't cope with the child, how can an inexperienced half-blind Yankee schoolgirl manage her?

[JAMES moves in with the trunk on his shoulder.]

JAMES. [easily] Great improvement. Now we have two of them to look after.

KELLER. You look after those strawberry plants!

[JAMES *stops with the trunk.* KELLER *turns from him without another word, and marches off.*]

JAMES. Nothing I say is right.

KATE. Why say anything?

[*She calls.*]

Don't be long, Captain, we'll have supper right away—

[*She goes into the house, and through the rear door of the family room.* JAMES *trudges in with the trunk, takes it up the steps to* ANNIE's *room, and sets it down outside the door. The lights elsewhere dim somewhat.*

Meanwhile, inside, ANNIE *has given* HELEN *a key; while* ANNIE *removes her bonnet,* HELEN *unlocks and opens the suitcase. The first thing she pulls out is a voluminous shawl. She fingers it until she perceives what it is; then she wraps it around her, and acquiring* ANNIE's *bonnet and smoked glasses as well, dons the lot: the shawl swamps her, and the bonnet settles down upon the glasses, but she stands before a mirror cocking her head to one side, then to the other, in a mockery of adult action.* ANNIE *is amused, and talks to her as one might to a kitten, with no trace of company manners.*]

ANNIE. All the trouble I went to and that's how I look?

[HELEN *then comes back to the suitcase, gropes for more, lifts out a pair of female drawers.*]

Oh, no. Not the drawers!

[*But* HELEN *discarding them comes to the elegant doll. Her fingers explore its features, and when she raises it and finds its eyes open and close, she is at first startled, then delighted. She picks it up, taps its head vigorously, taps her own chest, and nods questioningly.* ANNIE *takes her finger, points it to the doll, points it to* HELEN, *and touching it to her own face, also nods.* HELEN *sits back on her heels, clasps the doll to herself, and rocks it.* ANNIE *studies her, still in bonnet and smoked glasses like a caricature of herself, and addresses her humorously.*]

All right, Miss O'Sullivan. Let's begin with doll.

[*She takes* HELEN's *hand; in her palm* ANNIE's *forefinger points, thumb holding her other fingers clenched.*]

TAKE NOTES

DRAMA

TAKE NOTES

D.

[*Her thumb next holds all her fingers clenched, touching* HELEN's *palm.*]

O.

[*Her thumb and forefinger extended.*]

L.

[*Same contact repeated.*]

L.

[*She puts* HELEN's *hand to the doll.*]

Doll.

JAMES. You spell pretty well.

[ANNIE *in one hurried move gets the drawers swiftly back into the suitcase, the lid banged shut, and her head turned, to see* JAMES *leaning in the doorway.*]

Finding out if she's ticklish? She is.

[ANNIE *regards him stonily, but* HELEN *after a scowling moment tugs at her hand again, imperious.* ANNIE *repeats the letters, and* HELEN *interrupts her fingers in the middle, feeling each of them, puzzled.* ANNIE *touches* HELEN's *hand to the doll, and begins spelling into it again.*]

JAMES. What is it, a game?

ANNIE. [*curtly*] An alphabet.

JAMES. Alphabet?

ANNIE. For the deaf.

[HELEN *now repeats the finger movements in air, exactly, her head cocked to her own hand, and* ANNIE's *eyes suddenly gleam.*]

Ho. How *bright* she is!

JAMES. You think she knows what she's doing?

[*He takes* HELEN's *hand, to throw a meaningless gesture into it; she repeats this one too.*]

She imitates everything, she's a monkey.

ANNIE. [*very pleased*] Yes, she's a bright little monkey, all right.

[*She takes the doll from* HELEN, *and reaches for her hand;* HELEN *instantly grabs the doll back.* ANNIE *takes it again, and* HELEN's *hand next, but* HELEN *is incensed now; when* ANNIE *draws her hand to her face to shake her head no, then tries to spell to her,* HELEN *slaps at* ANNIE's *face.* ANNIE *grasps* HELEN *by both arms, and swings her into a chair, holding her pinned there, kicking, while glasses, doll, bonnet fly in various directions.* JAMES *laughs.*]

JAMES. She wants her doll back.

ANNIE. When she spells it.

JAMES. Spell, she doesn't know the thing has a name, even.

ANNIE. Of course not, who expects her to, now? All I want is her fingers to learn the letters.

JAMES. Won't mean anything to her.

[ANNIE *gives him a look. She then tries to form* HELEN's *fingers into the letters, but* HELEN *swings a haymaker[3] instead, which* ANNIE *barely ducks, at once pinning her down again.*]

Doesn't like that alphabet, Miss Sullivan. You invent it yourself?

[HELEN *is now in a rage, fighting tooth and nail to get out of the chair, and* ANNIE *answers while struggling and dodging her kicks.*]

ANNIE. Spanish monks under a—vow of silence. Which I wish *you'd* take!

[*And suddenly releasing* HELEN's *hands, she comes and shuts the door in* JAMES's *face.* HELEN *drops to the floor, groping around for the doll.* ANNIE *looks around desperately, sees her purse on the bed, rummages in it, and comes up with a battered piece of cake wrapped in newspaper; with her foot she moves the doll deftly out of the way of* HELEN's *groping, and going on her knee she lets* HELEN *smell the cake. When* HELEN *grabs for it,* ANNIE *removes the cake and spells quickly into the reaching hand.*]

Cake. From Washington up north, it's the best I can do.

---

3. **swings a haymaker** throws a punch

DRAMA

TAKE NOTES

[HELEN's hand waits, baffled. ANNIE repeats it.]

C, a, k, e. Do what my fingers do, never mind what it means.

[She touches the cake briefly to HELEN's nose, pats her hand, presents her own hand. HELEN spells the letters rapidly back. ANNIE pats her hand enthusiastically, and gives her the cake; HELEN crams it into her mouth with both hands. ANNIE watches her, with humor.]

Get it down fast, maybe I'll steal that back too. Now.

[She takes the doll, touches it to HELEN's nose, and spells again into her hand.]

D, o, l, l. Think it over.

[HELEN thinks it over, while ANNIE presents her own hand. Then HELEN spells three letters. ANNIE waits a second, then completes the word for Helen in her palm.]

L.

[She hands over the doll, and HELEN gets a good grip on its leg.]

Imitate now, understand later. End of the first les—

[She never finishes, because HELEN swings the doll with a furious energy, it hits ANNIE squarely in the face, and she falls back with a cry of pain, her knuckles up to her mouth. HELEN waits, tensed for further combat. When ANNIE lowers her knuckles she looks at blood on them; she works her lips, gets to her feet, finds the mirror, and bares her teeth at herself. Now she is furious herself.]

You little wretch, no one's taught you *any* manners? I'll—

[But rounding from the mirror she sees the door slam, HELEN and the doll are on the outside, and HELEN is turning the key in the lock. ANNIE darts over, to pull the knob, the door is locked fast. She yanks it again.]

Helen! Helen, let me out of—

[She bats her brow at the folly of speaking, but JAMES, now downstairs, hears her and turns to see HELEN with the key and doll groping her way down the steps. JAMES takes in the whole situation, makes a move to intercept HELEN, but then changes his mind, lets her pass, and

96 Close Reading Notebook • Unit 4

amusedly follows her out onto the porch. Upstairs ANNIE *meanwhile rattles the knob, kneels, peers through the keyhole, gets up. She goes to the window, looks down, frowns.* JAMES *from the yard sings gaily up to her:*]

JAMES.
> *Buffalo girl, are you coming out tonight,*
> *Coming out tonight,*
> *Coming out—*

[*He drifts back into the house.* ANNIE *takes a handkerchief, nurses her mouth, stands in the middle of the room, staring at door and window in turn, and so catches sight of herself in the mirror, her cheek scratched, her hair disheveled, her handkerchief bloody, her face disgusted with herself. She addresses the mirror, with some irony.*]

ANNIE. Don't worry. They'll find you, you're not lost. Only out of place.

[*But she coughs, spits something into her palm, and stares at it, outraged.*]

And toothless.

[*She winces.*]

Oo! It hurts.

. . . .

from Act III

At Annie's request, Annie and Helen have just spent two weeks alone in a separate building on the family's property. Annie thought she could make better progress with Helen without the interference of Helen's parents. Now, Helen and Annie return to the family home, where the family gathers for dinner. It soon becomes clear that Helen has still not learned how to behave at the table.

[. . . ANNIE, *with everyone now watching, for the third time puts the napkin on* HELEN. HELEN *yanks it off, and throws it down.* ANNIE *rises, lifts* HELEN'*s plate, and bears it away.* HELEN, *feeling it gone, slides down and commences to kick up under the table; the dishes jump.* ANNIE *contemplates this for a moment, then coming back takes* HELEN'*s wrists firmly and swings her off the chair.*

from The Miracle Worker **97**

DRAMA

TAKE NOTES

HELEN *struggling gets one hand free, and catches at her mother's skirt; when* KATE *takes her by the shoulders,* HELEN *hangs quiet.*]

KATE. Miss ANNIE.

ANNIE. No.

KATE. [*a pause*] It's a very special day.

ANNIE. [*grimly*] It will be, when I give in to that.

[*She tries to disengage* HELEN's *hand; Kate lays hers on* ANNIE's.]

KATE. Please. I've hardly had a chance to welcome her home—

ANNIE. Captain Keller.

KELLER. [*embarrassed*] Oh. Katie, we—had a little talk, Miss Annie feels that if we indulge Helen in these—

AUNT EV. But what's the child done?

ANNIE. She's learned not to throw things on the floor and kick. It took us the best part of two weeks and—

AUNT EV. But only a napkin, it's not as if it were breakable!

ANNIE. And everything she's learned *is*? Mrs. Keller, I don't think we should—play tug-of-war for her, either give her to me or you keep her from kicking.

KATE. What do you wish to do?

ANNIE. Let me take her from the table.

AUNT EV. Oh, let her stay, my goodness, she's only a child, she doesn't have to wear a napkin if she doesn't want to her first evening—

ANNIE. [*level*] And ask outsiders not to interfere.

AUNT EV. [*astonished*] Out—outsi— I'm the child's *aunt*!

KATE. [*distressed*] Will once hurt so much, Miss Annie? I've—made all Helen's favorite foods, tonight.

[*A pause*]

KELLER. [*gently*] It's a homecoming party, Miss Annie.

[ANNIE *after a moment releases* HELEN. *But she cannot accept it, at her own chair she shakes her head and turns back, intent on* KATE.]

ANNIE. She's testing you. You realize?

JAMES. [*to* ANNIE] She's testing you.

KELLER. Jimmie, be quiet.

[JAMES *sits, tense.*]

Now she's home, naturally she—

ANNIE. And wants to see what will happen. At your hands. I said it was my main worry, is this what you promised me not half an hour ago?

KELLER. [*reasonably*] But she's *not* kicking, now—

ANNIE. And not learning not to. Mrs. Keller, teaching her is bound to be painful, to everyone. I know it hurts to watch, but she'll live up to just what you demand of her, and no more.

JAMES. [*palely*] She's testing *you.*

KELLER. [*testily*] Jimmie.

JAMES. I have an opinion, I think I should—

KELLER. No one's interested in hearing your opinion.

ANNIE. *I'm* interested, of course she's testing me. Let me keep her to what she's learned and she'll go on learning from me. Take her out of my hands and it all comes apart.

[KATE *closes her eyes, digesting it;* ANNIE *sits again, with a brief comment for her.*]

Be bountiful, it's at her expense.

[*She turns to* JAMES, *flatly.*]

Please pass me more of—her favorite foods.

[*Then* KATE *lifts* HELEN's *hand, and turning her toward* ANNIE, *surrenders her;* HELEN *makes for her own chair.*]

KATE. [*low*] Take her, Miss Annie.

ANNIE. [*then*] Thank you.

[*But the moment* ANNIE *rising reaches for her hand,* HELEN *begins to fight and kick, clutching to the*

from The Miracle Worker

DRAMA

TAKE NOTES

tablecloth, and uttering laments. ANNIE again tries to loosen her hand, and KELLER rises.]

KELLER. [*tolerant*] I'm afraid you're the difficulty, Miss Annie. Now I'll keep her to what she's learned, you're quite right there—

[*He takes* HELEN's *hands from* ANNIE, *pats them;* HELEN *quiets down.*]

—but I don't see that we need send her from the table, after all, she's the guest of honor. Bring her plate back.

ANNIE. If she was a seeing child, none of you would tolerate one—

KELLER. Well, she's not, I think some compromise is called for. Bring her plate, please.

[ANNIE's *jaw sets, but she restores the plate, while* KELLER *fastens the napkin around* HELEN's *neck; she permits it.*]

There. It's not unnatural, most of us take some aversion to our teachers, and occasionally another hand can smooth things out.

[*He puts a fork in* HELEN's *hand;* HELEN *takes it. Genially:*]

Now. Shall we start all over?

[*He goes back around the table, and sits.* ANNIE *stands watching.* HELEN *is motionless, thinking things through, until with a wicked glee she deliberately flings the fork on the floor. After another moment she plunges her hand into her food, and crams a fistful into her mouth.*]

JAMES. [*wearily*] I think we've started all over—

[KELLER *shoots a glare at him, as* HELEN *plunges her other hand into* ANNIE's *plate.* ANNIE *at once moves in, to grasp her wrist, and* HELEN *flinging out a hand encounters the pitcher; she swings with it at* ANNIE; ANNIE *falling back blocks it with an elbow, but the water flies over her dress.* ANNIE *gets her breath, then snatches the pitcher away in one hand, hoists* HELEN *up bodily under the other arm, and starts to carry her out, kicking.* KELLER *stands.*]

ANNIE. [*savagely polite*] Don't get up!

Keller. Where are you going?

Annie. Don't smooth anything else out for me, don't interfere in any way! I treat her like a seeing child because I *ask* her to see, I *expect* her to see, don't undo what I do!

Keller. Where are you taking her?

Annie. To make her fill this pitcher again!

[*She thrusts out with* Helen *under her arm, but* Helen *escapes up the stairs and* Annie *runs after her.* Keller *stands rigid.* Aunt Ev *is astounded.*]

Aunt Ev. You let her speak to you like that, Arthur? A creature who *works* for you?

Keller. [*angrily*] No. I don't.

[*He is starting after* Annie *when* James, *on his feet with shaky resolve, interposes his chair between them in* Keller's *path.*]

James. Let her go.

Keller. What!

James. [*a swallow*] I said—let her go. She's right.

[Keller *glares at the chair and him.* James *takes a deep breath, then headlong:*]

She's right, Kate's right, I'm right, and you're wrong. If you drive her away from here it will be over my dead—chair, has it never occurred to you that on one occasion you might be consummately wrong?

[Keller's *stare is unbelieving, even a little fascinated.* Kate *rises in trepidation, to mediate.*]

Kate. Captain.

[Keller *stops her with his raised hand; his eyes stay on* James's *pale face, for a long hold. When he finally finds his voice, it is gruff.*]

Keller. Sit down, everyone.

[*He sits.* Kate *sits.* James *holds onto his chair.* Keller *speaks mildly.*]

Please sit down, Jimmie.

from The Miracle Worker

DRAMA

TAKE NOTES

[JAMES *sits, and a moveless silence prevails;* KELLER's *eyes do not leave him.*

ANNIE *has pulled* HELEN *downstairs again by one hand, the pitcher in her other hand, down the porch steps, and across the yard to the pump. She puts* HELEN's *hand on the pump handle, grimly.*]

ANNIE. All right. Pump.

[HELEN *touches her cheek, waits uncertainly.*]

No, she's not here. Pump!

[*She forces* HELEN's *hand to work the handle, then lets go. And* HELEN *obeys. She pumps till the water comes, then* ANNIE *puts the pitcher in her other hand and guides it under the spout, and the water tumbling half into and half around the pitcher douses* HELEN's *hand.* ANNIE *takes over the handle to keep water coming, and does automatically what she has done so many times before, spells into* HELEN's *free palm:*]

Water. W, a, t, e, r. *Water.* It has a—*name*—

[*And now the miracle happens.* HELEN *drops the pitcher on the slab under the spout, it shatters. She stands transfixed.* ANNIE *freezes on the pump handle: there is a change in the sundown light, and with it a change in* HELEN's *face, some light coming into it we have never seen there, some struggle in the depths behind it; and her lips tremble, trying to remember something the muscles around them once knew, till at last it finds its way out, painfully, a baby sound buried under the debris of years of dumbness.*]

HELEN. Wah. Wah.

[*And again, with great effort*]

Wah. Wah.

[HELEN *plunges her hand into the dwindling water, spells into her own palm. Then she gropes frantically,* ANNIE *reaches for her hand, and* HELEN *spells into* ANNIE's *hand.*]

ANNIE. [*whispering*] Yes.

[HELEN *spells into it again.*]

102 Close Reading Notebook • Unit 4

Yes!

[HELEN *grabs at the handle, pumps for more water, plunges her hand into its spurt and grabs* ANNIE's *to spell it again.*]

Yes! Oh, my dear—

[*She falls to her knees to clasp* HELEN's *hand, but* HELEN *pulls it free, stands almost bewildered, then drops to the ground, pats it swiftly, holds up her palm, imperious.* ANNIE *spells into it:*]

Ground.

[HELEN *spells it back.*]

Yes!

[HELEN *whirls to the pump, pats it, holds up her palm, and* ANNIE *spells into it.*]

Pump.

[HELEN *spells it back.*]

Yes! Yes!

[*Now* HELEN *is in such an excitement she is possessed, wild, trembling, cannot be still, turns, runs, falls on the porch steps, claps it, reaches out her palm, and* ANNIE *is at it instantly to spell:*]

Step.

[HELEN *has no time to spell back now, she whirls groping, to touch anything, encounters the trellis, shakes it, thrusts out her palm, and* ANNIE *while spelling to her cries wildly at the house.*]

Trellis. Mrs. Keller. *Mrs. Keller!*

from The Miracle Worker 103

The Diary of Anne Frank

by Frances Goodrich and Albert Hackett

Characters

Anne Frank	Mr. Kraler
Otto Frank	Mr. Dussel
Edith Frank	Peter Van Daan
Margot Frank	Mrs. Van Daan
Miep Gies	Mr. Van Daan

Act I

Scene 1

[*The scene remains the same throughout the play. It is the top floor of a warehouse and office building in Amsterdam, Holland. The sharply peaked roof of the building is outlined against a sea of other rooftops, stretching away into the distance. Nearby is the belfry of a church tower, the Westertoren, whose carillon[1] rings out the hours. Occasionally faint sounds float up from below: the voices of children playing in the street, the tramp of marching feet, a boat whistle from the canal.*

The three rooms of the top floor and a small attic space above are exposed to our view. The largest of the rooms is in the center, with two small rooms, slightly raised, on either side. On the right is a bathroom, out of sight. A narrow steep flight of stairs at the back leads up to the attic. The rooms are sparsely furnished with a few chairs, cots, a table or two. The windows are painted over, or covered with makeshift blackout curtains.[2] In the main room there is a sink, a gas ring for cooking and a woodburning stove for warmth.

The room on the left is hardly more than a closet. There is a skylight in the sloping ceiling. Directly under this room is a small steep stairwell, with steps leading down to a door. This is the only entrance from the building below. When the door is opened we see that it has been concealed on the outer side by a bookcase attached to it.

The curtain rises on an empty stage. It is late afternoon, November 1945.

---

1. **carillon** (karʹ ə länʹ) *n.* set of bells, each producing one note of the scale.
2. **blackout curtains** dark curtains that conceal all lights that might be visible to bombers from the air.

The rooms are dusty, the curtains in rags. Chairs and tables are overturned.

The door at the foot of the small stairwell swings open. Mr. Frank *comes up the steps into view. He is a gentle, cultured European in his middle years. There is still a trace of a German accent in his speech.*

He stands looking slowly around, making a supreme effort at self-control. He is weak, ill. His clothes are threadbare.

After a second he drops his rucksack on the couch and moves slowly about. He opens the door to one of the smaller rooms, and then abruptly closes it again, turning away. He goes to the window at the back, looking off at the Westertoren as its carillon strikes the hour of six, then he moves restlessly on.

From the street below we hear the sound of a barrel organ[3] and children's voices at play. There is a many-colored scarf hanging from a nail. Mr. Frank *takes it, putting it around his neck. As he starts back for his rucksack, his eye is caught by something lying on the floor. It is a woman's white glove. He holds it in his hand and suddenly all of his self-control is gone. He breaks down, crying.*

We hear footsteps on the stairs. Miep Gies *comes up, looking for* Mr. Frank. Miep *is a Dutch girl of about twenty-two. She wears a coat and hat, ready to go home. She is pregnant. Her attitude toward* Mr. Frank *is protective, compassionate.*]

Miep. Are you all right, Mr. Frank?

Mr. Frank. [*Quickly controlling himself*] Yes, Miep, yes.

Miep. Everyone in the office has gone home . . . It's after six. [*Then pleading*] Don't stay up here, Mr. Frank. What's the use of torturing yourself like this?

Mr. Frank. I've come to say good-bye . . . I'm leaving here, Miep.

Miep. What do you mean? Where are you going? Where?

Mr. Frank. I don't know yet. I haven't decided.

---

3. barrel organ mechanical musical instrument often played by street musicians in past decades.

MIEP. Mr. Frank, you can't leave here! This is your home! Amsterdam is your home. Your business is here, waiting for you . . . You're needed here . . . Now that the war is over, there are things that . . .

MR. FRANK. I can't stay in Amsterdam, Miep. It has too many memories for me. Everywhere there's something . . . the house we lived in . . . the school . . . that street organ playing out there . . . I'm not the person you used to know, Miep. I'm a bitter old man. [*Breaking off*] Forgive me. I shouldn't speak to you like this . . . after all that you did for us . . . the suffering . . .

MIEP. No. No. It wasn't suffering. You can't say we suffered. [*As she speaks, she straightens a chair which is overturned.*]

MR. FRANK. I know what you went through, you and Mr. Kraler. I'll remember it as long as I live. [*He gives one last look around.*] Come, Miep. [*He starts for the steps, then remembers his rucksack, going back to get it.*]

MIEP. [*Hurrying up to a cupboard*] Mr. Frank, did you see? There are some of your papers here. [*She brings a bundle of papers to him.*] We found them in a heap of rubbish on the floor after . . . after you left.

MR. FRANK. Burn them. [*He opens his rucksack to put the glove in it.*]

MIEP. But, Mr. Frank, there are letters, notes . . .

MR. FRANK. Burn them. All of them.

MIEP. Burn *this*? [*She hands him a paper-bound notebook.*]

MR. FRANK. [*Quietly*] Anne's diary. [*He opens the diary and begins to read.*] "Monday, the sixth of July, nineteen forty-two." [*To* MIEP] Nineteen forty-two. Is it possible, Miep? . . . Only three years ago. [*As he continues his reading, he sits down on the couch.*] "Dear Diary, since you and I are going to be great friends, I will start by telling you about myself. My name is Anne Frank. I am thirteen years old. I was born in Germany the twelfth of June, nineteen twenty-nine. As my family is Jewish, we emigrated to Holland when Hitler came to power."

[As Mr. Frank *reads on, another voice joins his, as if coming from the air. It is* Anne's Voice.]

Mr. Frank and Anne. "My father started a business, importing spice and herbs. Things went well for us until nineteen forty. Then the war came, and the Dutch capitulation,[4] followed by the arrival of the Germans. Then things got very bad for the Jews."

[Mr. Frank's Voice *dies out.* Anne's Voice *continues alone. The lights dim slowly to darkness. The curtain falls on the scene.*]

Anne's Voice. You could not do this and you could not do that. They forced Father out of his business. We had to wear yellow stars.[5] I had to turn in my bike. I couldn't go to a Dutch school any more. I couldn't go to the movies, or ride in an automobile, or even on a streetcar, and a million other things. But somehow we children still managed to have fun. Yesterday Father told me we were going into hiding. Where, he wouldn't say. At five o'clock this morning Mother woke me and told me to hurry and get dressed. I was to put on as many clothes as I could. It would look too suspicious if we walked along carrying suitcases. It wasn't until we were on our way that I learned where we were going. Our hiding place was to be upstairs in the building where Father used to have his business. Three other people were coming in with us . . . the Van Daans and their son Peter . . . Father knew the Van Daans but we had never met them . . .

[*During the last lines the curtain rises on the scene. The lights dim on.* Anne's Voice *fades out.*]

Scene 2

[*It is early morning, July 1942. The rooms are bare, as before, but they are now clean and orderly.*

Mr. Van Daan, *a tall, portly[6] man in his late forties, is in the main room, pacing up and down, nervously smoking a cigarette. His clothes and overcoat are expensive and well cut.*

---

4. **capitulation** (kə pich′ ə lā′ shən) *n.* surrender.
5. **yellow stars** Stars of David, the six-pointed stars that are symbols of Judaism. The Nazis ordered all Jews to wear them on their clothing.
6. **portly** (pôrt′ lē) *adj.* large and heavy.

MRS. VAN DAAN *sits on the couch, clutching her possessions, a hatbox, bags, etc. She is a pretty woman in her early forties. She wears a fur coat over her other clothes.*

PETER VAN DAAN *is standing at the window of the room on the right, looking down at the street below. He is a shy, awkward boy of sixteen. He wears a cap, a raincoat, and long Dutch trousers, like "plus fours."[7] At his feet is a black case, a carrier for his cat.*

The yellow Star of David is conspicuous on all of their clothes.]

MRS. VAN DAAN. [*Rising, nervous, excited*] Something's happened to them! I know it!

MR. VAN DAAN. Now, Kerli!

MRS. VAN DAAN. Mr. Frank said they'd be here at seven o'clock. He said . . .

MR. VAN DAAN. They have two miles to walk. You can't expect . . .

MRS. VAN DAAN. They've been picked up. That's what's happened. They've been taken . . .

[MR. VAN DAAN *indicates that he hears someone coming.*]

MR. VAN DAAN. You see?

[PETER *takes up his carrier and his schoolbag, etc., and goes into the main room as* MR. FRANK *comes up the stairwell from below.* MR. FRANK *looks much younger now. His movements are brisk, his manner confident. He wears an overcoat and carries his hat and a small cardboard box. He crosses to the* VAN DAANS, *shaking hands with each of them.*]

MR. FRANK. Mrs. Van Daan, Mr. Van Daan, Peter. [*Then, in explanation of their lateness*] There were too many of the Green Police[8] on the streets . . . we had to take the long way around.

[*Up the steps come* MARGOT FRANK, MRS. FRANK, MIEP *(not pregnant now) and* MR. KRALER. *All of them carry bags,*

---

7. **plus fours** *n.* loose knickers (short pants) worn for active sports.
8. **Green Police** the Dutch Gestapo, or Nazi police, who wore green uniforms and were known for their brutality. Those in danger of being arrested or deported feared the Gestapo, especially because of their practice of raiding houses to round up victims in the middle of the night—when people are most confused and vulnerable.

packages, and so forth. The Star of David is conspicuous on all of the FRANKS' *clothing.* MARGOT *is eighteen, beautiful, quiet, shy.* MRS. FRANK *is a young mother, gently bred, reserved. She, like* MR. FRANK, *has a slight German accent.* MR. KRALER *is a Dutchman, dependable, kindly.*

As MR. KRALER *and* MIEP *go upstage to put down their parcels,* MRS. FRANK *turns back to call* ANNE.]

MRS. FRANK. Anne?

[ANNE *comes running up the stairs. She is thirteen, quick in her movements, interested in everything, mercurial[9] in her emotions. She wears a cape, long wool socks and carries a schoolbag.*]

MR. FRANK. [*Introducing them*] My wife, Edith. Mr. and Mrs. Van Daan [MRS. FRANK *hurries over, shaking hands with them.*] . . . their son, Peter . . . my daughters, Margot and Anne.

[ANNE *gives a polite little curtsy as she shakes* MR. VAN DAAN'S *hand. Then she immediately starts off on a tour of investigation of her new home, going upstairs to the attic room.*]

MIEP *and* MR. KRALER *are putting the various things they have brought on the shelves.*]

MR. KRALER. I'm sorry there is still so much confusion.

MR. FRANK. Please. Don't think of it. After all, we'll have plenty of leisure to arrange everything ourselves.

MIEP. [*To* MRS. FRANK] We put the stores of food you sent in here. Your drugs are here . . . soap, linen here.

MRS. FRANK. Thank you, Miep.

MIEP. I made up the beds . . . the way Mr. Frank and Mr. Kraler said. [*She starts out.*] Forgive me. I have to hurry. I've got to go to the other side of town to get some ration books[10] for you.

MRS. VAN DAAN. Ration books? If they see our names on ration books, they'll know we're here.

MR. KRALER. There isn't anything . . .

---

9. **mercurial** (mər kyoor´ ē əl) *adj.* quick or changeable in behavior.
10. **ration** (rash´ ən) **books** *n.* books of stamps given to ensure the equal distribution of scarce items, such as meat or gasoline, in times of shortage.

DRAMA

TAKE NOTES

MIEP. Don't worry. Your names won't be on them. [*As she hurries out*] I'll be up later.

MR. FRANK. Thank you, Miep.

MRS. FRANK. [*To* MR. KRALER] It's illegal, then, the ration books? We've never done anything illegal.

MR. FRANK. We won't be living here exactly according to regulations.

[*As* MR. KRALER *reassures* MRS. FRANK, *he takes various small things, such as matches, soap, etc., from his pockets, handing them to her.*]

MR. KRALER. This isn't the black market,[11] Mrs. Frank. This is what we call the white market . . . helping all of the hundreds and hundreds who are hiding out in Amsterdam.

[*The carillon is heard playing the quarter-hour before eight.* MR. KRALER *looks at his watch.* ANNE *stops at the window as she comes down the stairs.*]

ANNE. It's the Westertoren!

MR. KRALER. I must go. I must be out of here and downstairs in the office before the workmen get here. [*He starts for the stairs leading out.*] Miep or I, or both of us, will be up each day to bring you food and news and find out what your needs are. Tomorrow I'll get you a better bolt for the door at the foot of the stairs. It needs a bolt that you can throw yourself and open only at our signal. [*To* MR. FRANK] Oh . . . You'll tell them about the noise?

MR. FRANK. I'll tell them.

MR. KRALER. Good-bye then for the moment. I'll come up again, after the workmen leave.

MR. FRANK. Good-bye, Mr. Kraler.

MRS. FRANK. [*Shaking his hand*] How can we thank you?

[*The others murmur their good-byes.*]

MR. KRALER. I never thought I'd live to see the day when a man like Mr. Frank would have to go into hiding. When you think—

---

11. **black market** illegal way of buying scarce items without ration stamps.

110 Close Reading Notebook • Unit 4

[*He breaks off, going out.* MR. FRANK *follows him down the steps, bolting the door after him. In the interval before he returns,* PETER *goes over to* MARGOT, *shaking hands with her. As* MR. FRANK *comes back up the steps,* MRS. FRANK *questions him anxiously.*]

MRS. FRANK. What did he mean, about the noise?

MR. FRANK. First let us take off some of these clothes.

[*They all start to take off garment after garment. On each of their coats, sweaters, blouses, suits, dresses, is another yellow Star of David.* MR. *and* MRS. FRANK *are underdressed quite simply. The others wear several things, sweaters, extra dresses, bathrobes, aprons, nightgowns, etc.*]

MR. VAN DAAN. It's a wonder we weren't arrested, walking along the streets . . . Petronella with a fur coat in July . . . and that cat of Peter's crying all the way.

ANNE. [*As she is removing a pair of panties*] A cat?

MRS. FRANK. [*Shocked*] Anne, please!

ANNE. It's alright. I've got on three more.

[*She pulls off two more. Finally, as they have all removed their surplus clothes, they look to* MR. FRANK, *waiting for him to speak.*]

MR. FRANK. Now. About the noise. While the men are in the building below, we must have complete quiet. Every sound can be heard down there, not only in the workrooms, but in the offices too. The men come at about eight-thirty, and leave at about five-thirty. So, to be perfectly safe, from eight in the morning until six in the evening we must move only when it is necessary, and then in stockinged feet. We must not speak above a whisper. We must not run any water. We cannot use the sink, or even, forgive me, the w.c.[12] The pipes go down through the workrooms. It would be heard. No trash . . .

[MR. FRANK *stops abruptly as he hears the sound of marching feet from the street below. Everyone is motionless, paralyzed with fear.* MR. FRANK *goes quietly into the room on the right to look down out of the window.*

---

12. w.c. water closet; bathroom.

ANNE *runs after him, peering out with him. The tramping feet pass without stopping. The tension is relieved.* MR. FRANK, *followed by* ANNE, *returns to the main room and resumes his instructions to the group.*] . . . No trash must ever be thrown out which might reveal that someone is living up here . . . not even a potato paring. We must burn everything in the stove at night. This is the way we must live until it is over, if we are to survive.

[*There is silence for a second.*]

MRS. FRANK. Until it is over.

MR. FRANK. [*Reassuringly*] After six we can move about . . . we can talk and laugh and have our supper and read and play games . . . just as we would at home. [*He looks at his watch.*] And now I think it would be wise if we all went to our rooms, and were settled before eight o'clock. Mrs. Van Daan, you and your husband will be upstairs. I regret that there's no place up there for Peter. But he will be here, near us. This will be our common room, where we'll meet to talk and eat and read, like one family.

MR. VAN DAAN. And where do you and Mrs. Frank sleep?

MR. FRANK. This room is also our bedroom.

[*Together*]
{ **MRS. VAN DAAN.** That isn't right. We'll sleep here and you take the room upstairs.
MR. VAN DAAN. It's your place.

MR. FRANK. Please. I've thought this out for weeks. It's the best arrangement. The only arrangement.

MRS. VAN DAAN. [*To* MR. FRANK] Never, never can we thank you. [*Then to* MRS. FRANK] I don't know what would have happened to us, if it hadn't been for Mr. Frank.

MR. FRANK. You don't know how your husband helped me when I came to this country . . . knowing no one . . . not able to speak the language. I can never repay him for that. [*Going to* VAN DAAN] May I help you with your things?

MR. VAN DAAN. No. No. [*To* MRS. VAN DAAN] Come along, liefje.[13]

---

13. *liefje* (lēf′ yə) Dutch for "little love."

Mrs. Van Daan. You'll be all right, Peter? You're not afraid?

Peter. [*Embarrassed*] Please, Mother.

[*They start up the stairs to the attic room above.* Mr. Frank *turns to* Mrs. Frank.]

Mr. Frank. You too must have some rest, Edith. You didn't close your eyes last night. Nor you, Margot.

Anne. I slept, Father. Wasn't that funny? I knew it was the last night in my own bed, and yet I slept soundly.

Mr. Frank. I'm glad, Anne. Now you'll be able to help me straighten things in here. [*To* Mrs. Frank *and* Margot] Come with me . . . You and Margot rest in this room for the time being.

[*He picks up their clothes, starting for the room on the right.*]

Mrs. Frank. You're sure . . . ? I could help . . . And Anne hasn't had her milk . . .

Mr. Frank. I'll give it to her. [*To* Anne *and* Peter] Anne, Peter . . . it's best that you take off your shoes now, before you forget.

[*He leads the way to the room, followed by* Margot.]

Mrs. Frank. You're sure you're not tired, Anne?

Anne. I feel fine. I'm going to help Father.

Mrs. Frank. Peter, I'm glad you are to be with us.

Peter. Yes, Mrs. Frank.

[Mrs. Frank *goes to join* Mr. Frank *and* Margot.]

[*During the following scene* Mr. Frank *helps* Margot *and* Mrs. Frank *to hang up their clothes. Then he persuades them both to lie down and rest. The* Van Daans *in their room above settle themselves. In the main room* Anne *and* Peter *remove their shoes.* Peter *takes his cat out of the carrier.*]

Anne. What's your cat's name?

Peter. Mouschi.

Anne. Mouschi! Mouschi! Mouschi! [*She picks up the cat, walking away with it. To* Peter] I love cats. I

The Diary of Anne Frank 113

have one . . . a darling little cat. But they made me leave her behind. I left some food and a note for the neighbors to take care of her . . . I'm going to miss her terribly. What is yours? A him or a her?

Peter. He's a tom. He doesn't like strangers. [*He takes the cat from her, putting it back in its carrier.*]

Anne. [*Unabashed*] Then I'll have to stop being a stranger, won't I? Is he fixed?

Peter. [*Startled*] Huh?

Anne. Did you have him fixed?

Peter. No.

Anne. Oh, you ought to have him fixed—to keep him from—you know, fighting. Where did you go to school?

Peter. Jewish Secondary.

Anne. But that's where Margot and I go! I never saw you around.

Peter. I used to see you . . . sometimes . . .

Anne. You did?

Peter. . . . In the school yard. You were always in the middle of a bunch of kids. [*He takes a penknife from his pocket.*]

Anne. Why didn't you ever come over?

Peter. I'm sort of a lone wolf. [*He starts to rip off his Star of David.*]

Anne. What are you doing?

Peter. Taking it off.

Anne. But you can't do that. They'll arrest you if you go out without your star.

[*He tosses his knife on the table.*]

Peter. Who's going out?

Anne. Why, of course! You're right! Of course we don't need them any more. [*She picks up his knife and starts to take her star off.*] I wonder what our friends will think when we don't show up today?

PETER. I didn't have any dates with anyone.

ANNE. Oh, I did. I had a date with Jopie to go and play ping-pong at her house. Do you know Jopie de Waal?

PETER. No.

ANNE. Jopie's my best friend. I wonder what she'll think when she telephones and there's no answer? . . . Probably she'll go over to the house . . . I wonder what she'll think . . . we left everything as if we'd suddenly been called away . . . breakfast dishes in the sink . . . beds not made . . . [*As she pulls off her star, the cloth underneath shows clearly the color and form of the star.*] Look! It's still there! [PETER *goes over to the stove with his star.*] What're you going to do with yours?

PETER. Burn it.

ANNE. [*She starts to throw hers in, and cannot.*] It's funny, I can't throw mine away. I don't know why.

PETER. You can't throw . . . ? Something they branded you with . . . ? That they made you wear so they could spit on you?

ANNE. I know. I know. But after all, it *is* the Star of David, isn't it?

[*In the bedroom, right,* MARGOT *and* MRS. FRANK *are lying down.* MR. FRANK *starts quietly out.*]

PETER. Maybe it's different for a girl.

[MR. FRANK *comes into the main room.*]

MR. FRANK. Forgive me, Peter. Now let me see. We must find a bed for your cat. [*He goes to a cupboard.*] I'm glad you brought your cat. Anne was feeling so badly about hers. [*Getting a used small washtub*] Here we are. Will it be comfortable in that?

PETER. [*Gathering up his things*] Thanks.

MR. FRANK. [*Opening the door of the room on the left*] And here is your room. But I warn you, Peter, you can't grow any more. Not an inch, or you'll have to sleep with your feet out of the skylight. Are you hungry?

TAKE NOTES

DRAMA

TAKE NOTES

PETER. No.

MR. FRANK. We have some bread and butter.

PETER. No, thank you.

MR. FRANK. You can have it for luncheon then. And tonight we will have a real supper . . . our first supper together.

PETER. Thanks. Thanks. [*He goes into his room. During the following scene he arranges his possessions in his new room.*]

MR. FRANK. That's a nice boy, Peter.

ANNE. He's awfully shy, isn't he?

MR. FRANK. You'll like him, I know.

ANNE. I certainly hope so, since he's the only boy I'm likely to see for months and months.

[MR. FRANK *sits down, taking off his shoes.*]

MR. FRANK. Annele,[14] there's a box there. Will you open it?

[*He indicates a carton on the couch.* ANNE *brings it to the center table. In the street below there is the sound of children playing.*]

ANNE. [*As she opens the carton*] You know the way I'm going to think of it here? I'm going to think of it as a boarding house. A very peculiar summer boarding house, like the one that we—[*She breaks off as she pulls out some photographs.*] Father! My movie stars! I was wondering where they were! I was looking for them this morning . . . and Queen Wilhelmina![15] How wonderful!

MR. FRANK. There's something more. Go on. Look further. [*He goes over to the sink, pouring a glass of milk from a thermos bottle.*]

ANNE. [*Pulling out a pasteboard-bound book*] A diary! [*She throws her arms around her father.*] I've never had a diary. And I've always longed for one. [*She looks around the room.*] Pencil, pencil, pencil, pencil.

---

14. **Annele** (än′ ə lə) another nickname for "Anne."
15. **Queen Wilhelmina** (vil′ hel mē′ nä) Queen of the Netherlands from 1890 to 1948.

116 Close Reading Notebook • Unit 4

[*She starts down the stairs.*] I'm going down to the office to get a pencil.

Mr. Frank. Anne! No! [*He goes after her, catching her by the arm and pulling her back.*]

Anne. [*Startled*] But there's no one in the building now.

Mr. Frank. It doesn't matter. I don't want you ever to go beyond that door.

Anne. [*Sobered*] Never . . . ? Not even at nighttime, when everyone is gone? Or on Sundays? Can't I go down to listen to the radio?

Mr. Frank. Never. I am sorry, Anneke.[16] It isn't safe. No, you must never go beyond that door.

[*For the first time* Anne *realizes what "going into hiding" means.*]

Anne. I see.

Mr. Frank. It'll be hard, I know. But always remember this, Anneke. There are no walls, there are no bolts, no locks that anyone can put on your mind. Miep will bring us books. We will read history, poetry, mythology. [*He gives her the glass of milk.*] Here's your milk. [*With his arm about her, they go over to the couch, sitting down side by side.*] As a matter of fact, between us, Anne, being here has certain advantages for you. For instance, you remember the battle you had with your mother the other day on the subject of overshoes? You said you'd rather die than wear overshoes? But in the end you had to wear them? Well now, you see, for as long as we are here you will never have to wear overshoes! Isn't that good? And the coat that you inherited from Margot, you won't have to wear that any more. And the piano! You won't have to practice on the piano. I tell you, this is going to be a fine life for you!

[Anne's *panic is gone.* Peter *appears in the doorway of his room, with a saucer in his hand. He is carrying his cat.*]

Peter. I . . . I . . . I thought I'd better get some water for Mouschi before . . .

---

16. Anneke (än´ ə kə) nickname for "Anne."

TAKE NOTES

The Diary of Anne Frank **117**

DRAMA

TAKE NOTES

Mr. Frank. Of course.

[*As he starts toward the sink the carillon begins to chime the hour of eight. He tiptoes to the window at the back and looks down at the street below. He turns to* Peter, *indicating in pantomime that it is too late.* Peter *starts back for his room. He steps on a creaking board. The three of them are frozen for a minute in fear. As* Peter *starts away again,* Anne *tiptoes over to him and pours some of the milk from her glass into the saucer for the cat.* Peter *squats on the floor, putting the milk before the cat.* Mr. Frank *gives* Anne *his fountain pen, and then goes into the room at the right. For a second* Anne *watches the cat, then she goes over to the center table, and opens her diary.*

In the room at the right, Mrs. Frank *has sat up quickly at the sound of the carillon.* Mr. Frank *comes in and sits down beside her on the settee, his arm comfortingly around her.*

Upstairs, in the attic room, Mr. *and* Mrs. Van Daan *have hung their clothes in the closet and are now seated on the iron bed.* Mrs. Van Daan *leans back exhausted.* Mr. Van Daan *fans her with a newspaper.*

Anne *starts to write in her diary. The lights dim out, the curtain falls.*

In the darkness Anne's Voice *comes to us again, faintly at first, and then with growing strength.*]

Anne's Voice. I expect I should be describing what it feels like to go into hiding. But I really don't know yet myself. I only know it's funny never to be able to go outdoors . . . never to breathe fresh air . . . never to run and shout and jump. It's the silence in the nights that frightens me most. Every time I hear a creak in the house, or a step on the street outside, I'm sure they're coming for us. The days aren't so bad. At least we know that Miep and Mr. Kraler are down there below us in the office. Our protectors, we call them. I asked Father what would happen to them if the Nazis found out they were hiding us. Pim said that they would suffer the same fate that we would . . . Imagine! They know this, and yet when they come up here, they're always cheerful and gay as if there were nothing in the world to bother them . . . Friday, the twenty-first of August,

118 Close Reading Notebook • Unit 4

nineteen forty-two. Today I'm going to tell you our general news. Mother is unbearable. She insists on treating me like a baby, which I loathe. Otherwise things are going better. The weather is . . .

[*As* Anne's Voice *is fading out, the curtain rises on the scene.*]

Scene 3

[*It is a little after six o'clock in the evening, two months later.*

Margot *is in the bedroom at the right, studying.* Mr. Van Daan *is lying down in the attic room above.*

The rest of the "family" is in the main room. Anne *and* Peter *sit opposite each other at the center table, where they have been doing their lessons.* Mrs. Frank *is on the couch.* Mrs. Van Daan *is seated with her fur coat, on which she has been sewing, in her lap. None of them are wearing their shoes.*

Their eyes are on Mr. Frank, *waiting for him to give them the signal which will release them from their day-long quiet.* Mr. Frank, *his shoes in his hand, stands looking down out of the window at the back, watching to be sure that all of the workmen have left the building below.*

After a few seconds of motionless silence, Mr. Frank *turns from the window.*]

Mr. Frank. [*Quietly, to the group*] It's safe now. The last workman has left.

[*There is an immediate stir of relief.*]

Anne. [*Her pent-up energy explodes.*] WHEE!

Mr. Frank. [*Startled, amused*] Anne!

Mrs. Van Daan. I'm first for the w.c.

[*She hurries off to the bathroom.* Mrs. Frank *puts on her shoes and starts up to the sink to prepare supper.* Anne *sneaks* Peter's *shoes from under the table and hides them behind her back.* Mr. Frank *goes in to* Margot's *room.*]

Mr. Frank. [*To* Margot] Six o'clock. School's over.

The Diary of Anne Frank **119**

TAKE NOTES

[MARGOT *gets up, stretching.* MR. FRANK *sits down to put on his shoes. In the main room* PETER *tries to find his.*]

PETER. [*To* ANNE] Have you seen my shoes?

ANNE. [*Innocently*] Your shoes?

PETER. You've taken them, haven't you?

ANNE. I don't know what you're talking about.

PETER. You're going to be sorry!

ANNE. Am I?

[PETER *goes after her.* ANNE, *with his shoes in her hand, runs from him, dodging behind her mother.*]

MRS. FRANK. [*Protesting*] Anne, dear!

PETER. Wait till I get you!

ANNE. I'm waiting!
 [PETER *makes a lunge for her. They both fall to the floor.* PETER *pins her down, wrestling with her to get the shoes.*]
 Don't! Don't! Peter, stop it. Ouch!

MRS. FRANK. Anne! . . . Peter!

[*Suddenly* PETER *becomes self-conscious. He grabs his shoes roughly and starts for his room.*]

ANNE. [*Following him*] Peter, where are you going? Come dance with me.

PETER. I tell you I don't know how.

ANNE. I'll teach you.

PETER. I'm going to give Mouschi his dinner.

ANNE. Can I watch?

PETER. He doesn't like people around while he eats.

ANNE. Peter, please.

PETER. No! [*He goes into his room.* ANNE *slams his door after him.*]

MRS. FRANK. Anne, dear, I think you shouldn't play like that with Peter. It's not dignified.

ANNE. Who cares if it's dignified? I don't want to be dignified.

120 Close Reading Notebook • Unit 4

[MR. FRANK *and* MARGOT *come from the room on the right.* MARGOT *goes to help her mother.* MR. FRANK *starts for the center table to correct* MARGOT'S *school papers.*]

MRS. FRANK. [*To* ANNE] You complain that I don't treat you like a grownup. But when I do, you resent it.

ANNE. I only want some fun . . . someone to laugh and clown with . . . After you've sat still all day and hardly moved, you've got to have some fun. I don't know what's the matter with that boy.

MR. FRANK. He isn't used to girls. Give him a little time.

ANNE. Time? Isn't two months time? I could cry. [*Catching hold of* MARGOT] Come on, Margot . . . dance with me. Come on, please.

MARGOT. I have to help with supper.

ANNE. You know we're going to forget how to dance . . . When we get out we won't remember a thing.

[*She starts to sing and dance by herself.* MR. FRANK *takes her in his arms, waltzing with her.* MRS. VAN DAAN *comes in from the bathroom.*]

MRS. VAN DAAN. Next? [*She looks around as she starts putting on her shoes.*] Where's Peter?

ANNE. [*As they are dancing*] Where would he be!

MRS. VAN DAAN. He hasn't finished his lessons, has he? His father'll kill him if he catches him in there with that cat and his work not done. [MR. FRANK *and* ANNE *finish their dance. They bow to each other with extravagant formality.*] Anne, get him out of there, will you?

ANNE. [*At* PETER'S *door*] Peter? Peter?

PETER. [*Opening the door a crack*] What is it?

ANNE. Your mother says to come out.

PETER. I'm giving Mouschi his dinner.

MRS. VAN DAAN. You know what your father says. [*She sits on the couch, sewing on the lining of her fur coat.*]

PETER. For heaven's sake, I haven't even looked at him since lunch.

TAKE NOTES

The Diary of Anne Frank **121**

DRAMA

TAKE NOTES

Mrs. Van Daan. I'm just telling you, that's all.

Anne. I'll feed him.

Peter. I don't want you in there.

Mrs. Van Daan. Peter!

Peter. [*To* Anne] Then give him his dinner and come right out, you hear?

[*He comes back to the table.* Anne *shuts the door of* Peter's *room after her and disappears behind the curtain covering his closet.*]

Mrs. Van Daan. [*To* Peter] Now is that any way to talk to your little girl friend?

Peter. Mother . . . for heaven's sake . . . will you please stop saying that?

Mrs. Van Daan. Look at him blush! Look at him!

Peter. Please! I'm not . . . anyway . . . let me alone, will you?

Mrs. Van Daan. He acts like it was something to be ashamed of. It's nothing to be ashamed of, to have a little girl friend.

Peter. You're crazy. She's only thirteen.

Mrs. Van Daan. So what? And you're sixteen. Just perfect. Your father's ten years older than I am. [*To* Mr. Frank] I warn you, Mr. Frank, if this war lasts much longer, we're going to be related and then . . .

Mr. Frank. *Mazeltov!*[17]

Mrs. Frank. [*Deliberately changing the conversation*] I wonder where Miep is. She's usually so prompt.

[*Suddenly everything else is forgotten as they hear the sound of an automobile coming to a screeching stop in the street below. They are tense, motionless in their terror. The car starts away. A wave of relief sweeps over them. They pick up their occupations again.* Anne *flings open the door of* Peter's *room, making a dramatic entrance. She is dressed in* Peter's *clothes.* Peter *looks at her in fury. The others are amused.*]

---

17. *Mazeltov* (mä′ zəl tōv′) "good luck" in Hebrew and Yiddish; a word used to offer congratulations.

ANNE. Good evening, everyone. Forgive me if I don't stay. [*She jumps up on a chair.*] I have a friend waiting for me in there. My friend Tom. Tom Cat. Some people say that we look alike. But Tom has the most beautiful whiskers, and I have only a little fuzz. I am hoping . . . in time . . .

PETER. All right, Mrs. Quack Quack!

ANNE. [*Outraged—jumping down*] Peter!

PETER. I heard about you . . . How you talked so much in class they called you Mrs. Quack Quack. How Mr. Smitter made you write a composition . . . "'Quack, Quack,' said Mrs. Quack Quack."

ANNE. Well, go on. Tell them the rest. How it was so good he read it out loud to the class and then read it to all his other classes!

PETER. Quack! Quack! Quack . . . Quack . . . Quack . . .

[ANNE *pulls off the coat and trousers.*]

ANNE. You are the most intolerable, insufferable boy I've ever met!

[*She throws the clothes down the stairwell.* PETER *goes down after them.*]

PETER. Quack, quack, quack!

MRS. VAN DAAN. [*To* ANNE] That's right, Anneke! Give it to him!

ANNE. With all the boys in the world . . . Why I had to get locked up with one like you! . . .

PETER. Quack, quack, quack, and from now on stay out of my room!

[*As* PETER *passes her,* ANNE *puts out her foot, tripping him. He picks himself up, and goes on into his room.*]

MRS. FRANK. [*Quietly*] Anne, dear . . . your hair. [*She feels* ANNE's *forehead.*] You're warm. Are you feeling all right?

ANNE. Please, Mother. [*She goes over to the center table, slipping into her shoes.*]

MRS. FRANK. [*Following her*] You haven't a fever, have you?

TAKE NOTES

DRAMA

TAKE NOTES

ANNE. [*Pulling away*] No. No.

MRS. FRANK. You know we can't call a doctor here, ever. There's only one thing to do . . . watch carefully. Prevent an illness before it comes. Let me see your tongue.

ANNE. Mother, this is perfectly absurd.

MRS. FRANK. Anne, dear, don't be such a baby. Let me see your tongue. [*As* ANNE *refuses,* MRS. FRANK *appeals to* MR. FRANK] Otto . . . ?

MR. FRANK. You hear your mother, Anne.

[ANNE *flicks out her tongue for a second, then turns away.*]

MRS. FRANK. Come on—open up! [*As* ANNE *opens her mouth very wide*] You seem all right . . . but perhaps an aspirin . . .

MRS. VAN DAAN. For heaven's sake, don't give that child any pills. I waited for fifteen minutes this morning for her to come out of the w.c.

ANNE. I was washing my hair!

MR. FRANK. I think there's nothing the matter with our Anne that a ride on her bike, or a visit with her friend Jopie de Waal wouldn't cure. Isn't that so, Anne?

[MR. VAN DAAN *comes down into the room. From outside we hear faint sounds of bombers going over and a burst of ack-ack.*][18]

MR. VAN DAAN. Miep not come yet?

MRS. VAN DAAN. The workmen just left, a little while ago.

MR. VAN DAAN. What's for dinner tonight?

MRS. VAN DAAN. Beans.

MR. VAN DAAN. Not again!

MRS. VAN DAAN. Poor Putti! I know. But what can we do? That's all that Miep brought us.

[MR. VAN DAAN *starts to pace, his hands behind his back.* ANNE *follows behind him, imitating him.*]

---

18. **ack-ack** (ak′ ak′) *n.* slang for an anti-aircraft gun's fire.

Anne. We are now in what is known as the "bean cycle." Beans boiled, beans en casserole, beans with strings, beans without strings . . .

[Peter *has come out of his room. He slides into his place at the table, becoming immediately absorbed in his studies.*]

Mr. Van Daan. [*To* Peter] I saw you . . . in there, playing with your cat.

Mrs. Van Daan. He just went in for a second, putting his coat away. He's been out here all the time, doing his lessons.

Mr. Frank. [*Looking up from the papers*] Anne, you got an excellent in your history paper today . . . and very good in Latin.

Anne. [*Sitting beside him*] How about algebra?

Mr. Frank. I'll have to make a confession. Up until now I've managed to stay ahead of you in algebra. Today you caught up with me. We'll leave it to Margot to correct.

Anne. Isn't algebra *vile*, Pim!

Mr. Frank. Vile!

Margot. [*To* Mr. Frank] How did I do?

Anne. [*Getting up*] Excellent, excellent, excellent, excellent!

Mr. Frank. [*To* Margot] You should have used the subjunctive[19] here . . .

Margot. Should I? . . . I thought . . . look here . . . I didn't use it here . . .

[*The two become absorbed in the papers.*]

Anne. Mrs. Van Daan, may I try on your coat?

Mrs. Frank. No, Anne.

Mrs. Van Daan. [*Giving it to* Anne] It's all right . . . but careful with it. [Anne *puts it on and struts with it.*] My father gave me that the year before he died. He always bought the best that money could buy.

---

19. subjunctive (səb juŋk′ tiv) *n.* form of a verb that is used to express doubt or uncertainty.

DRAMA

TAKE NOTES

ANNE. Mrs. Van Daan, did you have a lot of boy friends before you were married?

MRS. FRANK. Anne, that's a personal question. It's not courteous to ask personal questions.

MRS. VAN DAAN. Oh I don't mind. [*To* ANNE] Our house was always swarming with boys. When I was a girl we had . . .

MR. VAN DAAN. Oh, God. Not again!

MRS. VAN DAAN. [*Good-humored*] Shut up! [*Without a pause, to* ANNE, MR. VAN DAAN *mimics* MRS. VAN DAAN, *speaking the first few words in unison with her.*] One summer we had a big house in Hilversum. The boys came buzzing round like bees around a jam pot. And when I was sixteen! . . . We were wearing our skirts very short those days and I had good-looking legs. [*She pulls up her skirt, going to* MR. FRANK.] I still have 'em. I may not be as pretty as I used to be, but I still have my legs. How about it, Mr. Frank?

MR. VAN DAAN. All right. All right. We see them.

MRS. VAN DAAN. I'm not asking you. I'm asking Mr. Frank.

PETER. Mother, for heaven's sake.

MRS. VAN DAAN. Oh, I embarrass you, do I? Well, I just hope the girl you marry has as good. [*Then to* ANNE] My father used to worry about me, with so many boys hanging round. He told me, if any of them gets fresh, you say to him . . . "Remember, Mr. So-and-So, remember I'm a lady."

ANNE. "Remember, Mr. So-and-So, remember I'm a lady." [*She gives* MRS. VAN DAAN *her coat.*]

MR. VAN DAAN. Look at you, talking that way in front of her! Don't you know she puts it all down in that diary?

MRS. VAN DAAN. So, if she does? I'm only telling the truth!

[ANNE *stretches out, putting her ear to the floor, listening to what is going on below. The sound of the bombers fades away.*]

126 Close Reading Notebook • Unit 4

Mrs. Frank. [*Setting the table*] Would you mind, Peter, if I moved you over to the couch?

Anne. [*Listening*] Miep must have the radio on.

[Peter *picks up his papers, going over to the couch beside* Mrs. Van Daan.]

Mr. Van Daan. [*Accusingly, to* Peter] Haven't you finished yet?

Peter. No.

Mr. Van Daan. You ought to be ashamed of yourself.

Peter. All right. All right. I'm a dunce. I'm a hopeless case. Why do I go on?

Mrs. Van Daan. You're not hopeless. Don't talk that way. It's just that you haven't anyone to help you, like the girls have. [*To* Mr. Frank] Maybe you could help him, Mr. Frank?

Mr. Frank. I'm sure that his father . . . ?

Mr. Van Daan. Not me. I can't do anything with him. He won't listen to me. You go ahead . . . if you want.

Mr. Frank. [*Going to* Peter] What about it, Peter? Shall we make our school coeducational?

Mrs. Van Daan. [*Kissing* Mr. Frank] You're an angel, Mr. Frank. An angel. I don't know why I didn't meet you before I met that one there. Here, sit down, Mr. Frank . . . [*She forces him down on the couch beside* Peter.] Now, Peter, you listen to Mr. Frank.

Mr. Frank. It might be better for us to go into Peter's room.

[Peter *jumps up eagerly, leading the way.*]

Mrs. Van Daan. That's right. You go in there, Peter. You listen to Mr. Frank. Mr. Frank is a highly educated man.

[*As* Mr. Frank *is about to follow* Peter *into his room,* Mrs. Frank *stops him and wipes the lipstick from his lips. Then she closes the door after them.*]

Anne. [*On the floor, listening*] Shh! I can hear a man's voice talking.

Mr. Van Daan. [*To* Anne] Isn't it bad enough here without your sprawling all over the place?

TAKE NOTES

The Diary of Anne Frank **127**

DRAMA

[ANNE *sits up.*]

MRS. VAN DAAN. [*To* MR. VAN DAAN] If you didn't smoke so much, you wouldn't be so bad-tempered.

MR. VAN DAAN. Am I smoking? Do you see me smoking?

MRS. VAN DAAN. Don't tell me you've used up all those cigarettes.

MR. VAN DAAN. One package. Miep only brought me one package.

MRS. VAN DAAN. It's a filthy habit anyway. It's a good time to break yourself.

MR. VAN DAAN. Oh, stop it, please.

MRS. VAN DAAN. You're smoking up all our money. You know that, don't you?

MR. VAN DAAN. Will you shut up?
[*During this,* MRS. FRANK *and* MARGOT *have studiously kept their eyes down. But* ANNE, *seated on the floor, has been following the discussion interestedly.* MR. VAN DAAN *turns to see her staring up at him.*] And what are you staring at?

ANNE. I never heard grownups quarrel before. I thought only children quarreled.

MR. VAN DAAN. This isn't a quarrel! It's a discussion. And I never heard children so rude before.

ANNE. [*Rising, indignantly*] I, rude!

MR. VAN DAAN. Yes!

MRS. FRANK. [*Quickly*] Anne, will you get me my knitting? [ANNE *goes to get it.*] I must remember, when Miep comes, to ask her to bring me some more wool.

MARGOT. [*Going to her room*] I need some hairpins and some soap. I made a list. [*She goes into her bedroom to get the list.*]

MRS. FRANK. [*To* ANNE] Have you some library books for Miep when she comes?

ANNE. It's a wonder that Miep has a life of her own, the way we make her run errands for us. Please, Miep, get me some starch. Please take my hair out and have it cut. Tell me all the latest news, Miep. [*She goes over, kneeling on the couch beside* Mrs. Van Daan] Did you know she was engaged? His name is Dirk, and Miep's afraid the Nazis will ship him off to Germany to work in one of their war plants. That's what they're doing with some of the young Dutchmen . . . they pick them up off the streets—

Mr. Van Daan. [*Interrupting*] Don't you ever get tired of talking? Suppose you try keeping still for five minutes. Just five minutes.

[*He starts to pace again. Again* Anne *follows him, mimicking him.* Mrs. Frank *jumps up and takes her by the arm up to the sink, and gives her a glass of milk.*]

Mrs. Frank. Come here, Anne. It's time for your glass of milk.

Mr. Van Daan. Talk, talk, talk. I never heard such a child. Where is my . . . ? Every evening it's the same talk, talk, talk. [*He looks around.*] Where is my . . . ?

Mrs. Van Daan. What're you looking for?

Mr. Van Daan. My pipe. Have you seen my pipe?

Mrs. Van Daan. What good's a pipe? You haven't got any tobacco.

Mr. Van Daan. At least I'll have something to hold in my mouth! [*Opening* Margot's *bedroom door*] Margot, have you seen my pipe?

Margot. It was on the table last night.

[Anne *puts her glass of milk on the table and picks up his pipe, hiding it behind her back.*]

Mr. Van Daan. I know. I know. Anne, did you see my pipe? . . . Anne!

Mrs. Frank. Anne, Mr. Van Daan is speaking to you.

Anne. Am I allowed to talk now?

Mr. Van Daan. You're the most aggravating . . . The trouble with you is, you've been spoiled. What you need is a good old-fashioned spanking.

Anne. [*Mimicking* Mrs. Van Daan] "Remember, Mr. So-and-So, remember I'm a lady." [*She thrusts the pipe into his mouth, then picks up her glass of milk.*]

DRAMA

TAKE NOTES

Mr. Van Daan. [*Restraining himself with difficulty*] Why aren't you nice and quiet like your sister Margot? Why do you have to show off all the time? Let me give you a little advice, young lady. Men don't like that kind of thing in a girl. You know that? A man likes a girl who'll listen to him once in a while . . . a domestic girl, who'll keep her house shining for her husband . . . who loves to cook and sew and . . .

Anne. I'd cut my throat first! I'd open my veins! I'm going to be remarkable! I'm going to Paris . . .

Mr. Van Daan. [*Scoffingly*] Paris!

Anne. . . . to study music and art.

Mr. Van Daan. Yeah! Yeah!

Anne. I'm going to be a famous dancer or singer . . . or something wonderful.

[*She makes a wide gesture, spilling the glass of milk on the fur coat in* Mrs. Van Daan's *lap.* Margot *rushes quickly over with a towel.* Anne *tries to brush the milk off with her skirt.*]

Mrs. Van Daan. Now look what you've done . . . you clumsy little fool! My beautiful fur coat my father gave me . . .

Anne. I'm so sorry.

Mrs. Van Daan. What do you care? It isn't yours . . . So go on, ruin it! Do you know what that coat cost? Do you? And now look at it! Look at it!

Anne. I'm very, very sorry.

Mrs. Van Daan. I could kill you for this. I could just kill you!

[Mrs. Van Daan *goes up the stairs, clutching the coat.* Mr. Van Daan *starts after her.*]

Mr. Van Daan. Petronella . . . *liefje! Liefje!* . . . Come back . . . the supper . . . come back!

Mrs. Frank. Anne, you must not behave in that way.

Anne. It was an accident. Anyone can have an accident.

Mrs. Frank. I don't mean that. I mean the answering back. You must not answer back. They are our

130 Close Reading Notebook • Unit 4

guests. We must always show the greatest courtesy to them. We're all living under terrible tension. [*She stops as* Margot *indicates that* Van Daan *can hear. When he is gone, she continues.*] That's why we must control ourselves . . . You don't hear Margot getting into arguments with them, do you? Watch Margot. She's always courteous with them. Never familiar. She keeps her distance. And they respect her for it. Try to be like Margot.

Anne. And have them walk all over me, the way they do her? No, thanks!

Mrs. Frank. I'm not afraid that anyone is going to walk all over you, Anne. I'm afraid for other people, that you'll walk on them. I don't know what happens to you, Anne. You are wild, self-willed. If I had ever talked to my mother as you talk to me . . .

Anne. Things have changed. People aren't like that any more. "Yes, Mother." "No, Mother." "Anything you say, Mother." I've got to fight things out for myself! Make something of myself!

Mrs. Frank. It isn't necessary to fight to do it. Margot doesn't fight, and isn't she . . . ?

Anne. [*Violently rebellious*] Margot! Margot! Margot! That's all I hear from everyone . . . how wonderful Margot is . . . "Why aren't you like Margot?"

Margot. [*Protesting*] Oh, come on, Anne, don't be so . . .

Anne. [*Paying no attention*] Everything she does is right, and everything I do is wrong! I'm the goat around here! . . . You're all against me! . . . And you worst of all!

[*She rushes off into her room and throws herself down on the settee, stifling her sobs.* Mrs. Frank *sighs and starts toward the stove.*]

Mrs. Frank. [*To* Margot] Let's put the soup on the stove . . . if there's anyone who cares to eat. Margot, will you take the bread out? [Margot *gets the bread from the cupboard.*] I don't know how we can go on living this way . . . I can't say a word to Anne . . . she flies at me . . .

Margot. You know Anne. In half an hour she'll be out here, laughing and joking.

TAKE NOTES

TAKE NOTES

MRS. FRANK. And . . . [*She makes a motion upwards, indicating the* VAN DAANS.] . . . I told your father it wouldn't work . . . but no . . . no . . . he had to ask them, he said . . . he owed it to him, he said. Well, he knows now that I was right! These quarrels! . . . This bickering!

MARGOT. [*With a warning look*] Shush. Shush.

[*The buzzer for the door sounds.* MRS. FRANK *gasps, startled.*]

MRS. FRANK. Every time I hear that sound, my heart stops!

MARGOT. [*Starting for* PETER'S *door*] It's Miep. [*She knocks at the door.*] Father?

[MR. FRANK *comes quickly from* PETER'S *room.*]

MR. FRANK. Thank you, Margot. [*As he goes down the steps to open the outer door*] Has everyone his list?

MARGOT. I'll get my books. [*Giving her mother a list*] Here's your list.

[MARGOT *GOES INTO HER AND* ANNE'S *BEDROOM ON THE RIGHT.* ANNE *sits up, hiding her tears, as* MARGOT *comes in.*] Miep's here.

[MARGOT *PICKS UP HER BOOKS AND GOES BACK.* ANNE *hurries over to the mirror, smoothing her hair.*]

MR. VAN DAAN. [*Coming down the stairs*] Is it Miep?

MARGOT. Yes. Father's gone down to let her in.

MR. VAN DAAN. At last I'll have some cigarettes!

MRS. FRANK. [*To* MR. VAN DAAN] I can't tell you how unhappy I am about Mrs. Van Daan's coat. Anne should never have touched it.

MR. VAN DAAN. She'll be all right.

MRS. FRANK. Is there anything I can do?

MR. VAN DAAN. Don't worry.

[*He turns to meet* MIEP. *But it is not* MIEP *who comes up the steps. It is* MR. KRALER, *followed by* MR. FRANK. *Their faces are grave.* ANNE *comes from the bedroom.* PETER *comes from his room.*]

132 Close Reading Notebook • Unit 4

Mrs. Frank. Mr. Kraler!

Mr. Van Daan. How are you, Mr. Kraler?

Margot. This is a surprise.

Mrs. Frank. When Mr. Kraler comes, the sun begins to shine.

Mr. Van Daan. Miep is coming?

Mr. Kraler. Not tonight.

[Kraler *goes to* Margot *and* Mrs. Frank *and* Anne, *shaking hands with them.*]

Mrs. Frank. Wouldn't you like a cup of coffee? . . . Or, better still, will you have supper with us?

Mr. Frank. Mr. Kraler has something to talk over with us. Something has happened, he says, which demands an immediate decision.

Mrs. Frank. [*Fearful*] What is it?

[Mr. Kraler *sits down on the couch. As he talks he takes bread, cabbages, milk, etc., from his briefcase, giving them to* Margot *and* Anne *to put away.*]

Mr. Kraler. Usually, when I come up here, I try to bring you some bit of good news. What's the use of telling you the bad news when there's nothing that you can do about it? But today something has happened . . . Dirk . . . Miep's Dirk, you know, came to me just now. He tells me that he has a Jewish friend living near him. A dentist. He says he's in trouble. He begged me, could I do anything for this man? Could I find him a hiding place? . . . So I've come to you . . . I know it's a terrible thing to ask of you, living as you are, but would you take him in with you?

Mr. Frank. Of course we will.

Mr. Kraler. [*Rising*] It'll be just for a night or two . . . until I find some other place. This happened so suddenly that I didn't know where to turn.

Mr. Frank. Where is he?

Mr. Kraler. Downstairs in the office.

Mr. Frank. Good. Bring him up.

The Diary of Anne Frank 133

MR. KRALER. His name is Dussel . . . Jan Dussel.

MR. FRANK. Dussel . . . I think I know him.

MR. KRALER. I'll get him.

[*He goes quickly down the steps and out.* MR. FRANK *suddenly becomes conscious of the others.*]

MR. FRANK. Forgive me. I spoke without consulting you. But I knew you'd feel as I do.

MR. VAN DAAN. There's no reason for you to consult anyone. This is your place. You have a right to do exactly as you please. The only thing I feel . . . there's so little food as it is . . . and to take in another person . . .

[PETER *turns away, ashamed of his father.*]

MR. FRANK. We can stretch the food a little. It's only for a few days.

MR. VAN DAAN. You want to make a bet?

MRS. FRANK. I think it's fine to have him. But, Otto, where are you going to put him? Where?

PETER. He can have my bed. I can sleep on the floor. I wouldn't mind.

MR. FRANK. That's good of you, Peter. But your room's too small . . . even for *you*.

ANNE. I have a much better idea. I'll come in here with you and Mother, and Margot can take Peter's room and Peter can go in our room with Mr. Dussel.

MARGOT. That's right. We could do that.

MR. FRANK. No, Margot. You mustn't sleep in that room . . . neither you nor Anne. Mouschi has caught some rats in there. Peter's brave. He doesn't mind.

ANNE. Then how about *this?* I'll come in here with you and Mother, and Mr. Dussel can have my bed.

MRS. FRANK. *No. No. No!* Margot will come in here with us and he can have her bed. It's the only way. Margot, bring your things in here. Help her, Anne.

[MARGOT *hurries into her room to get her things.*]

ANNE. [*To her mother*] Why Margot? Why can't I come in here?

Mrs. Frank. Because it wouldn't be proper for Margot to sleep with a . . . Please, Anne. Don't argue. Please.

[Anne *starts slowly away.*]

Mr. Frank. [*To* Anne] You don't mind sharing your room with Mr. Dussel, do you, Anne?

Anne. No. No, of course not.

Mr. Frank. Good. [Anne *goes off into her bedroom, helping* Margot. Mr. Frank *starts to search in the cupboards.*] Where's the cognac?

Mrs. Frank. It's there. But, Otto, I was saving it in case of illness.

Mr. Frank. I think we couldn't find a better time to use it. Peter, will you get five glasses for me?

[Peter *goes for the glasses.* Margot *comes out of her bedroom, carrying her possessions, which she hangs behind a curtain in the main room.* Mr. Frank *finds the cognac and pours it into the five glasses that* Peter *brings him.* mr. van daan *stands looking on sourly.* Mrs. Van Daan *comes downstairs and looks around at all the bustle.*]

Mrs. Van Daan. What's happening? What's going on?

Mr. Van Daan. Someone's moving in with us.

Mrs. Van Daan. In here? You're joking.

Margot. It's only for a night or two . . . until Mr. Kraler finds him another place.

Mr. Van Daan. Yeah! Yeah!

[Mr. Frank *hurries over as* Mr. Kraler *and* Dussel *come up.* Dussel *is a man in his late fifties, meticulous, finicky . . . bewildered now. He wears a raincoat. He carries a briefcase, stuffed full, and a small medicine case.*]

Mr. Frank. Come in, Mr. Dussel.

Mr. Kraler. This is Mr. Frank.

Dussel. Mr. Otto Frank?

Mr. Frank. Yes. Let me take your things. [*He takes the hat and briefcase, but* Dussel *clings to his medicine case.*] This is my wife Edith . . . Mr. and Mrs. Van Daan . . . their son, Peter . . . and my daughters, Margot and Anne.

TAKE NOTES

The Diary of Anne Frank 135

DRAMA

TAKE NOTES

[DUSSEL *shakes hands with everyone.*]

MR. KRALER. Thank you, Mr. Frank. Thank you all. Mr. Dussel, I leave you in good hands. Oh . . . Dirk's coat.

[DUSSEL *hurriedly takes off the raincoat, giving it to* MR. KRALER. *Underneath is his white dentist's jacket, with a yellow Star of David on it.*]

DUSSEL. [*To* MR. KRALER] What can I say to thank you . . . ?

MRS. FRANK. [*To* DUSSEL] Mr. Kraler and Miep . . . They're our life line. Without them we couldn't live.

MR. KRALER. Please. Please. You make us seem very heroic. It isn't that at all. We simply don't like the Nazis. [*To* MR. FRANK, *who offers him a drink*] No, thanks. [*Then going on*] We don't like their methods. We don't like . . .

MR. FRANK. [*Smiling*] I know. I know. "No one's going to tell us Dutchmen what to do with our damn Jews!"

MR. KRALER. [*To* DUSSEL] Pay no attention to Mr. Frank. I'll be up tomorrow to see that they're treating you right. [*To* MR. FRANK] Don't trouble to come down again. Peter will bolt the door after me, won't you, Peter?

PETER. Yes, sir.

MR. FRANK. Thank you, Peter. I'll do it.

MR. KRALER. Good night. Good night.

GROUP. Good night, Mr. Kraler. We'll see you tomorrow, etc., etc.

[MR. KRALER *goes out with* MR. FRANK, MRS. FRANK *gives each one of the "grownups" a glass of cognac.*]

MRS. FRANK. Please, Mr. Dussel, sit down.

[MR. DUSSEL *sinks into a chair.* MRS. FRANK *gives him a glass of cognac.*]

DUSSEL. I'm dreaming. I know it. I can't believe my eyes. Mr. Otto Frank here! [*To* MRS. FRANK] You're not in Switzerland then? A woman told me . . . She said she'd gone to your house . . . the door was open, everything was in disorder, dishes in the

136 Close Reading Notebook • Unit 4

sink. She said she found a piece of paper in the wastebasket with an address scribbled on it . . . an address in Zurich. She said you must have escaped to Zurich.

Anne. Father put that there purposely . . . just so people would think that very thing!

Dussel. And you've been *here* all the time?

Mrs. Frank. All the time . . . ever since July.

[Anne *speaks to her father as he comes back.*]

Anne. It worked, Pim . . . the address you left! Mr. Dussel says that people believe we escaped to Switzerland.

Mr. Frank. I'm glad. . . . And now let's have a little drink to welcome Mr. Dussel.

[*Before they can drink,* Mr. Dussel *bolts his drink.* Mr. Frank *smiles and raises his glass.*]

To Mr. Dussel. Welcome. We're very honored to have you with us.

Mrs. Frank. To Mr. Dussel, welcome.

[*The* Van Daans *murmur a welcome. The "grownups" drink.*]

Mrs. Van Daan. Um. That was good.

Mr. Van Daan. Did Mr. Kraler warn you that you won't get much to eat here? You can imagine . . . three ration books among the seven of us . . . and now you make eight.

[Peter *walks away, humiliated. Outside a street organ is heard dimly.*]

Dussel. [*Rising*] Mr. Van Daan, you don't realize what is happening outside that you should warn me of a thing like that. You don't realize what's going on . . .

[*As* Mr. Van Daan *starts his characteristic pacing,* Dussel *turns to speak to the others.*]

Right here in Amsterdam every day hundreds of Jews disappear . . . They surround a block and search house by house. Children come home from school to find their parents gone. Hundreds are being deported . . . people that you and I know . . . the Hallensteins . . . the Wessels . . .

TAKE NOTES

Mrs. Frank. [*In tears*] Oh, no. No!

Dussel. They get their call-up notice . . . come to the Jewish theater on such and such a day and hour . . . bring only what you can carry in a rucksack. And if you refuse the call-up notice, then they come and drag you from your home and ship you off to Mauthausen.[20] The death camp!

Mrs. Frank. We didn't know that things had got so much worse.

Dussel. Forgive me for speaking so.

Anne. [*Coming to* Dussel] Do you know the de Waals? . . . What's become of them? Their daughter Jopie and I are in the same class. Jopie's my best friend.

Dussel. They are gone.

Anne. Gone?

Dussel. With all the others.

Anne. Oh, no. Not Jopie!

[*She turns away, in tears.* Mrs. Frank *motions to* Margot *to comfort her.* Margot *goes to* Anne, *putting her arms comfortingly around her.*]

Mrs. Van Daan. There were some people called Wagner. They lived near us . . . ?

Mr. Frank. [*Interrupting, with a glance at* Anne] I think we should put this off until later. We all have many questions we want to ask . . . But I'm sure that Mr. Dussel would like to get settled before supper.

Dussel. Thank you. I would. I brought very little with me.

Mr. Frank. [*Giving him his hat and briefcase*] I'm sorry we can't give you a room alone. But I hope you won't be too uncomfortable. We've had to make strict rules here . . . a schedule of hours . . . We'll tell you after supper. Anne, would you like to take Mr. Dussel to his room?

Anne. [*Controlling her tears*] If you'll come with me, Mr. Dussel? [*She starts for her room.*]

---

20. **Mauthausen** (mou´ tou´ zən) village in Austria that was the site of a Nazi concentration camp.

Dussel. [*Shaking hands with each in turn*] Forgive me if I haven't really expressed my gratitude to all of you. This has been such a shock to me. I'd always thought of myself as Dutch. I was born in Holland. My father was born in Holland, and my grandfather. And now . . . after all these years . . . [*He breaks off.*] If you'll excuse me.

[Dussel *gives a little bow and hurries off after* Anne. Mr. Frank *and the others are subdued.*]

Anne. [*Turning on the light*] Well, here we are.

[Dussel *looks around the room. In the main room* Margot *speaks to her mother.*]

Margot. The news sounds pretty bad, doesn't it? It's so different from what Mr. Kraler tells us. Mr. Kraler says things are improving.

Mr. Van Daan. I like it better the way Kraler tells it.

[*They resume their occupations, quietly.* Peter *goes off into his room. In* Anne's *room,* Anne *turns to* Dussel.]

Anne. You're going to share the room with me.

Dussel. I'm a man who's always lived alone. I haven't had to adjust myself to others. I hope you'll bear with me until I learn.

Anne. Let me help you. [*She takes his briefcase.*] Do you always live all alone? Have you no family at all?

Dussel. No one. [*He opens his medicine case and spreads his bottles on the dressing table.*]

Anne. How dreadful. You must be terribly lonely.

Dussel. I'm used to it.

Anne. I don't think I could ever get used to it. Didn't you even have a pet? A cat, or a dog?

Dussel. I have an allergy for fur-bearing animals. They give me asthma.

Anne. Oh, dear. Peter has a cat.

Dussel. Here? He has it here?

Anne. Yes. But we hardly ever see it. He keeps it in his room all the time. I'm sure it will be all right.

TAKE NOTES

DRAMA

TAKE NOTES

Dussel. Let us hope so. [*He takes some pills to fortify himself.*]

Anne. That's Margot's bed, where you're going to sleep. I sleep on the sofa there. [*Indicating the clothes hooks on the wall*] We cleared these off for your things. [*She goes over to the window.*] The best part about this room . . . you can look down and see a bit of the street and the canal. There's a houseboat . . . you can see the end of it . . . a bargeman lives there with his family . . . They have a baby and he's just beginning to walk and I'm so afraid he's going to fall into the canal some day. I watch him. . . .

Dussel. [*Interrupting*] Your father spoke of a schedule.

Anne. [*Coming away from the window*] Oh, yes. It's mostly about the times we have to be quiet. And times for the w.c. You can use it now if you like.

Dussel. [*Stiffly*] No, thank you.

Anne. I suppose you think it's awful, my talking about a thing like that. But you don't know how important it can get to be, especially when you're frightened . . . About this room, the way Margot and I did . . . she had it to herself in the afternoons for studying, reading . . . lessons, you know . . . and I took the mornings. Would that be all right with you?

Dussel. I'm not at my best in the morning.

Anne. You stay here in the mornings then. I'll take the room in the afternoons.

Dussel. Tell me, when you're in here, what happens to me? Where am I spending my time? In there, with all the people?

Anne. Yes.

Dussel. I see. I see.

Anne. We have supper at half past six.

Dussel. [*Going over to the sofa*] Then, if you don't mind . . . I like to lie down quietly for ten minutes before eating. I find it helps the digestion.

Anne. Of course. I hope I'm not going to be too much of a bother to you. I seem to be able to get everyone's back up.

[Dussel *lies down on the sofa, curled up, his back to her.*]

Dussel. I always get along very well with children. My patients all bring their children to me, because they know I get on well with them. So don't you worry about that.

[Anne *leans over him, taking his hand and shaking it gratefully.*]

Anne. Thank you. Thank you, Mr. Dussel.

[*The lights dim to darkness. The curtain falls on the scene.* Anne's Voice *comes to us faintly at first, and then with increasing power.*]

Anne's Voice. . . . And yesterday I finished Cissy Van Marxvelt's latest book. I think she is a first-class writer. I shall definitely let my children read her. Monday the twenty-first of September, nineteen forty-two. Mr. Dussel and I had another battle yesterday. Yes, Mr. Dussel! According to him, nothing, I repeat . . . nothing, is right about me . . . my appearance, my character, my manners. While he was going on at me I thought . . . sometime I'll give you such a smack that you'll fly right up to the ceiling! Why is it that every grownup thinks he knows the way to bring up children? Particularly the grownups that never had any. I keep wishing that Peter was a girl instead of a boy. Then I would have someone to talk to. Margot's a darling, but she takes everything too seriously. To pause for a moment on the subject of Mrs. Van Daan. I must tell you that her attempts to flirt with father are getting her nowhere. Pim, thank goodness, won't play.

[*As she is saying the last lines, the curtain rises on the darkened scene.* Anne's Voice *fades out.*]

Scene 4

[*It is the middle of the night, several months later. The stage is dark except for a little light which comes through the skylight in* Peter's *room.*

Everyone is in bed. Mr. *and* Mrs. Frank *lie on the couch in the main room, which has been pulled out to serve as a makeshift double bed.*

TAKE NOTES

The Diary of Anne Frank **141**

DRAMA

TAKE NOTES

[MARGOT *is sleeping on a mattress on the floor in the main room, behind a curtain stretched across for privacy. The others are all in their accustomed rooms.*

From outside we hear two drunken soldiers singing "Lili Marlene." A girl's high giggle is heard. The sound of running feet is heard coming closer and then fading in the distance. Throughout the scene there is the distant sound of airplanes passing overhead.

A match suddenly flares up in the attic. We dimly see MR. VAN DAAN. *He is getting his bearings. He comes quickly down the stairs, and goes to the cupboard where the food is stored. Again the match flares up, and is as quickly blown out. The dim figure is seen to steal back up the stairs.*

There is quiet for a second or two, broken only by the sound of airplanes, and running feet on the street below.

Suddenly, out of the silence and the dark, we hear ANNE *scream.*]

ANNE. [*Screaming*] No! No! Don't . . . don't take me!

[*She moans, tossing and crying in her sleep. The other people wake, terrified.* DUSSEL *sits up in bed, furious.*]

DUSSEL. Shush! Anne! Anne, for God's sake, shush!

ANNE. [*Still in her nightmare*] Save me! Save me!

[*She screams and screams.* DUSSEL *gets out of bed, going over to her, trying to wake her.*]

DUSSEL. For God's sake! Quiet! Quiet! You want someone to hear?

[*In the main room* MRS. FRANK *grabs a shawl and pulls it around her. She rushes in to* ANNE, *taking her in her arms.* MR. FRANK *hurriedly gets up, putting on his overcoat.* MARGOT *sits up, terrified.* PETER'S *light goes on in his room.*]

MRS. FRANK. [*To* ANNE, *in her room*] Hush, darling, hush. It's all right. It's all right. [*Over her shoulder to* DUSSEL] Will you be kind enough to turn on the light, Mr. Dussel? [*Back to* ANNE] It's nothing, my darling. It was just a dream.

[DUSSEL *turns on the light in the bedroom.* MRS. FRANK *holds* ANNE *in her arms. Gradually* ANNE *comes out of her nightmare still trembling with horror.* MR. FRANK *comes*

142 Close Reading Notebook • Unit 4

into the room, and goes quickly to the window, looking out to be sure that no one outside has heard ANNE'S *screams.* MRS. FRANK *holds* ANNE, *talking softly to her. In the main room* MARGOT *stands on a chair, turning on the center hanging lamp. A light goes on in the* VAN DAANS' *room overhead.* PETER *puts his robe on, coming out of his room.*]

DUSSEL. [*To* MRS. FRANK, *blowing his nose*] Something must be done about that child, Mrs. Frank. Yelling like that! Who knows but there's somebody on the streets? She's endangering all our lives.

MRS. FRANK. Anne, darling.

DUSSEL. Every night she twists and turns. I don't sleep. I spend half my night shushing her. And now it's nightmares!

[MARGOT *comes to the door of* ANNE'S *room, followed by* PETER. MR. FRANK *goes to them, indicating that everything is all right.* PETER *takes* MARGOT *back.*]

MRS. FRANK. [*To* ANNE] You're here, safe, you see? Nothing has happened. [*To* DUSSEL] Please, Mr. Dussel, go back to bed. She'll be herself in a minute or two. Won't you, Anne?

DUSSEL. [*Picking up a book and a pillow*] Thank you, but I'm going to the w.c. The one place where there's peace!

[*He stalks out.* MR. VAN DAAN, *in underwear and trousers, comes down the stairs.*]

MR. VAN DAAN. [*To* DUSSEL] What is it? What happened?

DUSSEL. A nightmare. She was having a nightmare!

MR. VAN DAAN. I thought someone was murdering her.

DUSSEL. Unfortunately, no.

[*He goes into the bathroom.* MR. VAN DAAN *goes back up the stairs.* MR. FRANK, *in the main room, sends* PETER *back to his own bedroom.*]

MR. FRANK. Thank you, Peter. Go back to bed.

[PETER *goes back to his room.* MR. FRANK *follows him, turning out the light and looking out the window. Then*

TAKE NOTES

The Diary of Anne Frank 143

DRAMA

TAKE NOTES

he goes back to the main room, and gets up on a chair, turning out the center hanging lamp.]

Mrs. Frank. [*To* Anne] Would you like some water? [Anne *shakes her head.*] Was it a very bad dream? Perhaps if you told me . . . ?

Anne. I'd rather not talk about it.

Mrs. Frank. Poor darling. Try to sleep then. I'll sit right here beside you until you fall asleep. [*She brings a stool over, sitting there.*]

Anne. You don't have to.

Mrs. Frank. But I'd like to stay with you . . . very much. Really.

Anne. I'd rather you didn't.

Mrs. Frank. Good night, then. [*She leans down to kiss* Anne. Anne *throws her arm up over her face, turning away.* Mrs. Frank, *hiding her hurt, kisses* Anne's *arm.*] You'll be all right? There's nothing that you want?

Anne. Will you please ask Father to come.

Mrs. Frank. [*After a second*] Of course, Anne dear. [*She hurries out into the other room.* Mr. Frank *comes to her as she comes in.*] *Sie verlangt nach Dir!*[21]

Mr. Frank. [*Sensing her hurt*] Edith, *Liebe, schau* . . .[22]

Mrs. Frank. *Es macht nichts! Ich danke dem lieben Herrgott, dass sie sich wenigstens an Dich wendet, wenn sie Trost braucht! Geh hinein, Otto, sie ist ganz hysterisch vor Angst.*[23]

[*As* Mr. Frank *hesitates*] *Geh zu ihr.*[24]

[*He looks at her for a second and then goes to get a cup of water for* Anne. Mrs. Frank *sinks down on the bed, her face in her hands, trying to keep from sobbing aloud.* Margot *comes over to her, putting her arms around her.*] She wants nothing of me. She pulled away when I leaned down to kiss her.

---

21. *Sie verlangt nach Dir* (sē fer´ laŋt´ näkh´ dir´) German for "She is asking for you."
22. *Liebe, schau* (lē´ bə shou´) German for "Dear, look."
23. *Es macht . . . vor Angst* German for "It's all right. I thank dear God that at least she turns to you when she needs comfort. Go in, Otto, she is hysterical because of fear."
24. *Geh zu ihr* (gā´ tsoo´ ēr´) German for "Go to her."

Margot. It's a phase . . . You heard Father . . . Most girls go through it . . . they turn to their fathers at this age . . . they give all their love to their fathers.

Mrs. Frank. You weren't like this. You didn't shut me out.

Margot. She'll get over it . . .

[*She smooths the bed for* Mrs. Frank *and sits beside her a moment as* Mrs. Frank *lies down. In* Anne's *room* Mr. Frank *comes in, sitting down by* Anne. Anne *flings her arms around him, clinging to him. In the distance we hear the sound of ack-ack.*]

Anne. Oh, Pim. I dreamed that they came to get us! The Green Police! They broke down the door and grabbed me and started to drag me out the way they did Jopie.

Mr. Frank. I want you to take this pill.

Anne. What is it?

Mr. Frank. Something to quiet you.

[*She takes it and drinks the water. In the main room* Margot *turns out the light and goes back to her bed.*]

Mr. Frank. [*To* Anne] Do you want me to read to you for a while?

Anne. No. Just sit with me for a minute. Was I awful? Did I yell terribly loud? Do you think anyone outside could have heard?

Mr. Frank. No. No. Lie quietly now. Try to sleep.

Anne. I'm a terrible coward. I'm so disappointed in myself. I think I've conquered my fear . . . I think I'm really grown-up . . . and then something happens . . . and I run to you like a baby . . . I love you, Father. I don't love anyone but you.

Mr. Frank. [*Reproachfully*] Annele!

Anne. It's true. I've been thinking about it for a long time. You're the only one I love.

Mr. Frank. It's fine to hear you tell me that you love me. But I'd be happier if you said you loved your mother as well . . . She needs your help so much . . . your love . . .

TAKE NOTES

DRAMA

TAKE NOTES

ANNE. We have nothing in common. She doesn't understand me. Whenever I try to explain my views on life to her she asks me if I'm constipated.

MR. FRANK. You hurt her very much just now. She's crying. She's in there crying.

ANNE. I can't help it. I only told the truth. I didn't want her here . . . [*Then, with sudden change*] Oh, Pim, I was horrible, wasn't I? And the worst of it is, I can stand off and look at myself doing it and know it's cruel and yet I can't stop doing it. What's the matter with me? Tell me. Don't say it's just a phase! Help me.

MR. FRANK. There is so little that we parents can do to help our children. We can only try to set a good example . . . point the way. The rest you must do yourself. You must build your own character.

ANNE. I'm trying. Really I am. Every night I think back over all of the things I did that day that were wrong . . . like putting the wet mop in Mr. Dussel's bed . . . and this thing now with Mother. I say to myself, that was wrong. I make up my mind, I'm never going to do that again. Never! Of course I may do something worse . . . but at least I'll never do *that* again! . . . I have a nicer side, Father . . . a sweeter, nicer side. But I'm scared to show it. I'm afraid that people are going to laugh at me if I'm serious. So the mean Anne comes to the outside and the good Anne stays on the inside, and I keep on trying to switch them around and have the good Anne outside and the bad Anne inside and be what I'd like to be . . . and might be . . . if only . . . only . . .

[*She is asleep.* MR. FRANK *watches her for a moment and then turns off the light, and starts out. The lights dim out. The curtain falls on the scene.* ANNE'S VOICE *is heard dimly at first, and then with growing strength.*]

ANNE'S VOICE. . . . The air raids are getting worse. They come over day and night. The noise is terrifying. Pim says it should be music to our ears. The more planes, the sooner will come the end of the war. Mrs. Van Daan pretends to be a fatalist. What will be, will be. But when the planes come over, who is

146 Close Reading Notebook • Unit 4

the most frightened? No one else but Petronella! . . . Monday, the ninth of November, nineteen forty-two. Wonderful news! The Allies have landed in Africa. Pim says that we can look for an early finish to the war. Just for fun he asked each of us what was the first thing we wanted to do when we got out of here. Mrs. Van Daan longs to be home with her own things, her needle-point chairs, the Beckstein piano her father gave her . . . the best that money could buy. Peter would like to go to a movie. Mr. Dussel wants to get back to his dentist's drill. He's afraid he is losing his touch. For myself, there are so many things . . . to ride a bike again . . . to laugh till my belly aches . . . to have new clothes from the skin out . . . to have a hot tub filled to overflowing and wallow in it for hours . . . to be back in school with my friends . . .

[As the last lines are being said, the curtain rises on the scene. The lights dim on as ANNE'S VOICE fades away.]

Scene 5

[It is the first night of the Hanukkah[25] celebration. MR. FRANK is standing at the head of the table on which is the Menorah.[26] He lights the Shamos,[27] or servant candle, and holds it as he says the blessing. Seated listening is all of the "family," dressed in their best. The men wear hats, PETER wears his cap.]

MR. FRANK. [Reading from a prayer book] "Praised be Thou, oh Lord our God, Ruler of the universe, who has sanctified us with Thy commandments and bidden us kindle the Hanukkah lights. Praised be Thou, oh Lord our God, Ruler of the universe, who has wrought wondrous deliverances for our fathers in days of old. Praised be Thou, oh Lord our God, Ruler of the universe, that Thou has given us life and sustenance and brought us to this happy season." [MR. FRANK lights the one candle of the Menorah as he continues.] "We kindle this Hanukkah light to celebrate the great and wonderful deeds wrought

TAKE NOTES

---

25. **Hanukkah** (khä′ noo kä′) n. Jewish celebration that lasts eight days.
26. **Menorah** (mə nō′ rə) n. candle holder with nine candles, used during Hanukkah.
27. **Shamos** (shä′ məs) n. candle used to light the others in a menorah.

through the zeal with which God filled the hearts of the heroic Maccabees, two thousand years ago. They fought against indifference, against tyranny and oppression, and they restored our Temple to us. May these lights remind us that we should ever look to God, whence cometh our help." Amen.

ALL. Amen.

[MR. FRANK *hands* MRS. FRANK *the prayer book.*]

MRS. FRANK. [*Reading*] "I lift up mine eyes unto the mountains, from whence cometh my help. My help cometh from the Lord who made heaven and earth. He will not suffer thy foot to be moved. He that keepeth thee will not slumber. He that keepeth Israel doth neither slumber nor sleep. The Lord is thy keeper. The Lord is thy shade upon thy right hand. The sun shall not smite thee by day, nor the moon by night. The Lord shall keep thee from all evil. He shall keep thy soul. The Lord shall guard thy going out and thy coming in, from this time forth and forevermore." Amen.

ALL. Amen.

[MRS. FRANK *puts down the prayer book and goes to get the food and wine.* MARGOT *helps her.* MR. FRANK *takes the men's hats and puts them aside.*]

DUSSEL. [*Rising*] That was very moving.

ANNE. [*Pulling him back*] It isn't over yet!

MRS. VAN DAAN. Sit down! Sit down!

ANNE. There's a lot more, songs and presents.

DUSSEL. Presents?

MRS. FRANK. Not this year, unfortunately.

MRS. VAN DAAN. But always on Hanukkah everyone gives presents . . . everyone!

DUSSEL. Like our St. Nicholas' Day.[28]

[*There is a chorus of "no's" from the group.*]

MRS. VAN DAAN. No! Not like St. Nicholas! What kind of a Jew are you that you don't know Hanukkah?

---

28. **St. Nicholas' Day** December 6, the day Christian children in the Netherlands receive gifts.

Mrs. Frank. [*As she brings the food*] I remember particularly the candles . . . First one, as we have tonight. Then the second night you light two candles, the next night three . . . and so on until you have eight candles burning. When there are eight candles it is truly beautiful.

Mrs. Van Daan. And the potato pancakes.

Mr. Van Daan. Don't talk about them!

Mrs. Van Daan. I make the best *latkes* you ever tasted!

Mrs. Frank. Invite us all next year . . . in your own home.

Mr. Frank. God willing!

Mrs. Van Daan. God willing.

Margot. What I remember best is the presents we used to get when we were little . . . eight days of presents . . . and each day they got better and better.

Mrs. Frank. [*Sitting down*] We are all here, alive. That is present enough.

Anne. No, it isn't. I've got something . . . [*She rushes into her room, hurriedly puts on a little hat improvised from the lamp shade, grabs a satchel bulging with parcels and comes running back.*]

Mrs. Frank. What is it?

Anne. Presents!

Mrs. Van Daan. Presents!

Dussel. Look!

Mr. Van Daan. What's she got on her head?

Peter. A lamp shade!

Anne. [*She picks out one at random.*] This is for Margot. [*She hands it to* Margot, *pulling her to her feet.*] Read it out loud.

Margot. [*Reading*]
"You have never lost your temper.
You never will, I fear,
You are so good.
But if you should,

The Diary of Anne Frank **149**

DRAMA

TAKE NOTES

Put all your cross words here."
[*She tears open the package.*] A new crossword puzzle book! Where did you get it?

ANNE. It isn't new. It's one that you've done. But I rubbed it all out, and if you wait a little and forget, you can do it all over again.

MARGOT. [*Sitting*] It's wonderful, Anne. Thank you. You'd never know it wasn't new.

[*From outside we hear the sound of a streetcar passing.*]

ANNE. [*With another gift*] Mrs. Van Daan.

MRS. VAN DAAN. [*Taking it*] This is awful . . . I haven't anything for anyone . . . I never thought . . .

MR. FRANK. This is all Anne's idea.

MRS. VAN DAAN. [*Holding up a bottle*] What is it?

ANNE. It's hair shampoo. I took all the odds and ends of soap and mixed them with the last of my toilet water.

MRS. VAN DAAN. Oh, Anneke!

ANNE. I wanted to write a poem for all of them, but I didn't have time. [*Offering a large box to* MR. VAN DAAN] Yours, Mr. Van Daan, is really something . . . something you want more than anything. [*As she waits for him to open it*] Look! Cigarettes!

MR. VAN DAAN. Cigarettes!

ANNE. Two of them! Pim found some old pipe tobacco in the pocket lining of his coat . . . and we made them . . . or rather, Pim did.

MRS. VAN DAAN. Let me see . . . Well, look at that! Light it, Putti! Light it.

[MR. VAN DAAN *hesitates.*]

ANNE. It's tobacco, really it is! There's a little fluff in it, but not much.

[*Everyone watches intently as* MR. VAN DAAN *cautiously lights it. The cigarette flares up. Everyone laughs.*]

PETER. It works!

MRS. VAN DAAN. Look at him.

150 Close Reading Notebook • Unit 4

Mr. Van Daan. [*Spluttering*] Thank you, Anne. Thank you.

[Anne *rushes back to her satchel for another present.*]

Anne. [*Handing her mother a piece of paper*] For Mother, Hanukkah greeting.

[*She pulls her mother to her feet.*]

Mrs. Frank. [*She reads*] "Here's an I.O.U. that I promise to pay. Ten hours of doing whatever you say. Signed, Anne Frank." [Mrs. Frank, *touched, takes* Anne *in her arms, holding her close.*]

Dussel. [*To* Anne] Ten hours of doing what you're told? Anything you're told?

Anne. That's right.

Dussel. You wouldn't want to sell that, Mrs. Frank?

Mrs. Frank. Never! This is the most precious gift I've ever had!

[*She sits, showing her present to the others.* Anne *hurries back to the satchel and pulls out a scarf, the scarf that* Mr. Frank *found in the first scene.*]

Anne. [*Offering it to her father*] For Pim.

Mr. Frank. Anneke . . . I wasn't supposed to have a present!

[*He takes it, unfolding it and showing it to the others.*]

Anne. It's a muffler . . . to put round your neck . . . like an ascot, you know. I made it myself out of odds and ends . . . I knitted it in the dark each night, after I'd gone to bed. I'm afraid it looks better in the dark!

Mr. Frank. [*Putting it on*] It's fine. It fits me perfectly. Thank you, Annele.

[Anne *hands* Peter *a ball of paper with a string attached to it.*]

Anne. That's for Mouschi.

Peter. [*Rising to bow*] On behalf of Mouschi, I thank you.

Anne. [*Hesitant, handing him a gift*] And . . . this is yours . . . from Mrs. Quack Quack. [*As he holds it gingerly in his hands*] Well . . . open it . . . Aren't you going to open it?

TAKE NOTES

DRAMA

TAKE NOTES

PETER. I'm scared to. I know something's going to jump out and hit me.

ANNE. No. It's nothing like that, really.

MRS. VAN DAAN. [*As he is opening it*] What is it, Peter? Go on. Show it.

ANNE. [*Excitedly*] It's a safety razor!

DUSSEL. A what?

ANNE. A razor!

MRS. VAN DAAN. [*Looking at it*] You didn't make that out of odds and ends.

ANNE. [*To* PETER] Miep got it for me. It's not new. It's second-hand. But you really do need a razor now.

DUSSEL. For what?

ANNE. Look on his upper lip . . . you can see the beginning of a mustache.

DUSSEL. He wants to get rid of that? Put a little milk on it and let the cat lick it off.

PETER. [*Starting for his room*] Think you're funny, don't you.

DUSSEL. Look! He can't wait! He's going in to try it!

PETER. I'm going to give Mouschi his present!

[*He goes into his room, slamming the door behind him.*]

MR. VAN DAAN. [*Disgustedly*] Mouschi, Mouschi, Mouschi.

[*In the distance we hear a dog persistently barking.* ANNE *brings a gift to* DUSSEL.]

ANNE. And last but never least, my roommate, Mr. Dussel.

DUSSEL. For me? You have something for me?

[*He opens the small box she gives him.*]

ANNE. I made them myself.

DUSSEL. [*Puzzled*] Capsules! Two capsules!

ANNE. They're ear-plugs!

DUSSEL. Ear-plugs?

152 Close Reading Notebook • Unit 4

Anne. To put in your ears so you won't hear me when I thrash around at night. I saw them advertised in a magazine. They're not real ones . . . I made them out of cotton and candle wax. Try them . . . See if they don't work . . . see if you can hear me talk . . .

Dussel. [*Putting them in his ears*] Wait now until I get them in . . . so.

Anne. Are you ready?

Dussel. Huh?

Anne. Are you ready?

Dussel. Good God! They've gone inside! I can't get them out! [*They laugh as* Mr. Dussel *jumps about, trying to shake the plugs out of his ears. Finally he gets them out. Putting them away*] Thank you, Anne! Thank you!

[*Together*]
- **Mr. Van Daan.** A real Hanukkah!
- **Mrs. Van Daan.** Wasn't it cute of her?
- **Mrs. Frank.** I don't know when she did it.
- **Margot.** I love my present.

Anne. [*Sitting at the table*] And now let's have the song, Father . . . please . . . [*To* Dussel] Have you heard the Hanukkah song, Mr. Dussel? The song is the whole thing! [*She sings.*] "Oh, Hanukkah! Oh, Hanukkah! The sweet celebration . . ."

Mr. Frank. [*Quieting her*] I'm afraid, Anne, we shouldn't sing that song tonight. [*To* Dussel] It's a song of jubilation, of rejoicing. One is apt to become too enthusiastic.

Anne. Oh, please, please. Let's sing the song. I promise not to shout!

Mr. Frank. Very well. But quietly now . . . I'll keep an eye on you and when . . .

[*As* Anne *starts to sing, she is interrupted by* Dussel, *who is snorting and wheezing.*]

Dussel. [*Pointing to* Peter] You . . . You! [Peter *is coming from his bedroom, ostentatiously holding a bulge in his coat as if he were holding his cat, and dangling* Anne's *present before it.*] How many times . . . I told you . . . Out! Out!

DRAMA

TAKE NOTES

Mr. Van Daan. [*Going to* Peter] What's the matter with you? Haven't you any sense? Get that cat out of here.

Peter. [*Innocently*] Cat?

Mr. Van Daan. You heard me. Get it out of here!

Peter. I have no cat. [*Delighted with his joke, he opens his coat and pulls out a bath towel. The group at the table laugh, enjoying the joke.*]

Dussel. [*Still wheezing*] It doesn't need to be the cat . . . his clothes are enough . . . when he comes out of that room . . .

Mr. Van Daan. Don't worry. You won't be bothered any more. We're getting rid of it.

Dussel. At last you listen to me. [*He goes off into his bedroom.*]

Mr. Van Daan. [*Calling after him*] I'm not doing it for you. That's all in your mind . . . all of it! [*He starts back to his place at the table.*] I'm doing it because I'm sick of seeing that cat eat all our food.

Peter. That's not true! I only give him bones . . . scraps . . .

Mr. Van Daan. Don't tell me! He gets fatter every day! Damn cat looks better than any of us. Out he goes tonight!

Peter. No! No!

Anne. Mr. Van Daan, you can't do that! That's Peter's cat. Peter loves that cat.

Mrs. Frank. [*Quietly*] Anne.

Peter. [*To* Mr. Van Daan] If he goes, I go.

Mr. Van Daan. Go! Go!

Mrs. Van Daan. You're not going and the cat's not going! Now please . . . this is Hanukkah . . . Hanukkah . . . this is the time to celebrate . . . What's the matter with all of you? Come on, Anne. Let's have the song.

Anne. [*Singing*]
"Oh, Hanukkah! Oh, Hanukkah! The sweet celebration."

154 Close Reading Notebook • Unit 4

Mr. Frank. [*Rising*] I think we should first blow out the candle . . . then we'll have something for tomorrow night.

Margot. But, Father, you're supposed to let it burn itself out.

Mr. Frank. I'm sure that God understands shortages. [*Before blowing it out*] "Praised be Thou, oh Lord our God, who hast sustained us and permitted us to celebrate this joyous festival."

[*He is about to blow out the candle when suddenly there is a crash of something falling below. They all freeze in horror, motionless. For a few seconds there is complete silence.* Mr. Frank *slips off his shoes. The others noiselessly follow his example.* Mr. Frank *turns out a light near him. He motions to* Peter *to turn off the center lamp.* Peter *tries to reach it, realizes he cannot and gets up on a chair. Just as he is touching the lamp he loses his balance. The chair goes out from under him. He falls. The iron lamp shade crashes to the floor. There is a sound of feet below, running down the stairs.*]

Mr. Van Daan. [*Under his breath*] God Almighty! [*The only light left comes from the Hanukkah candle.* Dussel *comes from his room.* Mr. Frank *creeps over to the stairwell and stands listening. The dog is heard barking excitedly.*] Do you hear anything?

Mr. Frank. [*In a whisper*] No. I think they've gone.

Mrs. Van Daan. It's the Green Police. They've found us.

Mr. Frank. If they had, they wouldn't have left. They'd be up here by now.

Mrs. Van Daan. I know it's the Green Police. They've gone to get help. That's all. They'll be back!

Mr. Van Daan. Or it may have been the Gestapo,[29] looking for papers . . .

Mr. Frank. [*Interrupting*] Or a thief, looking for money.

Mrs. Van Daan. We've got to do something . . . Quick! Quick! Before they come back.

Mr. Van Daan. There isn't anything to do. Just wait.

---

29. **Gestapo** (gə stä′ pō) *n.* secret police force of Nazi Germany, known for its brutality.

TAKE NOTES

DRAMA

TAKE NOTES

[MR. FRANK *holds up his hand for them to be quiet. He is listening intently. There is complete silence as they all strain to hear any sound from below. Suddenly* ANNE *begins to sway. With a low cry she falls to the floor in a faint.* MRS. FRANK *goes to her quickly, sitting beside her on the floor and taking her in her arms.*]

MRS. FRANK. Get some water, please! Get some water!

[MARGOT *starts for the sink.*]

MR. VAN DAAN. [*Grabbing* MARGOT] No! No! No one's going to run water!

MR. FRANK. If they've found us, they've found us. Get the water. [MARGOT *starts again for the sink.* MR. FRANK, *getting a flashlight*] I'm going down.

[MARGOT *rushes to him, clinging to him.* ANNE *struggles to consciousness.*]

MARGOT. No, Father, no! There may be someone there, waiting . . . It may be a trap!

MR. FRANK. This is Saturday. There is no way for us to know what has happened until Miep or Mr. Kraler comes on Monday morning. We cannot live with this uncertainty.

MARGOT. Don't go, Father!

MRS. FRANK. Hush, darling, hush. [MR. FRANK *slips quietly out, down the steps and out through the door below.*] Margot! Stay close to me. [MARGOT *goes to her mother.*]

MR. VAN DAAN. Shush! Shush!

[MRS. FRANK *whispers to* MARGOT *to get the water.* MARGOT *goes for it.*]

MRS. VAN DAAN. Putti, where's our money? Get our money. I hear you can buy the Green Police off, so much a head. Go upstairs quick! Get the money!

MR. VAN DAAN. Keep still!

MRS. VAN DAAN. [*Kneeling before him, pleading*] Do you want to be dragged off to a concentration camp? Are you going to stand there and wait for them to come up and get you? Do something, I tell you!

156 Close Reading Notebook • Unit 4

Mr. Van Daan. [*Pushing her aside*] Will you keep still!

[*He goes over to the stairwell to listen.* Peter *goes to his mother, helping her up onto the sofa. There is a second of silence, then* Anne *can stand it no longer.*]

Anne. Someone go after Father! Make Father come back!

Peter. [*Starting for the door*] I'll go.

Mr. Van Daan. Haven't you done enough?

[*He pushes* Peter *roughly away. In his anger against his father* Peter *grabs a chair as if to hit him with it, then puts it down, burying his face in his hands.* Mrs. Frank *begins to pray softly.*]

Anne. Please, please, Mr. Van Daan. Get Father.

Mr. Van Daan. Quiet! Quiet!

[Anne *is shocked into silence.* Mrs. Frank *pulls her closer, holding her protectively in her arms.*]

Mrs. Frank. [*Softly, praying*] "I lift up mine eyes unto the mountains, from whence cometh my help. My help cometh from the Lord who made heaven and earth. He will not suffer thy foot to be moved . . . He that keepeth thee will not slumber . . ."

[*She stops as she hears someone coming. They all watch the door tensely.* Mr. Frank *comes quietly in.* Anne *rushes to him, holding him tight.*]

Mr. Frank. It was a thief. That noise must have scared him away.

Mrs. Van Daan. Thank God.

Mr. Frank. He took the cash box. And the radio. He ran away in such a hurry that he didn't stop to shut the street door. It was swinging wide open. [*A breath of relief sweeps over them.*] I think it would be good to have some light.

Margot. Are you sure it's all right?

Mr. Frank. The danger has passed. [Margot *goes to light the small lamp.*] Don't be so terrified, Anne. We're safe.

Dussel. Who says the danger has passed? Don't you realize we are in greater danger than ever?

TAKE NOTES

The Diary of Anne Frank **157**

DRAMA

TAKE NOTES

Mr. Frank. Mr. Dussel, will you be still!

[Mr. Frank *takes* Anne *back to the table, making her sit down with him, trying to calm her.*]

Dussel. [*Pointing to* Peter] Thanks to this clumsy fool, there's someone now who knows we're up here! Someone now knows we're up here, hiding!

Mrs. Van Daan. [*Going to* Dussel] Someone knows we're here, yes. But who is the someone? A thief! A thief! You think a thief is going to go to the Green Police and say . . . I was robbing a place the other night and I heard a noise up over my head? You think a thief is going to do that?

Dussel. Yes. I think he will.

Mrs. Van Daan. [*Hysterically*] You're crazy!

[*She stumbles back to her seat at the table.* Peter *follows protectively, pushing* Dussel *aside.*]

Dussel. I think some day he'll be caught and then he'll make a bargain with the Green Police . . . if they'll let him off, he'll tell them where some Jews are hiding!

[*He goes off into the bedroom. There is a second of appalled silence.*]

Mr. Van Daan. He's right.

Anne. Father, let's get out of here! We can't stay here now . . . Let's go . . .

Mr. Van Daan. Go! Where?

Mrs. Frank. [*Sinking into her chair at the table*] Yes. Where?

Mr. Frank. [*Rising, to them all*] Have we lost all faith? All courage? A moment ago we thought that they'd come for us. We were sure it was the end. But it wasn't the end. We're alive, safe.

[Mr. Van Daan *goes to the table and sits.* Mr. Frank *prays.*] "We thank Thee, oh Lord our God, that in Thy infinite mercy Thou hast again seen fit to spare us." [*He blows out the candle, then turns to* Anne.] Come on, Anne. The song! Let's have the song!

158 Close Reading Notebook • Unit 4

[*He starts to sing.* Anne *finally starts falteringly to sing, as* Mr. Frank *urges her on. Her voice is hardly audible at first.*]

Anne. [*Singing*]
"Oh, Hanukkah! Oh, Hanukkah! The sweet . . . celebration . . ."

[*As she goes on singing, the others gradually join in, their voices still shaking with fear.* Mrs. Van Daan *sobs as she sings.*]

Group. Around the feast . . . we . . . gather
In complete . . . jubilation . . .
Happiest of sea . . . sons
Now is here.
Many are the reasons for good cheer.

[Dussel *comes from the bedroom. He comes over to the table, standing beside* Margot, *listening to them as they sing.*]

"Together/We'll weather/Whatever tomorrow may bring."

[*As they sing on with growing courage, the lights start to dim.*]

"So hear us rejoicing/And merrily voicing/The Hanukkah song that we sing./Hoy!"

[*The lights are out. The curtain starts slowly to fall.*]

"Hear us rejoicing/And merrily voicing/The Hanukkah song that we sing."

[*They are still singing, as the curtain falls.*]

TAKE NOTES

The Governess

by Neil Simon

Mistress. Julia! [*Calls again*] Julia!

[*A young governess,* Julia, *comes rushing in. She stops before the desk and curtsies.*]

Julia. [*Head down*] Yes, madame?

Mistress. Look at me, child. Pick your head up. I like to see your eyes when I speak to you.

Julia. [*Lifts her head up*] Yes, madame. [*But her head has a habit of slowly drifting down again.*]

Mistress. And how are the children coming along with their French lessons?

Julia. They're very bright children, madame.

Mistress. Eyes up . . . They're bright, you say. Well, why not? And mathematics? They're doing well in mathematics, I assume?

Julia. Yes, madame. Especially Vanya.

Mistress. Certainly. I knew it. I excelled in mathematics. He gets that from his mother, wouldn't you say?

Julia. Yes, madame.

Mistress. Head up . . . [*She lifts head up.*] That's it. Don't be afraid to look people in the eyes, my dear. If you think of yourself as inferior, that's exactly how people will treat you.

Julia. Yes, ma'am.

Mistress. A quiet girl, aren't you? . . . Now then, let's settle our accounts. I imagine you must need money, although you never ask me for it yourself. Let's see now, we agreed on thirty rubles[1] a month, did we not?

Julia. [*Surprised*] Forty, ma'am.

Mistress. No, no, thirty. I made a note of it. [*Points to the book*] I always pay my governesses thirty . . . Who told you forty?

---

1. **rubles** (roo´ bəlz) *n.* Russian currency; similar to U.S. dollars.

Julia. You did, ma'am. I spoke to no one else concerning money . . .

Mistress. Impossible. Maybe you *thought* you heard forty when I said thirty. If you kept your head up, that would never happen. Look at me again and I'll say it clearly. *Thirty rubles a month.*

Julia. If you say so, ma'am.

Mistress. Settled. Thirty a month it is . . . Now then, you've been here two months exactly.

Julia. Two months and five days.

Mistress. No, no. Exactly two months. I made a note of it. You should keep books the way I do so there wouldn't be these discrepancies. So—we have two months at thirty rubles a month . . . comes to sixty rubles. Correct?

Julia. [*Curtsies*] Yes, ma'am. Thank you, ma'am.

Mistress. Subtract nine Sundays . . . We did agree to subtract Sundays, didn't we?

Julia. No, ma'am.

Mistress. Eyes! Eyes! . . . Certainly we did. I've always subtracted Sundays. I didn't bother making a note of it because I always do it. Don't you recall when I said we will subtract Sundays?

Julia. No, ma'am.

Mistress. Think.

Julia. [*Thinks*] No, ma'am.

Mistress. You weren't thinking. Your eyes were wandering. Look straight at my face and look hard . . . Do you remember now?

Julia. [*Softly*] Yes, ma'am.

Mistress. I didn't hear you, Julia.

Julia. [*Louder*] Yes, ma'am.

Mistress. Good. I was sure you'd remember . . . Plus three holidays. Correct?

Julia. Two, ma'am. Christmas and New Year's.

TAKE NOTES

The Governess 161

DRAMA

TAKE NOTES

MISTRESS. And your birthday. That's three.

JULIA. I worked on my birthday, ma'am.

MISTRESS. You did? There was no need to. My governesses never worked on their birthdays . . .

JULIA. But I did work, ma'am.

MISTRESS. But that's not the question, Julia. We're discussing financial matters now. I will, however, only count two holidays if you insist . . . Do you insist?

JULIA. I did work, ma'am.

MISTRESS. Then you *do* insist.

JULIA. No, ma'am.

MISTRESS. Very well. That's three holidays, therefore we take off twelve rubles. Now then, four days little Kolya was sick, and there were no lessons.

JULIA. But I gave lessons to Vanya.

MISTRESS. True. But I engaged you to teach two children, not one. Shall I pay you in full for doing only half the work?

JULIA. No, ma'am.

MISTRESS. So we'll deduct it . . . Now, three days you had a toothache and my husband gave you permission not to work after lunch. Correct?

JULIA. After four. I worked until four.

MISTRESS. [*Looks in the book*] I have here: "Did not work after lunch." We have lunch at one and are finished at two, not at four, correct?

JULIA. Yes, ma'am. But I—

MISTRESS. That's another seven rubles . . . Seven and twelve is nineteen . . . Subtract . . . that leaves . . . forty-one rubles . . . Correct?

JULIA. Yes, ma'am. Thank you, ma'am.

MISTRESS. Now then, on January fourth you broke a teacup and saucer, is that true?

JULIA. Just the saucer, ma'am.

Mistress. What good is a teacup without a saucer, eh? . . . That's two rubles. The saucer was an heirloom.[2] It cost much more, but let it go. I'm used to taking losses.

Julia. Thank you, ma'am.

Mistress. Now then, January ninth, Kolya climbed a tree and tore his jacket.

Julia. I forbid him to do so, ma'am.

Mistress. But he didn't listen, did he? . . . Ten rubles . . . January fourteenth, Vanya's shoes were stolen . . .

Julia. But the maid, ma'am. You discharged her yourself.

Mistress. But you get paid good money to watch everything. I explained that in our first meeting. Perhaps you weren't listening. Were you listening that day, Julia, or was your head in the clouds?

Julia. Yes, ma'am.

Mistress. Yes, your head was in the clouds?

Julia. No, ma'am. I was listening.

Mistress. Good girl. So that means another five rubles off [*Looks in the book*] . . . Ah, yes . . . The sixteenth of January I gave you ten rubles.

Julia. You didn't.

Mistress. But I made a note of it. Why would I make a note of it if I didn't give it to you?

Julia. I don't know, ma'am.

Mistress. That's not a satisfactory answer, Julia . . . Why would I make a note of giving you ten rubles if I did not in fact give it to you, eh? . . . No answer? . . . Then I must have given it to you, mustn't I?

Julia. Yes, ma'am. If you say so, ma'am.

Mistress. Well, certainly I say so. That's the point of this little talk. To clear these matters up. Take

TAKE NOTES

---

2. heirloom (er´ lo͞om´) *n.* treasured possession passed down from generation to generation.

The Governess **163**

DRAMA

TAKE NOTES

twenty-seven from forty-one, that leaves . . . fourteen, correct?

Julia. Yes, ma'am. [*She turns away, softly crying.*]

Mistress. What's this? Tears? Are you crying? Has something made you unhappy, Julia? Please tell me. It pains me to see you like this. I'm so sensitive to tears. What is it?

Julia. Only once since I've been here have I ever been given any money and that was by your husband. On my birthday he gave me three rubles.

Mistress. Really? There's no note of it in my book. I'll put it down now. [*She writes in the book.*] Three rubles. Thank you for telling me. Sometimes I'm a little lax with my accounts . . . Always shortchanging myself. So then, we take three more from fourteen . . . leaves eleven . . . Do you wish to check my figures?

Julia. There's no need to, ma'am.

Mistress. Then we're all settled. Here's your salary for two months, dear. Eleven rubles. [*She puts the pile of coins on the desk.*] Count it.

Julia. It's not necessary, ma'am.

Mistress. Come, come. Let's keep the records straight. Count it.

Julia. [*Reluctantly counts it*] One, two, three, four, five, six, seven, eight, nine, ten . . . ? There's only ten, ma'am.

Mistress. Are you sure? Possibly you dropped one . . . Look on the floor, see if there's a coin there.

Julia. I didn't drop any, ma'am. I'm quite sure.

Mistress. Well, it's not here on my desk, and I *know* I gave you eleven rubles. Look on the floor.

Julia. It's all right, ma'am. Ten rubles will be fine.

Mistress. Well, keep the ten for now. And if we don't find it on the floor later, we'll discuss it again next month.

164 Close Reading Notebook • Unit 4

Julia. Yes, ma'am. Thank you, ma'am. You're very kind, ma'am.

[*She curtsies and then starts to leave.*]

Mistress. Julia!

[Julia *stops, turns.*]

Come back here.

[*She goes back to the desk and curtsies again.*]

Why did you thank me?

Julia. For the money, ma'am.

Mistress. For the money? . . . But don't you realize what I've done? I've cheated you . . . *Robbed* you! I have no such notes in my book. I made up whatever came into my mind. Instead of the eighty rubles which I owe you, I gave you only ten. I have actually stolen from you and you still thank me . . . Why?

Julia. In the other places that I've worked, they didn't give me anything at all.

Mistress. Then they cheated you even worse than I did . . . I was playing a little joke on you. A cruel lesson just to teach you. You're much too trusting, and in this world that's very dangerous . . . I'm going to give you the entire eighty rubles. [*Hands her an envelope*] It's all ready for you. The rest is in this envelope. Here, take it.

Julia. As you wish, ma'am. [*She curtsies and starts to go again.*]

Mistress. Julia! [Julia *stops.*] Is it possible to be so spineless? Why don't you protest? Why don't you speak up? Why don't you cry out against this cruel and unjust treatment? Is it really possible to be so guileless, so innocent, such a—pardon me for being so blunt—such a simpleton?

Julia. [*The faintest trace of a smile on her lips*] Yes, ma'am . . . it's possible.

[*She curtsies again and runs off. The* Mistress *looks after her a moment, a look of complete bafflement on her face. The lights fade.*]

DRAMA

TAKE NOTES

from Kindertransport
by Diane Samuels

You are about to read an excerpt from the drama Kindertransport. In the preceding section of the play, two stories have unfolded side by side. In one story, set in the 1930s, Helga prepares her nine-year-old daughter, Eva, to leave Germany for England, where Eva will live with a foster family. Eva must flee Germany because she and her family are Jews, their lives endangered by Nazi persecution. When she arrives in England, she is taken in by Lil, who raises Eva as her own child.

The preceding section of the play also tells a second story, set in the present. Evelyn, Eva's grown self, is helping her own daughter, Faith, prepare to leave home. Exploring the storage room in their home, Faith discovers evidence of Evelyn's German Jewish past—a past Evelyn has never shared with Faith. Faith flares up in anger at her mother.

This excerpt from the play opens as Lil, Evelyn's adoptive mother and Faith's grandmother, attempts to help Evelyn deal with the crisis. As you read, note ways in which the drama shifts between the two stories—Eva's and Evelyn's.

Characters

EVELYN: English middle-class woman. In her fifties.

FAITH: Evelyn's only child. In her early twenties.

EVA: Evelyn's younger self. She starts the play at 9 years old and finishes it at 17 years old. Jewish German becoming increasingly English.

HELGA: German Jewish woman of the late 1930s. In her early thirties. Eva/Evelyn's mother.

LIL: Eva/Evelyn's English foster mother. In her eighties.

The Ratcatcher: *A mythical character who also plays:* The Nazi Border Official, The English Organizer, The Postman, The Station Guard.

[*The play takes place in a spare storage room in Evelyn's house in an outer London suburb in recent times.*]

from Scene 1

Evelyn. What shall I do with the papers?

Lil. You should've known she'd find them one day.

Evelyn. She's never searched in here in her life.

Lil. Burying's not enough, love. You have to get rid.

Evelyn. How could I get rid of them? There are documents in there that prove I have a right to be here. Papers that will stop them from sending me away.

Lil. Who'd want to send you away?

Evelyn. Someone. Anyone. You can never tell. Who knows what they may be thinking.

Lil. Who for [goodness] sake!

Evelyn. The authorities.

Lil. Your passport's not in there is it?

Evelyn. Not my current one.

Lil. And your naturalization papers?

Evelyn. The first entry permit is. There might be other documents.

Lil. Dig them out then.

Evelyn. I don't want to touch those letters and pictures.

Lil. I'll help.

[Evelyn *pulls back.*]

Lil. Don't you trust me?

Evelyn. Yes.

Lil. I'll sort them out with you.

[Lil *brings the box of papers over and takes out a letter. She holds it out to* Evelyn.]

TAKE NOTES

LIL. Do you want to keep this?

[EVELYN *looks at the letter.*]

LIL. It's personal not official.

EVELYN. No.

LIL. What shall I do with it?

EVELYN. [*taking it*] I'll rip it up.

[EVELYN *holds it.*]

LIL. If you're going to do it, do it.

[EVELYN *is still.*]

What're you waiting for? Get tearing.

[EVELYN *looks at the paper.*]

LIL. Go on.

EVELYN. Why are you so keen for me to destroy everything?

LIL. I thought you wanted shut of it.

EVELYN. I do . . . I just . . .

LIL. Here love, let me.

EVELYN. No.

LIL. If you can't, I will.

EVELYN. It's mine not yours.

LIL. Don't be so daft.

EVELYN. You've always done too much.

LIL. How could I ever do enough?

EVELYN. You took too much.

LIL. How did I take?

EVELYN. Too much of me. You took me away.

LIL. What d'you mean by that?

EVELYN. I wasn't your child.

LIL. As good as . . .

EVELYN. You made me betray her.

LIL. I got you through it. Never forget that, Evelyn.

Evelyn. You made me betray them all.

Lil. I was with you and I put up with you and I stuck by you. That's what mothering's all about. Being there when it counts. No one else was there, were they? And good or bad, I'm still here. Who else have you got?

Evelyn. No one.

Lil. That's right, Evelyn, no one.

Evelyn. And isn't that what you always wanted?

Lil. Did I start the war? Am I Hitler?

Evelyn. You might as well have been.

Lil. What have I done to you that wasn't done in love?

Evelyn. What are you? Some saint? . . .

Lil. I didn't have to take you in . . .

Evelyn. Some savior to all the world's poor little orphans?

Lil. I could've starved you or worked you . . .

Evelyn. And what do I have to pay?

Lil. I could've hit you . . .

Evelyn. What's your price?

Lil. I saved you.

Evelyn. Part of me is dead because of you.

Lil. Nothing you say will make me walk out that door.

Evelyn. Murderer.

Lil. I kept you alive. More than alive.

Evelyn. Child-stealer.

Lil. Go on then. Bare your grudges at me. What else do you want to blame me for? What other ills in your life are all down to me?

Evelyn. Shut up.

Lil. I'm waiting.

Evelyn. I don't want to blame you.

from Kindertransport

DRAMA

TAKE NOTES

Lil. What do you want?

Evelyn. I want it never to have happened.

Lil. Well it did.

[*Pause.*]

Lil. Now what?

Evelyn. Enough.

[Evelyn *tears up the letter into small pieces. She and* Lil *proceed to destroy each item in the box.*]

[Station Guard *enters.*]

Guard. [*to* Eva] Can I help you, love?

Eva. What?

Guard. You waiting for someone?

Eva. Two people.

Guard. What do they look like, love?

[Eva *takes out a photo and shows it.*]

Guard. Well-heeled.

Eva. Mother knows a good cobbler.

Guard. Right. Is that them?

Eva. No.

Guard. They your parents are they?

Eva. Yes.

[*They look.*]

Guard. [*pointing*] What about those two?

Eva. No.

Guard. You're not here on your own to meet them are you?

Eva. Mrs. Miller has just gone to cloakroom.

Guard. Who's that then?

Eva. She looks after me.

Guard. She knows where to find you?

Eva. Oh yes.

Guard. What about that woman there?

Eva. No.

Guard. Live in Manchester[1] do you?

Eva. Yes.

Guard. Not been evacuated then?

Eva. No.

[*They look.*]

Guard. Well, I'm afraid they don't seem to be here, your Mam and Dad.

Eva. They will come.

Guard. You sure they were on this train?

Eva. They write that they come to me on September 9th.

Guard. But, it's September 11th today.

Eva. They must to come soon.

Guard. Look. Are you certain they were traveling from London?

Eva. Yes . . . it must be . . . I got here from there.

Guard. You see there's no more trains today from London.

Eva. Are you sure?

Guard. Course I am.

Eva. It can't be.

Guard. [*suspicious*] Where are you from?

Eva. 72 Mulberry Road . . .

Guard. No. I mean, what's your nationality?

Eva. My?

Guard. What country you from?

Eva. [*worried*] I don't live there any more.

Guard. Where don't you live any more?

Eva. It does not matter so much.

---

1. **Manchester** (man´ ches´ tər) city in northwest England.

from Kindertransport

TAKE NOTES

Guard. And where's this lady who's looking after you? She's left you a long time on your own hasn't she?

Eva. I don't know.

Guard. [*taking her by the arm*] I think that you'd better come with me young lady.

[Lil *runs up to* Eva.]

Lil. Eva! Eva! Where [. . .] did you go!

Guard. Are you supposed to be looking after her?

Lil. I just went to the cloakroom.

Guard. You should take better care of her. Can't leave a girl of her age on her own. Specially nowadays. Could be an air raid warning any minute.

Lil. She ran off. [*to* Eva] What d'you do that for? You had me frantic. D'you think I like pacing platforms looking for you!

Guard. And what's this about her being a foreigner?

Lil. [*to* Eva] The last train's been and gone, love.

Eva. We cannot to give up yet.

Lil. We've been here three days on the trot.[2]

Eva. Please can we come back tomorrow.

Lil. I don't think they're coming. [*to* Guard] I'll take her now.

Guard. I asked you about her being a foreigner?

Lil. [*to* Guard] Don't worry yourself about it.

Guard. Got to look out for spies we have.

Lil. She's not a spy. She's ten years old.

Guard. What about them parents she's waiting for?

Lil. Her parents are still in Germany.

Eva. No, they're not!

Guard. Are they indeed?

Lil. Just leave it to me, will you. [*to* Eva] I did warn you that this would happen.

---

2. **three days on the trot** British English idiom meaning "three days straight."

Guard. What's she doing here then? She should be in Germany with them.

Eva. Maybe they're in London.

Lil. Eva. They're not coming.

Eva. They keep their promises. Always.

Lil. Wars break promises.

Eva. They must be coming some different way. They have their visas got by now . . . they have written to us that they come this week . . .

Lil. They wrote that before the war started. If it'd broke out a fortnight[3] later . . .

Eva. I want them to come. I got permits!

Lil. Believe me, Eva love, I want them to come too.

Guard. Well, I don't.

Eva. You are wrong! You are wrong! They will come!

Lil. There's no way through.

Eva. There is!

Lil. There isn't.

Guard. If they put one foot into this country, they'll be interned[4] straight off. Got to protect ourselves.

Eva. No!

Lil. Oh Eva.

Eva. No! No! No! No! No!

Lil. I know. I know.

Eva. No!

[Eva *shakes with distress.*]

Guard. [*exiting*] Should've stayed where she belongs.

Lil. We can go to church and pray for them.

Eva. I don't know how to pray in a church.

Lil. It's a lot easier to learn than English.

Eva. I'll never see them again, will I?

---

3. **fortnight** (fôrt′ nīt′) *n.* period of two weeks.
4. **interned** (in turnd′) *v.* confined, especially during war.

from Kindertransport

DRAMA

TAKE NOTES

Lil. They've got as much chance of surviving as we have. And I'm not dying and neither are you.

[Eva *takes off two rings, a charm bracelet, a watch, and a chain with a Star of David on it.*]

Lil. What're you doing?

Eva. I don't want these on me any more.

Lil. Why on earth not?

Eva. I don't like them.

Lil. We'll put them away safe at home.

Eva. How much longer can I stay with you?

Lil. Don't ask stupid questions.

[Lil *takes* Eva's *arm.* Eva *slowly moves with her.*]

[Evelyn *rips. Lil picks up the "Rattenfänger"[5] book and starts to tear out the first page.*]

Evelyn. No. Not that.

Lil. It's in German. Horrible pictures.

Evelyn. You can't damage a book. I'll give it to a second-hand shop.

Lil. [*picking up the Haggadah*[6]] What about this?

Evelyn. That too.

[Evelyn *puts the books to the side.* Lil *opens a letter.*]

[Evelyn *picks up the mouth organ. She doesn't recognize it. She puts it with the books.*]

[Lil *reads the letter in her hand intently.*]

Evelyn. Is it important?

Lil. It's them changing their mind about letting you stay on at school after we fought them . . .

Evelyn. Rip it up.

Lil. "We accept Eva's proven brilliancy . . ."

---

5. **Rattenfänger** (rät′ ən fen′ ər) *German for "Rat-Catcher." Rattenfänger* is a name for the Pied Piper of Hamelin, a character in folklore who rid the city of Hamelin of its rats by luring them away with a flute. When the people failed to pay him for his service, he lured away their children as well.
6. **Haggadah** (hə gä′ də) book containing a narrative of the biblical story of Exodus, the story of the Jews' captivity in Egypt and of their liberation by Moses. It is read at the Seder meal during Passover, a Jewish holiday.

174 Close Reading Notebook • Unit 4

Evelyn. Mum.[7]

Lil. Can't we save it?

Evelyn. What did you say about destroying?

[Lil *withholds it.*]

Evelyn. You were absolutely right. All this unpleasantness could have been avoided. I should have sifted through all these years ago. It's only paper.

Lil. I suppose.

Evelyn. What's done is done, Mum.

[Evelyn *takes the letter and tears it.*]

Evelyn. Let's get back to normal shall we?

Lil. You've got over worse.

Evelyn. I've made a good life. All I can do is live it and count my blessings.

Lil. And make up with your daughter.

Evelyn. We'll see.

Lil. You always have to make an effort with your children. No matter what.

Evelyn. All our children leave us. And one day they never come back. I can't stop her.

Lil. You and I are still close.

Evelyn. You and I are different.

Lil. She's more like you than you think.

Evelyn. I don't want her to be like me.

Lil. She's herself too. Every child's their own person.

Evelyn. Was I?

Lil. And how.

Evelyn. Not any more. The older I get the less of myself I become.

Lil. The things you come out with.

Evelyn. I always knew she'd go. Didn't the German woman realize that too?

---

7. **mum** British English for "mom."

from Kindertransport **175**

DRAMA

TAKE NOTES

Lil. You mean your first mother?

Evelyn. She wanted me to be hers forever.

Lil. I thought you'd forgotten her.

Evelyn. It doesn't matter. I have.

[Evelyn *continues to tear.*]

[*Soundtrack of a newsreel about the liberation of Belsen.*[8]]

[Lil *and* Eva (*now fifteen*) *watch. Suddenly* Lil *throws a handkerchief over* Eva's *face and bundles her away.*]

Lil. They should have a warning about what's in them newsreels. No children should see such pictures.

Eva. [*taking the handkerchief off her face*] I'm not a child. I'm fifteen.

Lil. Especially not you. No matter how old you are.

Eva. It can't be kept from me forever.

Lil. D'you want to go back in then?

[*Pause.*]

Eva. No.

Lil. What you don't see can't come back to haunt you.

Eva. I suppose so.

Lil. Thank [goodness] I had my handkerchief.

Eva. The soldiers had them over their noses and mouths.

Lil. Don't think of it.

Eva. Can a handkerchief keep out the smell of all those bodies?

Lil. It couldn't hold all the tears that want crying.

[*Pause.*]

Eva. I don't want to cry.

Lil. Far too shocking.

Eva. Should I want to cry? Is it callous of me?

---

8. **Belsen** (bel′ zən) another name for Bergen-Belsen, a Nazi concentration camp in Germany.

Lil. You react as you react.

Eva. We can still go in to see the main feature, can't we?

Lil. Do you want to?

Eva. Yes. Is that wrong?

Lil. It was our treat.

Eva. There's no reason why we should miss our treat is there? I mean, it wouldn't make any difference to anything else would it?

Lil. Sure you're in the mood?

Eva. I have been looking forward to it.

Lil. I don't know if I'm in the mood now.

Eva. You've already paid for the tickets and we won't have another chance before it finishes.

Lil. All right.

[*Knocking on the door.*]

Faith. [*off*] Gran? Mum?

[Evelyn *shakes her head.*]

Lil. Go on down, Faith, love.

Faith. [*off*] What are you doing?

Lil. Let me sort it out.

Faith. [*off*] Let me in.

Lil. We'll be out soon. Promise.

Faith. [*off*] How soon?

Lil. Not long.

Faith. [*off*] I'll wait here.

[Eva *stands on a box.* Lil *starts to fix her skirt hem.*]

Eva. Thank you for helping.

Lil. [*to* Eva] You can do your own hem next time.

Eva. You know I'm no good at sewing.

Lil. You'll have to learn sooner or later.

from Kindertransport 177

DRAMA

TAKE NOTES

Eva. [*taking the gold watch and jewelry out of her pocket*] How much d'you think they're worth?

Lil. What's worth?

Eva. Two rings. A charm bracelet. Gold. A chain with a Star of David. A watch. All gold.

Lil. Don't ask me. I'm not a jeweler.

Eva. It'd be quite a lot, wouldn't it?

[*Eva peers at the jewelry.*]

Lil. Why d'you want to know?

Eva. I was thinking of selling them.

Lil. What d'you want to sell them for?

Eva. I'm fed up of hiding the watch under my socks to stop hearing the ticking at night.

Lil. It's bad luck to sell a keepsake.

Eva. I'd rather have the money.

Lil. Money's nothing. You purse it, you spend it. Those are more.

Eva. If they're mine, I can do what I want with them.

Lil. Are they yours?

Eva. My mother from Germany gave them to me.

Lil. To look after for her or have for yourself?

Eva. Same difference now.

Lil. We're still trying to track them down, aren't we? Still writing all those letters. Why are you so keen to give up?

Eva. It was all over a long time ago.

Lil. It isn't over till you know for sure.

Eva. I do know for sure.

Lil. Miracles can happen.

Eva. I don't believe in miracles.

Lil. It sounds to me like you don't want to.

Eva. I will sell them, Mum. There's better things the money could be spent on.

Lil. Like what?

Eva. I want to pay my way for myself as much as I can.

Lil. And I want to keep you. Like no one ever kept me. I don't care if it's hard. I'll do right by you. Somebody has to in this [. . .] world.

Eva. You've already done more than all right by me.

Lil. I've not finished yet.

Eva. D'you mind if I go now?

Lil. Just make sure no one [cheats] you.

[*Knocking on the door.*]

Faith. [*off*] Let me in. Please, let me in.

[Evelyn *nods.* Lil *opens the door.* Faith *enters.*]

Faith. My [goodness].

Evelyn. We're going to clean this room up now.

Faith. I didn't mean to shout at you like that.

Evelyn. It's over and done with.

Faith. I'm sorry.

Evelyn. It's forgotten.

[Lil *tidies around the box of torn papers.*]

Faith. What are those?

Evelyn. I've put an end to the trouble.

Faith. You've torn up those letters and photos . . .

Evelyn. It's the only way forward.

Faith. [*to* Lil] How could you let her do this?

Lil. It's what we both think is best.

[Faith *kneels down and stares at the pieces. She tries to gather and fit them together.*]

Evelyn. Don't get yourself all worked up now darling.

Faith. Weren't these family documents . . . I mean . . . more than that . . .

Evelyn. I know what they were.

Lil. [*to* Evelyn] No one's accusing you, love.

TAKE NOTES

from Kindertransport **179**

DRAMA

TAKE NOTES

Faith. But . . . weren't these things . . . sort of . . . entrusted to you? Why didn't you look after them?

[Evelyn *is silent.*]

Faith. Why didn't you pass them on to me?

Evelyn. I can do what I want with my own property.

Faith. But how do I know what went before without them? How does anyone know? What proof is there? It could all be make-believe, couldn't it?

Lil. [*to Faith*] You're not doing a very good job of making up, Faith.

Faith. [*picking up scraps of paper from the floor*] Look at these remains. Where's the body for these feet? The hand for these fingers? Now they're just lost in the millions.

Evelyn. You know, Faith, there are hundreds of books on the subject. Read some of those if you must have a morbid interest in past events.

Faith. Who's going to be able to take care of their memory?

Evelyn. Are you going to go on at me about this for the rest of our lives?

Faith. Did they die for you to forget?

Evelyn. Why are you being so cruel?

Faith. Destroying these was crueler.

Evelyn. Do you think I don't know that.

Faith. Why did you do it then?

Evelyn. Because—and I don't expect you to begin to understand this—it helps me? It gives me something I can do in the face of it all.

Faith. It can't change what happened though, can it?

Evelyn. Do you want to draw blood?

Faith. Not blood.

Evelyn. Well, blood is all I have left. Gallons and gallons of the freezing stuff stuck in my veins. One prick, Faith, and I might bleed forever.

Faith. Mother, don't . . .

Evelyn. Do you still want to know about my childhood, about my origins, about my parents?

Faith. Yes.

Evelyn. Well, let me tell you. Let me tell you what little remains in my brain. And if I do, will you leave me alone afterwards. Will you please leave me alone?

Faith. If that's what you want.

Evelyn. My father was called Werner Schlesinger. My mother was called Helga. They lived in Hamburg. They were Jews. I was an only child. I think I must have loved them a lot at one time. One forgets what these things feel like. Other feelings displace the original ones. I remember a huge cone of sweets that I had on my first day at school. There were a lot of toffees . . .

Faith. What else?

Lil. Faith.

Faith. What else do you remember?

Evelyn. Books. Rows and rows . . . a whole house built of books and some of them were mine. A storybook filled with dreadful pictures: a terrifying man with razor eyes, long, long fingernails, hair like rats' tails who could see wherever you were, whatever you did, no matter how careful you tried to be, who could get in through sealed windows and closed doors . . .

Faith. Go on.

Evelyn. The only other thing is a boy with a squint on the train I came away on. I kept trying not to look at him. Please believe me, Faith, there is nothing else in my memory from that time. It honestly is blank.

Faith. What happened to your parents?

Evelyn. They died.

Faith. In a concentration camp?

Evelyn. Yes. In Auschwitz.

from Kindertransport 181

TAKE NOTES

Lil. When did you find that out?

Faith. When did they die?

Evelyn. My father died in 1943. He was gassed soon after arrival.

Faith. What about your mother?

Evelyn. My mother . . . she was . . . she was not gassed.

Faith. What happened to her?

[Helga *enters. She is utterly transformed—thin, wizened, old-looking. Her hair is thin and short.*]

Helga. Ist das Eva? (*Is it Eva?*)

[Eva *is speechless.*]

Helga. Bist Du das, Eva? (*Is that you, Eva?*)

Eva. Mother?

[Helga *approaches Eva and hugs her.* Eva *tries to hug back but is clearly very uncomfortable.*]

Helga. Ich hätte Dich nicht erkannt. (*How much you have changed.*)

Eva. I'm sorry. I don't quite understand.

Helga. How much you have changed.

Eva. So have you.

Helga. You are sixteen now.

Eva. Seventeen.

Helga. Blue is suiting to you. A lovely dress.

Eva. Thank you.

Helga. You are very pretty.

Eva. This is a nice hotel. I can't believe you're here.

Helga. I promised I would come, Eva.

Eva. I'm called Evelyn now.

Helga. What is Evelyn?

Eva. I changed my name.

Helga. Why?

Eva. I wanted an English name.

182 Close Reading Notebook • Unit 4

Helga. Eva was the name of your great-grandmother.

Eva. I didn't mean any disrespect.

Helga. No. Of course not.

Eva. I'm sorry.

Helga. Nothing is the same any more.

Eva. It's just that I've settled down now.

Helga. These are the pieces of my life.

Eva. There were no letters for all those years and then I saw the newsreels and newspapers . . .

Helga. I am putting them all back together again.

Eva. I thought the worst.

Helga. I always promised that I would come and get you.

Eva. I was a little girl then.

Helga. I am sorry that there has been such a delay. It was not of my making. [*pause*] I am your Mutti, Eva.

Eva. Evelyn.

Helga. Eva. Now I am here, you have back your proper name.

Eva. Evelyn is on my naturalization papers.

Helga. Naturalized as English?

Eva. And adopted by Mr. and Mrs. Miller.

Helga. How can you be adopted when your own mother is alive for you?

Eva. I thought that you were not alive.

Helga. Never mind it. We have all done bad things in the last years that we regret. That is how we survive.

Eva. What did you do?

Helga. I was right to send you here, yes? It is good to survive. Is it not, Eva?

Eva. Please call me Evelyn.

TAKE NOTES

from Kindertransport

DRAMA

TAKE NOTES

HELGA. Now we must put our lives right again. We will go to New York where your Onkel Klaus will help us to make a beginning.

EVA. All the way to New York?

HELGA. Who is here for us? No one. The remains of our family is in America.

EVA. I have a family here.

HELGA. These people were just a help to you in bad times. You can to leave them now behind. The bad times are finished. I know it.

EVA. I like it here.

HELGA. You will like it better in America.

EVA. Do I have to go away with you?

HELGA. That is what I came for.

[RATCATCHER *music*]

Scene 2

[*The torn papers and their box have been cleared away.*]

[HELGA, *holding a suitcase, stands in a corner.*]

[EVELYN *has open the box of glasses. She rubs one with a tea towel.*]

[FAITH *watches.*]

EVELYN. [*holding up a glass*] Will these be of any use?

FAITH. Aren't they a bit precious?

EVELYN. You can have them if you want them.

FAITH. If you're sure . . .

EVELYN. Yes or no?

FAITH. Yes.

EVELYN. Good. That's glasses done.

[FAITH *picks up the box and puts it by the door.*]

[EVELYN *moves on to another box.*]

[LIL *enters. She is wearing a coat.*]

184 Close Reading Notebook • Unit 4

Lil. I'm off out now.

Evelyn. Will you be back for dinner?

Lil. Yes.

Faith. Do you want me to give you a lift to the station tomorrow?

Evelyn. I said that I would.

Faith. You hate driving into town.

Lil. [*to* Faith] I told her she didn't have to.

Evelyn. [*to* Lil] I want to take you to the station.

Lil. You don't need to make anything up to me. I told you. It's all right.

Evelyn. Maybe I feel less all right about it than you do.

Lil. Don't be silly.

Evelyn. Just let me take you.

Lil. All right, take me.

Evelyn. I'll find out about departure times.

Lil. I've already got a timetable.

Evelyn. Fine.

Lil. See you later then.

Evelyn. See you later.

Faith. Bye.

[Lil *exits.*]

[Faith *starts to search through some boxes.*]

Evelyn. Don't you do a thing. You'll only cause a muddle. [*opening a box*] Do you need cutlery?

Faith. What sort?

Evelyn. [*pushing the box to her*] Look at it and decide.

Faith. This is silver.

Evelyn. I don't like it.

Faith. Why not?

Evelyn. The design's far too fussy.

Faith. I like it.

from **Kindertransport** 185

DRAMA

TAKE NOTES

Evelyn. Take it.

Faith. Thanks.

Evelyn. Not at all.

[Faith *puts the box by the door.*]

[Evelyn *continues to check boxes.*]

Faith. Gran didn't know that your mother survived did she?

Evelyn. If she had known, she would have made me go with her.

Faith. To New York?

Evelyn. She would have handed me back like a borrowed package.

Faith. She might not.

Evelyn. You know your gran as well as I do, Faith.

Faith. Did you ever see her after she left?

Evelyn. No.

Faith. Was she still alive when I was born?

Evelyn. Yes.

Faith. When did she die?

Evelyn. In 1969.

Faith. She lived a long time.

Evelyn. She was a very strong woman.

Faith. Didn't you ever want to be with her?

Evelyn. We didn't get on.

Faith. You stopped me from knowing her.

Evelyn. I have tried to do my best for you. Please believe that.

Faith. You stopped her from knowing me.

Evelyn. I wish it could have been simpler. But it wasn't.

Faith. I just feel that I've lost out on so much.

Evelyn. Don't hanker after the past. It's done.

Faith. It's still a part of our lives.

186 Close Reading Notebook • Unit 4

Evelyn. It is an abyss.

Faith. Before, all I knew was a blank space. Now, it's beginning to fill up. I have a background, a context.

Evelyn. All you have now is a pile of ashes.

Faith. There's far more than ashes, Mum.

Evelyn. [*opening out two boxes*] Crockery?[9]

Faith. [*looking at it*] It's beautiful.

Evelyn. A collection.

Faith. Why don't you use it.

Evelyn. I prefer the Royal Crescent set downstairs. That's an old fancy. I've outgrown it.

Faith. I'll probably break it all.

Evelyn. I hope you won't.

Faith. I was joking.

Evelyn. You will take care of this home of yours won't you?

Faith. Of course, I will.

Evelyn. Do you have enough storage space?

Faith. There's lots of empty cupboards. [*pause*] Am I Jewish?

Evelyn. You've been baptized.

Faith. Wouldn't the Nazis have said that I was?

Evelyn. You can't let people who hate you tell you what you are.

Faith. I want to know what it means.

Evelyn. I'm afraid that I can't help.

Faith. Don't you feel at all Jewish?

Evelyn. I was baptized when I was eighteen. I was cleansed that day. Purified.

Faith. How can you say that?

Evelyn. I have been a great deal happier for it.

Faith. What about being German?

---

9. **crockery** (kräk´ ər ē) *n.* earthenware pots, dishes, and so on.

DRAMA

TAKE NOTES

Evelyn. Germany spat me out. England took me in. I love this place: the language, the countryside, the buildings, the sense of humor, even the food. I danced and sang when I got my first British passport. I was so proud of it. My certificate of belonging. You can't imagine what it was like.

Faith. Why didn't you tell Dad?

Evelyn. Is it so wrong to want a decent, ordinary life?

Faith. It's hard starting from scratch.

Evelyn. You can carry on from where you are.

Faith. Where I am has changed a lot in the last week.

Evelyn. There's a portable television somewhere.

Faith. This is what you're best at.

Evelyn. What is?

Faith. Providing for me.

Evelyn. You're hardly able to do it all for yourself yet.

Faith. I think I'll manage.

Evelyn. Not in the manner to which you have always been accustomed. [*pulling out a desk lamp*] What about a desk lamp?

Faith. Does it work?

Evelyn. There's no bulb.

Faith. That's no problem.

[Faith *turns to pick up a box.*]

Faith. I'll start taking it all down.

[Evelyn *pulls out the Haggadah and the "Rattenfänger" books.*]

Evelyn. [*holding them out to* Faith] There are these too.

Faith. [*putting down the box*] You said everything had been destroyed.

Evelyn. They're just books. You might not want them . . .

Faith. [*taking the books*] Of course I want them.

Evelyn. One is the storybook and the other is for some Jewish festival.

Faith. Thank you.

[Evelyn *picks up the mouth organ.*]

Evelyn. And this. It must have come with me.

[Faith *takes the mouth organ and lays it on top of a box.*]

Faith. I'd better start taking these down.

[Faith *picks up a box and starts to exit.*]

Evelyn. Leave it to the left of the door in the hallway, not the right.

[Faith *exits.*]

[Evelyn *carefully sorts through boxes.*]

[*Sounds of a quayside. A boat is about to leave.*]

[Eva *enters.*]

Helga. Where have you been?

Eva. I said. In the lavatory.

Helga. For half an hour in the lavatory?

Eva. I was being sick.

Helga. Sick?

Eva. I'm all right now.

Helga. Are you sure?

Eva. Yes.

Helga. You should change your mind and come with me.

Eva. I haven't got a case.

Helga. You could have your things sent on.

Eva. You said it was all right to come later.

Helga. I said I would prefer you to come now. There is enough money from Onkel Klaus for a ticket.

Eva. I can't just leave.

Helga. Why do you not want to be with your mother Eva?

from Kindertransport

DRAMA

TAKE NOTES

Eva. Evelyn. My name is Evelyn.

Helga. Why are you so cold to me?

Eva. I don't mean to be cold.

Helga. We have been together a week and you are still years away.

Eva. I can't help it.

[*Boat's hooter sounds.*]

Helga. Boats do not wait for people.

Eva. I hope you have a safe trip.

Helga. When is "later" when you are coming?

Eva. In a month or two.

Helga. Just get on the boat with me. Do it now.

Eva. I'm not ready yet. Not at all.

Helga. You're making a mistake.

Eva. You're making me . . .

Helga. What am I making you do! I am your mother. I love you. We must be together.

Eva. We've not been together for too long.

Helga. That is why it is even more important now.

Eva. I can't leave home yet.

Helga. Home is inside you. Inside me and you. It is not a place.

Eva. I don't understand what you mean.

Helga. You are wasting a chance hardly anyone else has been given.

Eva. I will come.

Helga. Will you?

Eva. If you want me to.

Helga. If I want you to?

Eva. Just not yet.

Helga. Do you want to come to make a new life with me?

190 Close Reading Notebook • Unit 4

Eva. You keep asking me that.

Helga. Do you?

Eva. It's hard for me.

Helga. I lost your father. He was sick and they put him in line for the showers. I saw it. You know what I say to you. I lost him. But I did not lose myself. Nearly, a million times over, right on the edge of life, but I held on with my bones rattling inside me. Why have you lost yourself, Eva?

[*Ship's horn sounds out.*]

Helga. I am going to start again. I want my daughter Eva with me. If you find her, Evelyn, by any chance, send her over to find me.

[Helga *embraces Eva who stands stock still.*]

[Helga *picks up her case and starts to walk away.*]

Evelyn. [*quietly*] There are four types of daughters: wise, bad, stupid, and the ones who do not know what to ask.

Helga. [*turning round*] Which are you?

Evelyn. Don't look at the razor eyes. Whatever you do.

[*She looks at Helga.*]

Why do you only ever stare at me like that? Are those the only eyes you have? Didn't you have others once? Eyes which didn't burn?

Evelyn. I wish you had died.

Helga. I wish you had lived.

Evelyn. I did my best.

Helga. Hitler started the job and you finished it.

Evelyn. Why does it have to be my fault?

Helga. You cut off my fingers and pulled out my hair one strand at a time.

Evelyn. You were the Ratcatcher. Those were his eyes, his face . . .

Helga. You hung me out of the window by my ears and broke my soul into shreds.

from Kindertransport

DRAMA

TAKE NOTES

Evelyn. You threw me into the sea with all your baggage on my shoulders.

Helga. You can never excuse yourself.

Evelyn. How could I swim ashore with so much heaviness on me? I was drowning in leagues and leagues of salty water.

Helga. I have bled oceans out of my eyes.

Evelyn. I had to let go to float.

Helga. Snake. Slithering out of yourself like it was an unwanted skin. Worm.

Evelyn. What right have you got to accuse me? You kept saying something. What was it? Over and over? Yes. "No," you said. That was all. "No. I won't help you. You have to be able to manage on your own. Take the needle. Sew the button and it's time to go. You don't need me. See. It's good." Was it really so very good, Mutti? Was it really what you wanted? It wasn't what I wanted.

Helga. My suffering is monumental. Yours is personal.

[Eva *exits*.]

Evelyn. What about what you did to me? You should have hung onto me and never let me go. Why did you send me away when you were in danger? No one made you. You chose to do it. Didn't it ever occur to you that I might have wanted to die with you. Because I did. I never wanted to live without you and you made me. What is more cruel than that? Except for coming back from the dead and punishing me for surviving on my own.

[Evelyn *sobs. Faith enters*.]

Faith. [*to* Evelyn] Are you crying?

[Faith *tries to get close to* Evelyn. Evelyn *does not turn to face* Faith.]

Faith. What can I do for you? Please tell me what I can do to help?

Evelyn. Stay my little girl forever.

Faith. I can't.

Evelyn. Then there's nothing you can do.

Faith. I'm going to find out what everything means. Get in touch with my relatives. I want to meet them.

Evelyn. You'll find them very different.

Faith. I'm sure they'd love to see you too.

Evelyn. I have nothing in common with them and neither do you.

Faith. I want to put that right.

Evelyn. I don't want you to bring trouble onto yourself.

Faith. There won't be any trouble.

Evelyn. You don't know . . .

Faith. We can do this together. It would make us closer to each other.

Evelyn. I'd rather die than go back.

Faith. You might change your mind . . .

Evelyn. I can't.

[Helga and Eva *exit.*]

Faith. Can I have my toys?

Evelyn. Surely you can leave those here.

Faith. I want to take them with me.

Evelyn. I'd like to keep something from when you were little.

Faith. They mean a lot to me.

Evelyn. Take them.

[Faith *picks up the box of toys.*]

Evelyn. Have you got everything you need now?

Faith. More or less.

Evelyn. All done in here then.

Faith. Yes we are.

[Faith *exits.*]

[*The shadow of the* Ratcatcher *covers the stage.*]

[The End.]

DIARY ENTRIES

TAKE NOTES

from Anne Frank: The Diary of a Young Girl

Saturday, 20 June, 1942

. . . There is a saying that "paper is more patient than man"; it came back to me on one of my slightly melancholy days, while I sat chin in hand, feeling too bored and limp even to make up my mind whether to go out or stay at home. Yes, there is no doubt that paper is patient and as I don't intend to show this cardboard-covered notebook, bearing the proud name of "diary," to anyone, unless I find a real friend, boy or girl, probably nobody cares. And now I come to the root of the matter, the reason for my starting a diary: it is that I have no such real friend.

Let me put it more clearly, since no one will believe that a girl of thirteen feels herself quite alone in the world, nor is it so. I have darling parents and a sister of sixteen. I know about thirty people whom one might call friends—I have strings of boy friends, anxious to catch a glimpse of me and who, failing that, peep at me through mirrors in class. I have relations, aunts and uncles, who are darlings too, a good home, no—I don't seem to lack anything. But it's the same with all my friends, just fun and joking, nothing more. I can never bring myself to talk of anything outside the common round. We don't seem to be able to get any closer, that is the root of the trouble. Perhaps I lack confidence, but anyway, there it is, a stubborn fact and I don't seem to be able to do anything about it.

Hence, this diary. In order to enhance in my mind's eye the picture of the friend for whom I have waited so long, I don't want to set down a series of bald facts in a diary like most people do, but I want this diary itself to be my friend, and I shall call my friend Kitty. No one will grasp what I'm talking about if I begin my letters to Kitty just out of the blue, so, albeit[1] unwillingly, I will start by sketching in brief the story of my life.

---

1. albeit (ôl bē´ it) *conj.* although.

194 Close Reading Notebook • Unit 4

My father was thirty-six when he married my mother, who was then twenty-five. My sister Margot was born in 1926 in Frankfort-on-Main, I followed on June 12, 1929, and, as we are Jewish, we emigrated to Holland in 1933, where my father was appointed Managing Director of Travies N.V. This firm is in close relationship with the firm of Kolen & Co. in the same building, of which my father is a partner.

The rest of our family, however, felt the full impact of Hitler's anti-Jewish laws, so life was filled with anxiety. In 1938 after the pogroms,[2] my two uncles (my mother's brothers) escaped to the U.S.A. My old grandmother came to us, she was then seventy-three. After May 1940 good times rapidly fled: first the war, then the capitulation,[3] followed by the arrival of the Germans, which is when the sufferings of us Jews really began. Anti-Jewish decrees followed each other in quick succession. Jews must wear a yellow star, Jews must hand in their bicycles, Jews are banned from trains and are forbidden to drive. Jews are only allowed to do their shopping between three and five o'clock and then only in shops which bear the placard "Jewish shop." Jews must be indoors by eight o'clock and cannot even sit in their own gardens after that hour. Jews are forbidden to visit theaters, cinemas, and other places of entertainment. Jews may not take part in public sports. Swimming baths, tennis courts, hockey fields, and other sports grounds are all prohibited to them. Jews may not visit Christians. Jews must go to Jewish schools, and many more restrictions of a similar kind.

So we could not do this and were forbidden to do that. But life went on in spite of it all. Jopie[4] used to say to me, "You're scared to do anything, because it may be forbidden." Our freedom was strictly limited. Yet things were still bearable.

Granny died in January 1942; no one will ever know how much she is present in my thoughts and how much I love her still.

In 1934 I went to school at the Montessori Kindergarten and continued there. It was at the end of the school year, I was in form 6B, when I had to

---

2. **pogroms** (pō´ grəmz) *n.* organized killings and other persecution of Jews.
3. **capitulation** (kə pich´ yōō lā´ shən) *n.* act of surrendering.
4. **Jopie** (yō´ pē) Jacqueline van Maarsen, Anne's best friend.

from Anne Frank: The Diary of a Young Girl

DIARY ENTRIES

TAKE NOTES

say good-by to Mrs. K. We both wept, it was very sad. In 1941 I went, with my sister Margot, to the Jewish Secondary School, she into the fourth form[5] and I into the first.

So far everything is all right with the four of us and here I come to the present day.

Thursday, 19 November, 1942

Dear Kitty,

Dussel is a very nice man, just as we had all imagined. Of course he thought it was all right to share my little room.

Quite honestly I'm not so keen that a stranger should use my things, but one must be prepared to make some sacrifices for a good cause, so I shall make my little offering with a good will. "If we can save someone, then everything else is of secondary importance," says Daddy, and he's absolutely right.

The first day that Dussel was here, he immediately asked me all sorts of questions: When does the charwoman[6] come? When can one use the bathroom? When is one allowed to use the lavatory?[7] You may laugh, but these things are not so simple in a hiding place. During the day we mustn't make any noise that might be heard downstairs; and if there is some stranger—such as the charwoman for example—then we have to be extra careful. I explained all this carefully to Dussel. But one thing amazed me: he is very slow on the uptake. He asks everything twice over and still doesn't seem to remember. Perhaps that will wear off in time, and it's only that he's thoroughly upset by the sudden change.

Apart from that, all goes well. Dussel has told us a lot about the outside world, which we have missed for so long now. He had very sad news. Countless friends and acquaintances have gone to a terrible fate. Evening after evening the green and gray army lorries trundle past.[8] The Germans ring at every front door to inquire if there are any Jews living in the house. If there are,

---

5. **fourth form** here, a grade in secondary school.
6. **charwoman** *n.* cleaning woman.
7. **lavatory** *n.* toilet.
8. **lorries trundle past** trucks move along.

196 Close Reading Notebook • Unit 4

then the whole family has to go at once. If they don't find any, they go on to the next house. No one has a chance of evading them unless one goes into hiding. Often they go around with lists, and only ring when they know they can get a good haul. Sometimes they let them off for cash—so much per head. It seems like the slave hunts of olden times. But it's certainly no joke; it's much too tragic for that. In the evenings when it's dark, I often see rows of good, innocent people accompanied by crying children, walking on and on, in charge of a couple of these chaps, bullied and knocked about until they almost drop. No one is spared—old people, babies, expectant mothers, the sick—each and all join in the march of death.

How fortunate we are here, so well cared for and undisturbed. We wouldn't have to worry about all this misery were it not that we are so anxious about all those dear to us whom we can no longer help.

I feel wicked sleeping in a warm bed, while my dearest friends have been knocked down or have fallen into a gutter somewhere out in the cold night. I get frightened when I think of close friends who have now been delivered into the hands of the cruelest brutes that walk the earth. And all because they are Jews!

Yours, Anne

Water Names
by Lan Samantha Chang

Summertime at dusk we'd gather on the back porch, tired and sticky from another day of fierce encoded quarrels, nursing our mosquito bites and frail dignities, sisters in name only. At first we'd pinch and slap each other, fighting for the best—least ragged—folding chair. Then we'd argue over who would sit next to our grandmother. We were so close together on the tiny porch that we often pulled our own hair by mistake. Forbidden to bite, we planted silent toothmarks on each others' wrists. We ignored the bulk of house behind us, the yard, the fields, the darkening sky. We even forgot about our grandmother. Then suddenly we'd hear her old, dry voice, very close, almost on the backs of our necks.

"*Xiushila!* Shame on you. Fighting like a bunch of chickens."

And Ingrid, the oldest, would freeze with her thumb and forefinger right on the back of Lily's arm. I would slide my hand away from the end of Ingrid's braid. Ashamed, we would shuffle our feet while Waipuo calmly found her chair.

On some nights she sat with us in silence. But on some nights she told us stories, "just to keep up your Chinese," she said.

"In these prairie crickets I often hear the sound of rippling waters, of the Yangtze River," she said. "Granddaughters, you are descended on both sides from people of the water country, near the mouth of the great Chang Jiang, as it is called, where the river is so grand and broad that even on clear days you can scarcely see the other side.

"The Chang Jiang runs four thousand miles, originating in the Himalaya mountains where it crashes, flecked with gold dust, down steep cliffs so perilous and remote that few humans have ever seen them. In central China, the river squeezes through deep gorges, then widens in its last thousand miles to the sea. Our ancestors have lived near the mouth of this river, the ever-changing delta, near a city called Nanjing, for more than a thousand years."

"A thousand years," murmured Lily, who was only ten. When she was younger she had sometimes burst into nervous crying at the thought of so many years. Her small insistent fingers grabbed my fingers in the dark.

"Through your mother and I you are descended from a line of great men and women. We have survived countless floods and seasons of ill-fortune because we have the spirit of the river in us. Unlike mountains, we cannot be powdered down or broken apart. Instead, we run together, like raindrops. Our strength and spirit wear down mountains into sand. But even our people must respect the water."

She paused. "When I was young, my own grandmother once told me the story of Wen Zhiqing's daughter. Twelve hundred years ago the civilized parts of China still lay to the north, and the Yangtze valley lay unspoiled. In those days lived an ancestor named Wen Zhiqing, a resourceful man, and proud. He had been fishing for many years with trained cormorants, which you girls of course have never seen. Cormorants are sleek, black birds with long, bending necks which the fishermen fitted with metal rings so the fish they caught could not be swallowed. The birds would perch on the side of the old wooden boat and dive into the river." We had only known blue swimming pools, but we tried to imagine the sudden shock of cold and the plunge, deep into water.

"Now, Wen Zhiqing had a favorite daughter who was very beautiful and loved the river. She would beg to go out on the boat with him. This daughter was a restless one, never contented with their catch, and often she insisted they stay out until it was almost dark. Even then, she was not satisfied. She had been spoiled by her father, kept protected from the river, so she could not see its danger. To this young woman, the river was as familiar as the sky. It was a bright, broad road stretching out to curious lands. She did not fully understand the river's depths.

"One clear spring evening, as she watched the last bird dive off into the blackening waters, she said, 'If

FICTION

TAKE NOTES

only this catch would bring back something more than another fish!'

"She leaned over the side of the boat and looked at the water. The stars and moon reflected back at her. And it is said that the spirits living underneath the water looked up at her as well. And the spirit of a young man who had drowned in the river many years before saw her lovely face."

We had heard about the ghosts of the drowned, who wait forever in the water for a living person to pull down instead. A faint breeze moved through the mosquito screens and we shivered.

"The cormorant was gone for a very long time," Waipuo said, "so long that the fisherman grew puzzled. Then, suddenly, the bird emerged from the waters, almost invisible in the night. Wen Zhiqing grasped his catch, a very large fish, and guided the boat back to shore. And when Wen reached home, he gutted the fish and discovered, in its stomach, a valuable pearl ring."

"From the man?" said Lily.

"Sshh, she'll tell you."

Waipuo ignored us. "His daughter was delighted that her wish had been fulfilled. What most excited her was the idea of an entire world like this, a world where such a beautiful ring would be only a bauble![1] For part of her had always longed to see faraway things and places. The river had put a spell on her heart. In the evenings she began to sit on the bank, looking at her own reflection in the water. Sometimes she said she saw a handsome young man looking back at her. And her yearning for him filled her heart with sorrow and fear, for she knew that she would soon leave her beloved family.

"'It's just the moon,' said Wen Zhiqing, but his daughter shook her head. 'There's a kingdom under the water,' she said. 'The prince is asking me to marry him. He sent the ring as an offering to you.' 'Nonsense,' said her father, and he forbade her to sit by the water again.

"For a year things went as usual, but the next spring there came a terrible flood that swept away almost everything. In the middle of a torrential rain, the family

---

1. **bauble** (bô′ bəl) *n.* trinket.

200 Close Reading Notebook • Unit 5

noticed that the daughter was missing. She had taken advantage of the confusion to hurry to the river and visit her beloved. The family searched for days but they never found her."

Her smoky, rattling voice came to a stop.

"What happened to her?" Lily said.

"It's okay, stupid," I told her. "She was so beautiful that she went to join the kingdom of her beloved. Right?"

"Who knows?" Waipuo said. "They say she was seduced by a water ghost. Or perhaps she lost her mind to desiring."

"What do you mean?" asked Ingrid.

"I'm going inside," Waipuo said, and got out of her chair with a creak. A moment later the light went on in her bedroom window. We knew she stood before the mirror, combing out her long, wavy silver-gray hair, and we imagined that in her youth she too had been beautiful.

We sat together without talking. We had gotten used to Waipuo's abruptness, her habit of creating a question and leaving without answering it, as if she were disappointed in the question itself. We tried to imagine Wen Zhiqing's daughter. What did she look like? How old was she? Why hadn't anyone remembered her name?

While we weren't watching, the stars had emerged. Their brilliant pinpoints mapped the heavens. They glittered over us, over Waipuo in her room, the house, and the small city we lived in, the great waves of grass that ran for miles around us, the ground beneath as dry and hard as bone.

TAKE NOTES

MEXICAN AMERICAN CUENTO

Chicoria

by Rudolfo A. Anaya and José Griego y Maestas

There were once many big ranches in California, and many New Mexicans went to work there. One day one of the big ranch owners asked his workers if there were any poets in New Mexico.

"Of course, we have many fine poets," they replied. "We have old Vilmas, Chicoria, Cinfuegos, to say nothing of the poets of Cebolleta and the Black Poet."

"Well, when you return next season, why don't you bring one of your poets to compete with Gracia—here none can compare with him!"

When the harvest was done the New Mexicans returned home. The following season when they returned to California they took with them the poet Chicoria, knowing well that in spinning a rhyme or in weaving wit there was no *Californio*[1] who could beat him.

As soon as the rancher found out that the workers had brought Chicoria with them, he sent his servant to invite his good neighbor and friend to come and hear the new poet. Meanwhile, the cooks set about preparing a big meal. When the maids began to dish up the plates of food, Chicoria turned to one of the servers and said, "Ah, my friends, it looks like they are going to feed us well tonight!"

The servant was surprised. "No, my friend," he explained, "the food is for *them*. We don't eat at the master's table. It is not permitted. We eat in the kitchen."

"Well, I'll bet I can sit down and eat with them," Chicoria boasted.

"If you beg or if you ask, perhaps, but if you don't ask they won't invite you," replied the servant.

"I never beg," the New Mexican answered. "The master will invite me of his own accord, and I'll bet you twenty dollars he will!"

---

1. ***Californio*** (kä′ lē fôr′ nyō) term for any one of the Spanish-speaking colonists who established ranches in California under Spanish and Mexican rule.

So they made a twenty-dollar bet and they instructed the serving maid to watch if this self-confident New Mexican had to ask the master for a place at the table. Then the maid took Chicoria into the dining room. Chicoria greeted the rancher cordially, but the rancher appeared haughty and did not invite Chicoria to sit with him and his guest at the table. Instead, he asked that a chair be brought and placed by the wall where Chicoria was to sit. The rich ranchers began to eat without inviting Chicoria.

So it is just as the servant predicted, Chicoria thought. The poor are not invited to share the rich man's food!

Then the master spoke: "Tell us about the country where you live. What are some of the customs of New Mexico?"

"Well, in New Mexico when a family sits down to eat each member uses one spoon for each biteful of food," Chicoria said with a twinkle in his eyes.

The ranchers were amazed that the New Mexicans ate in that manner, but what Chicoria hadn't told them was that each spoon was a piece of tortilla:[2] one fold and it became a spoon with which to scoop up the meal.

"Furthermore," he continued, "our goats are not like yours."

"How are they different?" the rancher asked.

"Here your nannies[3] give birth to two kids, in New Mexico they give birth to three!"

"What a strange thing!" the master said. "But tell us, how can the female nurse three kids?"

"Well, they do it exactly as you're doing it now: While two of them are eating the third one looks on."

The rancher then realized his lack of manners and took Chicoria's hint. He apologized and invited his New Mexico guest to dine at the table. After dinner, Chicoria sang and recited his poetry, putting Gracia to shame. And he won his bet as well.

---

2. **tortilla** (tôr tē′ yə) *n.* thin, round pancake of cornmeal or flour.
3. **nannies** (nan′ ēz) *n.* female goats.

TAKE NOTES

Chicoria 203

POEM

from **The People, Yes**

by Carl Sandburg

They have yarns[1]
Of a skyscraper so tall they had to put hinges
On the two top stories so to let the moon go by,
Of one corn crop in Missouri when the roots
5 Went so deep and drew off so much water
The Mississippi riverbed that year was dry,
Of pancakes so thin they had only one side,
Of "a fog so thick we shingled the barn and six feet
    out on the fog,"
Of Pecos Pete straddling a cyclone in Texas and
    riding it to the west coast where "it rained out
    under him,"
10 Of the man who drove a swarm of bees across the
    Rocky Mountains and the Desert "and didn't lose
    a bee,"
Of a mountain railroad curve where the engineer
    in his cab can touch the caboose and spit in the
    conductor's eye,
Of the boy who climbed a cornstalk growing so fast
    he would have starved to death if they hadn't
    shot biscuits up to him,
Of the old man's whiskers: "When the wind was
    with him his whiskers arrived a day before
    he did,"
Of the hen laying a square egg and cackling,
    "Ouch!" and of hens laying eggs with the dates
    printed on them,
15 Of the ship captain's shadow: it froze to the deck
    one cold winter night,
Of mutineers on that same ship put to chipping
    rust with rubber hammers,
Of the sheep counter who was fast and accurate: "I
    just count their feet and divide by four,"
Of the man so tall he must climb a ladder to shave
    himself,

---

1. **yarns** (yärnz) *n.* tall tales that depend on humor and exaggeration.

Of the runt so teeny-weeny it takes two men and a boy to see him,
20 Of mosquitoes: one can kill a dog, two of them a man,
Of a cyclone that sucked cookstoves out of the kitchen, up the chimney flue, and on to the next town,
Of the same cyclone picking up wagon-tracks in Nebraska and dropping them over in the Dakotas,
Of the hook-and-eye snake unlocking itself into forty pieces, each piece two inches long, then in nine seconds flat snapping itself together again,
Of the watch swallowed by the cow—when they butchered her a year later the watch was running and had the correct time,
25 Of horned snakes, hoop snakes that roll themselves where they want to go, and rattlesnakes carrying bells instead of rattles on their tails,
Of the herd of cattle in California getting lost in a giant redwood tree that had hollowed out,
Of the man who killed a snake by putting its tail in its mouth so it swallowed itself,
Of railroad trains whizzing along so fast they reach the station before the whistle,
Of pigs so thin the farmer had to tie knots in their tails to keep them from crawling through the cracks in their pens,
30 Of Paul Bunyan's big blue ox, Babe, measuring between the eyes forty-two ax-handles and a plug of Star tobacco exactly,
Of John Henry's hammer and the curve of its swing and his singing of it as "a rainbow round my shoulder."

TAKE NOTES

from The People, Yes

An Episode of War

by Stephen Crane

The lieutenant's rubber blanket lay on the ground, and upon it he had poured the company's supply of coffee. Corporals and other representatives of the grimy and hot-throated men who lined the breast-work[1] had come for each squad's portion.

The lieutenant was frowning and serious at this task of division. His lips pursed as he drew with his sword various crevices in the heap, until brown squares of coffee, astoundingly equal in size, appeared on the blanket. He was on the verge of a great triumph in mathematics, and the corporals were thronging forward, each to reap a little square, when suddenly the lieutenant cried out and looked quickly at a man near him as if he suspected it was a case of personal assault. The others cried out also when they saw blood upon the lieutenant's sleeve.

He had winced like a man stung, swayed dangerously, and then straightened. The sound of his hoarse breathing was plainly audible. He looked sadly, mystically, over the breast-work at the green face of a wood, where now were many little puffs of white smoke. During this moment the men about him gazed statuelike and silent, astonished and awed by this catastrophe which happened when catastrophes were not expected—when they had leisure to observe it.

As the lieutenant stared at the wood, they too swung their heads, so that for another instant all hands, still silent, contemplated the distant forest as if their minds were fixed upon the mystery of a bullet's journey.

The officer had, of course, been compelled to take his sword into his left hand. He did not hold it by the hilt. He gripped it at the middle of the blade, awkwardly. Turning his eyes from the hostile wood, he looked at the sword as he held it there, and seemed puzzled as

---

1. **breast-work** *n.* low wall put up quickly as a defense in battle.

to what to do with it, where to put it. In short, this weapon had of a sudden become a strange thing to him. He looked at it in a kind of stupefaction, as if he had been endowed with a trident, a sceptre, or a spade.[2]

Finally he tried to sheathe it. To sheathe a sword held by the left hand, at the middle of the blade, in a scabbard hung at the left hip, is a feat worthy of a sawdust ring.[3] This wounded officer engaged in a desperate struggle with the sword and the wobbling scabbard, and during the time of it breathed like a wrestler.

But at this instant the men, the spectators, awoke from their stone-like poses and crowded forward sympathetically. The orderly-sergeant took the sword and tenderly placed it in the scabbard. At the time, he leaned nervously backward, and did not allow even his finger to brush the body of the lieutenant. A wound gives strange dignity to him who bears it. Well men shy from his new and terrible majesty. It is as if the wounded man's hand is upon the curtain which hangs before the revelations of all existence—the meaning of ants, potentates,[4] wars, cities, sunshine, snow, a feather dropped from a bird's wing; and the power of it sheds radiance upon a bloody form, and makes the other men understand sometimes that they are little. His comrades look at him with large eyes thoughtfully. Moreover, they fear vaguely that the weight of a finger upon him might send him headlong, precipitate the tragedy, hurl him at once into the dim, grey unknown. And so the orderly-sergeant, while sheathing the sword, leaned nervously backward.

There were others who proffered assistance. One timidly presented his shoulder and asked the lieutenant if he cared to lean upon it, but the latter waved him away mournfully. He wore the look of one who knows he is the victim of a terrible disease and understands his helplessness. He again stared over the breast-work at the forest, and then, turning, went

TAKE NOTES

---

2. **a trident, a sceptre, or a spade** A trident is a three-pronged fishing spear; a sceptre is a decorative ceremonial staff; and a spade is a heavy, flat-bladed digging tool. Any of these three implements would probably be out of place in the lieutenant's hand.
3. **sawdust ring** *n.* ring in which circus acts are performed.
4. **potentates** (pōt´ 'n tāts´) *n.* rulers; powerful people.

An Episode of War 207

slowly rearward. He held his right wrist tenderly in his left hand as if the wounded arm was made of very brittle glass. •

And the men in silence stared at the wood, then at the departing lieutenant; then at the wood, then at the lieutenant.

As the wounded officer passed from the line of battle, he was enabled to see many things which as a participant in the fight were unknown to him. He saw a general on a black horse gazing over the lines of blue infantry at the green woods which veiled his problems. An aide galloped furiously, dragged his horse suddenly to a halt, saluted, and presented a paper. It was, for a wonder, precisely like a historical painting.

To the rear of the general and his staff a group, composed of a bugler, two or three orderlies, and the bearer of the corps standard,[5] all upon maniacal horses, were working like slaves to hold their ground, preserve their respectful interval, while the shells boomed in the air about them, and caused their chargers to make furious quivering leaps.

A battery, a tumultuous and shining mass, was swirling toward the right. The wild thud of hoofs, the cries of the riders shouting blame and praise, menace and encouragement, and, last, the roar of the wheels, the slant of the glistening guns, brought the lieutenant to an intent pause. The battery[6] swept in curves that stirred the heart; it made halts as dramatic as the crash of a wave on the rocks, and when it fled onward this aggregation of wheels, levers, motors had a beautiful unity, as if it were a missile. The sound of it was a war-chorus that reached into the depths of man's emotion.

The lieutenant, still holding his arm as if it were of glass, stood watching this battery until all detail of it was lost, save the figures of the riders, which rose and fell and waved lashes over the black mass.

Later, he turned his eyes toward the battle, where the shooting sometimes crackled like bush-fires, sometimes sputtered with exasperating irregularity, and sometimes reverberated like the thunder. He saw the smoke rolling upward and saw crowds of men

---

5. **corps** (kôr) **standard** *n.* flag or banner representing a military unit.
6. **battery** (bat´ ər ē) *n.* military unit of men and cannons.

who ran and cheered, or stood and blazed away at the inscrutable distance.

He came upon some stragglers, and they told him how to find the field hospital. They described its exact location. In fact, these men, no longer having part in the battle, knew more of it than others. They told the performance of every corps, every division, the opinion of every general. The lieutenant, carrying his wounded arm rearward, looked upon them with wonder.

At the roadside a brigade was making coffee and buzzing with talk like a girls' boarding-school. Several officers came out to him and inquired concerning things of which he knew nothing. One, seeing his arm, began to scold. "Why, man, that's no way to do. You want to fix that thing." He appropriated the lieutenant and the lieutenant's wound. He cut the sleeve and laid bare the arm, every nerve of which softly fluttered under his touch. He bound his handkerchief over the wound, scolding away in the meantime. His tone allowed one to think that he was in the habit of being wounded every day. The lieutenant hung his head, feeling, in this presence, that he did not know how to be correctly wounded. •

The low white tents of the hospital were grouped around an old schoolhouse. There was here a singular commotion. In the foreground two ambulances interlocked wheels in the deep mud. The drivers were tossing the blame of it back and forth, gesticulating and berating,[7] while from the ambulances, both crammed with wounded, there came an occasional groan. An interminable crowd of bandaged men were coming and going. Great numbers sat under the trees nursing heads or arms or legs. There was a dispute of some kind raging on the steps of the schoolhouse. Sitting with his back against a tree a man with a face as grey as a new army blanket was serenely smoking a corncob pipe. The lieutenant wished to rush forward and inform him that he was dying.

A busy surgeon was passing near the lieutenant. "Good-morning," he said, with a friendly smile. Then he caught sight of the lieutenant's arm, and his face

TAKE NOTES

---

7. **gesticulating** (jes tik´ yoo lāt´ iŋ) **and berating** (bē rāt´ iŋ) *v.* waving arms about wildly and scolding.

An Episode of War 209

SHORT STORY

TAKE NOTES

at once changed. "Well, let's have a look at it." He seemed possessed suddenly of a great contempt for the lieutenant. This wound evidently placed the latter on a very low social plane. The doctor cried out impatiently, "What mutton-head had tied it up that way anyhow?" The lieutenant answered, "Oh, a man."

When the wound was disclosed the doctor fingered it disdainfully. "Humph," he said. "You come along with me and I'll 'tend to you." His voice contained the same scorn as if he were saying: "You will have to go to jail."

The lieutenant had been very meek, but now his face flushed, and he looked into the doctor's eyes. "I guess I won't have it amputated," he said.

"Nonsense, man! Nonsense! Nonsense!" cried the doctor. "Come along, now. I won't amputate it. Come along. Don't be a baby."

"Let go of me," said the lieutenant, holding back wrathfully, his glance fixed upon the door of the old schoolhouse, as sinister to him as the portals of death.

And this is the story of how the lieutenant lost his arm. When he reached home, his sisters, his mother, his wife, sobbed for a long time at the sight of the flat sleeve. "Oh, well," he said, standing shamefaced amid these tears, "I don't suppose it matters so much as all that."

210 Close Reading Notebook • Unit 5

PERSUASIVE SPEECH

from The American Dream

by Martin Luther King, Jr.

June 6, 1961

America is essentially a dream, a dream as yet unfulfilled. It is a dream of a land where men of all races, of all nationalities and of all creeds[1] can live together as brothers. The substance of the dream is expressed in these sublime words, words lifted to cosmic proportions: "We hold these truths to be self-evident, that all men are created equal; that they are endowed by their Creator with certain unalienable rights; that among these are life, liberty, and the pursuit of happiness."[2] This is the dream.

One of the first things we notice in this dream is an amazing universalism. It does not say some men, but it says all men. It does not say all white men, but it says all men, which includes black men. It does not say all Gentiles, but it says all men, which includes Jews. It does not say all Protestants, but it says all men, which includes Catholics.

And there is another thing we see in this dream that ultimately distinguishes democracy and our form of government from all of the totalitarian regimes[3] that emerge in history. It says that each individual has certain basic rights that are neither conferred by nor derived from the state. To discover where they came from it is necessary to move back behind the dim mist of eternity, for they are God-given. Very seldom if ever in the history of the world has a sociopolitical document expressed in such profoundly eloquent and unequivocal language the dignity and the worth of human personality. The American dream reminds us that every man is heir to the legacy of worthiness.

---

1. **creeds** (krēdz) *n.* systems of belief.
2. **"We hold these truths . . . pursuit of happiness."** opening words of the Declaration of Independence, which asserted the American colonies' independence from Great Britain in 1776.
3. **totalitarian** (tō tal′ ə ter′ ē ən) **regimes** (rə zhēmz′) countries in which those in power control every aspect of citizens' lives.

TAKE NOTES

PERSUASIVE SPEECH

TAKE NOTES

Ever since the Founding Fathers of our nation dreamed this noble dream, America has been something of a schizophrenic[4] personality, tragically divided against herself. On the one hand we have proudly professed the principles of democracy, and on the other hand we have sadly practiced the very antithesis of those principles. Indeed slavery and segregation have been strange paradoxes in a nation founded on the principle that all men are created equal. This is what the Swedish sociologist, Gunnar Myrdal, referred to as the American dilemma.

But the shape of the world today does not permit us the luxury of an anemic democracy. The price America must pay for the continued exploitation of the Negro and other minority groups is the price of its own destruction. The hour is late; the clock of destiny is ticking out. It is trite, but urgently true, that if America is to remain a first-class nation she can no longer have second-class citizens. Now, more than ever before, America is challenged to bring her noble dream into reality, and those who are working to implement the American dream are the true saviors of democracy.

Now may I suggest some of the things we must do if we are to make the American dream a reality. First I think all of us must develop a world perspective if we are to survive. The American dream will not become a reality devoid of the larger dream of a world of brotherhood and peace and good will. The world in which we live is a world of geographical oneness and we are challenged now to make it spiritually one.

Man's scientific genius and technological ingenuity has dwarfed distance and placed time in chains. Jet planes have compressed into minutes distances that once took days and months to cover. It is not common for a preacher to be quoting Bob Hope, but I think he has aptly described this jet age in which we live. If, on taking off on a nonstop flight from Los Angeles to New York City, you develop hiccups, he said, you will hic in Los Angeles and cup in New York City. That is really *moving*. If you take a flight from Tokyo, Japan, on Sunday morning, you will arrive in Seattle,

---

4. **schizophrenic** (skit′ sə fren′ ik) *adj.* characterized by a fragmented personality and hallucinations, a disorder sometimes known popularly as "split personality."

Washington, on the preceding Saturday night. When your friends meet you at the airport and ask you when you left Tokyo, you will have to say, "I left tomorrow." This is the kind of world in which we live. Now this is a bit humorous but I am trying to laugh a basic fact into all of us: the world in which we live has become a single neighborhood.

Through our scientific genius we have made of this world a neighborhood; now through our moral and spiritual development we must make of it a brotherhood. In a real sense, we must all learn to live together as brothers, or we will all perish together as fools. We must come to see that no individual can live alone; no nation can live alone. We must all live together; we must all be concerned about each other.

TAKE NOTES

from The American Dream

HISTORICAL ESSAY

TAKE NOTES

Emancipation *from* Lincoln: A Photobiography

by Russell Freedman

The toughest decision facing Lincoln[1] . . . was the one he had to make about slavery. Early in the war, he was still willing to leave slavery alone in the South, if only he could restore the Union. Once the rebellion was crushed, slavery would be confined to the Southern states, where it would gradually die out. "We didn't go into the war to put down slavery, but to put the flag back," Lincoln said. "To act differently at this moment would, I have no doubt, not only weaken our cause, but smack of bad faith."

Abolitionists were demanding that the president free the slaves at once, by means of a wartime proclamation. "Teach the rebels and traitors that the price they are to pay for the attempt to abolish this Government must be the abolition of slavery," said Frederick Douglass, the famous black editor and reformer. "Let the war cry be down with treason, and down with slavery, the cause of treason!"

But Lincoln hesitated. He was afraid to alienate the large numbers of Northerners who supported the Union but opposed emancipation. And he worried about the loyal, slaveholding border states—Kentucky, Missouri, Maryland, and Delaware—that had refused to join the Confederacy. Lincoln feared that emancipation might drive those states into the arms of the South.

Yet slavery was the issue that had divided the country, and the president was under mounting pressure to do something about it. At first he supported a voluntary plan that would free the slaves gradually and compensate their owners with money from the federal treasury. Emancipation would begin in the loyal border states and be extended into the

---

1. **Lincoln** Abraham Lincoln (1809–1865), sixteenth president of the United States (1861–1865), and leader of the North during the Civil War.

South as the rebel states were conquered. Perhaps then the liberated slaves could be resettled in Africa or Central America.

Lincoln pleaded with the border-state congressmen to accept his plan, but they turned him down. They would not part with their slave property or willingly change their way of life. "Emancipation in the cotton states is simply an absurdity," said a Kentucky congressman. "There is not enough power in the world to compel it to be done."

Lincoln came to realize that if he wanted to attack slavery, he would have to act more boldly. A group of powerful Republican senators had been urging him to act. It was absurd, they argued, to fight the war without destroying the institution that had caused it. Slaves provided a vast pool of labor that was crucial to the South's war effort. If Lincoln freed the slaves, he could cripple the Confederacy and hasten the end of the war. If he did not free them, then the war would settle nothing. Even if the South agreed to return to the Union, it would start another war as soon as slavery was threatened again.

Besides, enslaved blacks were eager to throw off their shackles and fight for their own freedom. Thousands of slaves had already escaped from behind Southern lines. Thousands more were ready to enlist in the Union armies. "You need more men," Senator Charles Sumner told Lincoln, "not only at the North, but at the South, in the rear of the rebels. You need the slaves."

All along, Lincoln had questioned his authority as president to abolish slavery in those states where it was protected by law. His Republican advisors argued that in time of war, with the nation in peril, the president *did* have the power to outlaw slavery. He could do it in his capacity as commander in chief of the armed forces. Such an act would be justified as a necessary war measure, because it would weaken the enemy. If Lincoln really wanted to save the Union, Senator Sumner told him, he must act now. He must wipe out slavery.

The war had become an endless nightmare of bloodshed and bungling generals. Lincoln doubted if the Union could survive without bold and drastic

TAKE NOTES

HISTORICAL ESSAY

measures. By the summer of 1862, he had worked out a plan that would hold the loyal slave states in the Union, while striking at the enemies of the Union.

On July 22, 1862, he revealed his plan to his cabinet. He had decided, he told them, that emancipation was "a military necessity, absolutely essential to the preservation of the Union." For that reason, he intended to issue a proclamation freeing all the slaves in rebel states that had not returned to the Union by January 1, 1863. The proclamation would be aimed at the Confederate South only. In the loyal border states, he would continue to push for gradual, compensated emancipation.

Some cabinet members warned that the country wasn't ready to accept emancipation. But most of them nodded their approval, and in any case, Lincoln had made up his mind. He did listen to the objection of William H. Seward, his secretary of state. If Lincoln published his proclamation now, Seward argued, when Union armies had just been defeated in Virginia, it would seem like an act of desperation, "the last shriek on our retreat." The president must wait until the Union had won a decisive military victory in the East. Then he could issue his proclamation from a position of strength. Lincoln agreed. For the time being, he filed the document away in his desk.

A month later, in the war's second battle at Bull Run, Union forces commanded by General John Pope suffered another humiliating defeat. "We are whipped again," Lincoln moaned. He feared now that the war was lost. Rebel troops under Robert E. Lee were driving north. Early in September, Lee invaded Maryland and advanced toward Pennsylvania.

Lincoln again turned to General George McClellan— Who else do I have? he asked—and ordered him to repel the invasion. The two armies met at Antietam Creek in Maryland on September 17 in the bloodiest single engagement of the war. Lee was forced to retreat back to Virginia. But McClellan, cautious as ever, held his position and failed to pursue the defeated rebel army. It wasn't the decisive victory Lincoln had hoped for, but it would have to do.

On September 22, Lincoln read the final wording of his Emancipation Proclamation to his cabinet. If the rebels did not return to the Union by January 1, the president would free "thenceforward and forever" all the slaves everywhere in the Confederacy. Emancipation would become a Union war objective. As Union armies smashed their way into rebel territory, they would annihilate slavery once and for all.

The next day, the proclamation was released to the press. Throughout the North, opponents of slavery hailed the measure, and black people rejoiced. Frederick Douglass, the black abolitionist, had criticized Lincoln severely in the past. But he said now: "We shout for joy that we live to record this righteous decree."

When Lincoln delivered his annual message to Congress on December 1, he asked support for his program of military emancipation:

"Fellow citizens, *we* cannot escape history. We of this Congress and this administration, will be remembered in spite of ourselves. . . . In *giving* freedom to the *slave*, we *assure* freedom to the *free*—honorable alike in what we give, and what we preserve."

On New Year's Day, after a fitful night's sleep, Lincoln sat at his White House desk and put the finishing touches on his historic decree. From this day forward, all slaves in the rebel states were "forever free." Blacks who wished to could now enlist in the Union army and sail on Union ships. Several all-black regiments were formed immediately. By the end of the war, more than 180,000 blacks—a majority of them emancipated slaves—had volunteered for the Union forces. They manned military garrisons and served as front-line combat troops in every theatre of the war.

The traditional New Year's reception was held in the White House that morning. Mary appeared at an official gathering for the first time since Willie's death,[2] wearing garlands in her hair and a black shawl about her head.

During the reception, Lincoln slipped away and retired to his office with several cabinet members and other officials for the formal signing of the proclamation. He looked tired. He had been shaking

TAKE NOTES

---

2. **Mary appeared . . . Willie's death** Mary Todd Lincoln was President Lincoln's wife. The couple's son William died in 1862 at age eleven.

Emancipation *from* Lincoln: A Photobiography

HISTORICAL ESSAY

TAKE NOTES

hands all morning, and now his hand trembled as he picked up a gold pen to sign his name.

Ordinarily he signed "A. Lincoln." But today, as he put pen to paper, he carefully wrote out his full name. "If my name ever goes into history," he said then, "it will be for this act."

ACKNOWLEDGMENTS

Grateful acknowledgment is made to the following for copyrighted material:

Ashabranner, Brent "Always to Remember: The Vision of Maya Ying Lin" by Brent Ashabranner from *Always to Remember*. Copyright © 1988. Used by permission of Brent Ashabranner.

Bantam Books From *The Miracle Worker* by William Gibson. Copyright © 1975. Bantam Books.

Berkley Books From *A Small Enough Team to Do the Job* by Andrew Mishkin from *Sojourner*. Copyright © 2003 by Andrew Mishkin.

Clarion Books, a division of Houghton Mifflin Excerpt from "Emancipation" from *Lincoln: A Photobiography*. Copyright © 1987 by Russell Freedman. Reproduced by permission of Clarion Books, an imprint of Houghton Mifflin Company.

Curtis Brown London "Who Can Replace a Man" by Brian Aldiss from *Masterpieces: The Best Science Fiction of the Century*. Copyright © 1966 by Brian Aldiss. Reproduced with permission of Curtis Brown Group Ltd, London on behalf of Brian Aldiss.

Gary N. DaSilva for Neil Simon "The Governess" from *The Good Doctor* © 1974 by Neil Simon. Copyright renewed © 2002 by Neil Simon. Used by permission. CAUTION: Professionals and amateurs are hereby warned that *The Good Doctor* is fully protected under the Berne Convention and the Universal Copyright Convention and is subject to royalty. All rights, including without limitation professional, amateur, motion picture, television, radio, recitation, lecturing, public reading and foreign translation rights, computer media rights and the right of reproduction, and electronic storage or retrieval, in whole or in part and in any form, are strictly reserved and none of these rights can be exercised or used without written permission from the copyright owner. Inquiries for stock and amateur performances should be addressed to Samuel French, Inc., 45 West 25th Street, New York, NY 10010. All other inquiries should be addressed to Gary N. DaSilva, 111 N. Sepulveda Blvd., Suite 250, Manhattan Beach, CA 90266-6850.

Doubleday From *The Diary of a Young Girl: The Definitive Edition* by Anne Frank, edited by Otto H. Frank and Mirjam Pressler. Translated by Susan Massotty. Copyright © 1995 by Doubleday, a division of Random House, Inc. Used by permission of Doubleday, a division of Random House, Inc.

Richard Garcia "The City is So Big" by Richard Garcia from *The City Is So Big*.

Harcourt, Inc. "Choice: A Tribute to Martin Luther King, Jr." by Alice Walker from *In Search Of Our Mothers' Gardens: Womanist Prose*. Copyright © 1983 by Alice Walker.

"For My Sister Molly Who in the Fifties" from *Revolutionary Petunias & Other Poems*, copyright © 1972 and renewed 2000 by Alice Walker. Excerpt from *The People, Yes* by Carl Sandburg, copyright © 1936 by Harcourt, Inc. and renewed 1964 by Carl Sandburg.

Nick Hern Books Ltd. From *Kindertransport* by Diane Samuels. Copyright © 2002. London. Nick Hern Books.

Gelston Hinds, Jr. o/b/o Amy Ling "Grandma Ling" by Amy Ling from *Bridge: An Asian American Perspective, Vol. 7, No. 3*. Copyright © 1980 by Amy Ling. Used by permission of the author's husband.

Holiday House "January" from *A Child's Calendar* by John Updike. Text copyright © 1965, 1999 by John Updike. All rights reserved. Used by permission of Holiday House, Inc.

The Estate of Dr. Martin Luther King, Jr. c/o Writer's House LLC "The American Dream" by Dr. Martin Luther King, Jr. from *A Testament Of Hope: The Essential Writings Of Martin Luther King, Jr.* Copyright © 1961 Martin Luther King Jr.; Copyright © renewed 1989 Coretta Scott King. Used by arrangement with The Heirs to the Estate of Martin Luther King Jr., c/o Writers House as agent for the proprietor New York, N.Y.

Alfred A. Knopf, Inc. "Harlem Night Song" from *The Collected Poems of Langston Hughes* by Langston Hughes, edited by Arnold Rampersad with David Roessel, Associate Editor, copyright © 1994 by The Estate of Langston Hughes.

Liveright Publishing Corporation "your little voice/Over the wires came leaping" copyright © 1923, 1951, 1991 by the Trustees for the E. E. Cummings Trust. Copyright © 1976 by George James Firmage, from *Complete Poems: 1904-1962* by E. E. Cummings, edited by George J. Firmage.

Robert MacNeil "The Trouble with Television" by Robert MacNeil condensed from a speech, *November 1984 at President Leadership Forum, SUNY*. Copyright © 1985 by Reader's Digest and Robert MacNeil. Used by permission of Robert MacNeil.

Eve Merriam c/o Marian Reiner "Thumbprint" from *A Sky Full of Poems* by Eve Merriam. Copyright © 1964, 1970, 1973, 1986 by Eve Merriam. Used by permission of Marian Reiner.

N. Scott Momaday "New World" by N. Scott Momaday from *The Gourd Dancers*. Used with the permission of Navarre Scott Momaday.

Museum of New Mexico Press "Chicoria" by Jose Griego Y Maestas y Rudolfo Anaya from *Cuentos: Tales from the Hispanic Southwest*. Reproduced by permission of Museum of New Mexico Press.

ACKNOWLEDGMENTS

Harold Ober Associates, Inc. "Cat!" by Eleanor Farjeon from *Poems For Children*. Copyright © 1938 by Eleanor Farjeon, renewed 1966 by Gervase Farjeon. Used by permission of Harold Ober Associates Incorporated. All rights reserved.

Penguin Group (USA), Inc. "Kindertransport" by Diane Samuels from *Plume*. Copyright © Diane Samuels, 1995. All rights reserved.

G.P. Putnam's Sons "Describe Somebody," and "Almost Summer Sky" from *Locomotion* by Jacqueline Woodson, copyright © 2003 by Jacqueline Woodson. Used by permission of G.P. Putnam's Sons, A Division of Penguin Young Readers Group, A Member of Penguin Group (USA) Inc., 345 Hudson Street, New York, NY 10014. All rights reserved.

Random House, Inc. "Raymond's Run" by Toni Cade Bambara from *Gorilla, My Love*. Copyright © 1971 by Toni Cade Bambara. *The Diary of Anne Frank* by Frances Goodrich and Albert Hackett. Copyright © 1956 by Albert Hackett, Frances Goodrich Hackett and Otto Frank. CAUTION: Professionals and amateurs are hereby warned that *The Diary of Anne Frank*, being fully protected under the copyright Laws of the United States of America, the British Empire, including the Dominion of Canada, and all other countries of the Universal Copyright and Berne Conventions, are subject to royalty. All rights, including professional, amateur, motion picture, recitation, lecturing, public reading, radio and television broadcasting, and the rights of translation into foreign languages, are strictly reserved. All inquiries should be addressed to Random House, Inc. Used by permission of Random House, Inc.

Marian Reiner, Literary Agent "Concrete Mixers" by Patricia Hubbell from *8 A.M. Shadows*. Copyright © 1965 Patricia Hubbell. Copyright renewed © 1993 Patricia Hubbell. Used by permission of Marian Reiner on behalf of the author.

Maria Teresa Sanchez "Old Man" by Ricardo Sanchez from *Selected Poems*. Used by permission of Maria Teresa Sanchez for the Estate of Dr. Ricardo Sanchez.

Scholastic Inc. "An Hour with Abuelo" from *An Island Like You: Stories of the Barrio* by Judith Ortiz Cofer. Published by Orchard Books/Scholastic Inc. Copyright © 1995 by Judith Ortiz Cofer. Used by permission of Scholastic Inc.

The Society of Authors "Silver" by Walter de la Mare from *The Complete Poems of Walter de la Mare 1901-1918*. Used by permission of The Literary Trustees of Walter de la Mare and the Society of Authors as their representative.

University of Southern California Viterbi School of Engineering "Robots Get a Feel for the World at USC Viterbi," University of Southern California Viterbi School of Engineering. © 2012, U.S.C. Viterbi School of Engineering.

Viking Penguin, Inc. Excerpt from *Travels with Charley* by John Steinbeck, copyright © 1961, 1962 by The Curtis Publishing Co., © 1962 by John Steinbeck, renewed © 1990 by Elaine Steinbeck, Thom Steinbeck and John Steinbeck IV. Used by permission of Viking Penguin, a division of Penguin Group (USA) Inc.

W. W. Norton & Company, Inc. "Water Names" from *Hunger* by Lan Samantha Chang. Copyright © 1998 by Lan Samantha Chang.